RADICAL ARAB NATIONALISM
and POLITICAL ISLAM

RADICAL ARAB NATIONALISM and POLITICAL ISLAM

LAHOUARI ADDI

Translated by Anthony Roberts

Georgetown University Press / Washington, DC
and
The Center for Contemporary Arab Studies, Georgetown University

Library of Congress Cataloging-in-Publication Data

Names: Addi, Lahouari, 1949- author. | Roberts, Anthony (Translator), translator.
Title: Radical Arab nationalism and political Islam / Lahouari Addi ; translated by Anthony Roberts.
Description: Washington, D.C. : Georgetown University Press : Center for Contemporary Arab Studies, Georgetown University, 2017. | Includes bibliographical references and index. | Description based on print version record and CIP data provided by publisher; resource not viewed.
Identifiers: LCCN 2017006997 (print) | LCCN 2017018127 (ebook) | ISBN 9781626164499 (hc : alk. paper) | ISBN 9781626164505 (pb : alk. paper) | ISBN 9781626164512 (eb)
Subjects: LCSH: Arab nationalism. | Islam and politics--Arab countries. | Arab countries--Politics and government.
Classification: LCC DS63.6 (ebook) | LCC DS63.6 .A36 2017 (print) | DDC 320.540917/4927--dc23
LC record available at https://lccn.loc.gov/2017006997

18 17   9 8 7 6 5 4 3 2 First printing

Printed in the United States of America

Cover design by Jeremy John Parker. Cover image courtesy of Beshr Abdulhadi/ Flickr, "Minaret of the Great Mosque in Ar-raqqah City."

To Molly and Adam
for their support and their love

Contents

List of Boxes   ix

Preface   xi

Introduction   1

Part I. Origins and Perspectives of Arab Nationalism   11

1   The Emergence and Development of Arab Nationalism   15

    Wahhabism as a Proto-Nationalism   18

    Liberal Nationalism in Egypt   28

    From Liberal Arabism to Radical Arab Nationalism   34

2   The Ideological Limitations of Radical Arab Nationalism   45

    Radical Arab Nationalism against the Market Economy   47

    Populism against Society   60

    Economism as a Response to Cultural Crisis   72

3   Nationalism and Nation   83

    The Militarization of Politics   87

    The Aggressive Nature of Nationalism   98

    What Is a Nation if Its People Are Not Sovereign?   109

CONTENTS

Part II. The Ideological and Political Dynamics of Islamism   **121**

4   Islamism as Cultural Representation and Ideological Will   **125**

The Cultural Roots of Islamism   127

The Making of Islamist Ideology: Sayyid Qutb and

Abul A'la Mawdudi   138

Toward Post-Islamism?   153

5   Islamism and Democracy   **171**

Democracy and Political Participation   172

The *Al hakimiyya li Allah* Slogan   184

The Question of Sharia   200

6   The Ideological and Political Perspectives of Islamism   **217**

The Cultural Heterogeneity of Contemporary Arab Society   218

Al-Nahda, Sufism, and Islamism   231

Eventful Regression   240

Conclusion   **251**

Index   255

About the Author   275

Boxes

What Is Wahhabism?   26

Political Economy as a Social and Historical Science   56

Social Differentiation as an Ineluctable Trend   70

The Nation, Kant, and Gellner   108

The Historical Dimension of the Concept of Sovereignty   197

Three Currents of Religious Muslim Thought   237

Preface

THIS BOOK is the offshoot of my teaching work at the Institut d'études politiques, University of Lyon, France, and of a project undertaken at my research center (Triangle UMR-CNRS). I address the political regimes of the Arab world and the two great ideologies, radical nationalism and political Islam, that played an important role in the postcolonial era. My approach is analytical and critical, aiming to shed light on the logic and contradictions of a political field marked by heavy expectations—sometimes utopian in nature—of peoples in search of dignity and identity within an international framework rife with conflict. To some extent my analysis draws on history to pinpoint events that have brought about this state of affairs. Nevertheless, my principal emphasis is on political sociology and the crucial concept of representation, which alone can give legitimacy to the political order longed for by so many. A theoretical framework of this kind may provide the key to understanding the geopolitical development of a region that is strategically vital to the West on account of its oil reserves and that has been a highly sensitive issue ever since the foundation of Israel in 1948. The disintegration of the Ottoman Empire, along with Western colonial domination and the resistance it provoked, gave birth to states that took the form of monarchies after World War I, and of republics after World War II. All the republics except Tunisia opted for a socialist agenda, giving to the states an important role in the process of economic development. They used revolutionary rhetoric to denounce the West's domination of the region, accusing the monarchies of betraying the "Arab Nation." To survive, the monarchies fell back on religious symbolism while placing themselves under the protection of the Western powers. In this way the logic of the Cold War between East and West was reproduced throughout the region.

This book is an attempt to shed light on the contradictory socio-ideological dynamics sweeping over Arab societies today, confronted as they are by a process of modernization that is at once rejected and longed for. I have assembled it at the invitation of the Center for Contemporary Arab Studies (CCAS) at Georgetown University, where I was Carnegie Centennial Fellow during the 2013–14 academic year. I would like to thank Osama Abi-Mershed, director of the CCAS, for offering me this opportunity. I also wish to express my gratitude to the IEP, University of Lyon, France, for facilitating my tenure at Georgetown University for one year, and to Triangle, my research center to which I submitted a project on this subject. I would like also to thank the CCAS for the financial support for the translation of the French version of the manuscript.

Introduction

THE ANALYSIS OFFERED in this book focuses on a couple of ideologies that are both twins and rivals: Radical Arab nationalism and Islamism, both of which began with popular upheavals to change the status quo. The text demonstrates how the two ideologies are anchored in the histories and cultures of societies aspiring to modernity, with all their frustrations and contradictory expectations. The Arab world carries the burden of a rich religious past; because of this, it must face the complex question of secularization, which nationalism had thought to outflank with economic development directed by a state reduced to the status of a mere administrative framework. Islamism's response to this is to Islamize secularization, affirming that the separation of religion and state is heresy. Yet it offers no plan for government and its popularity is the consequence of radical nationalism's progressive weakening and failure ever since the late 1960s. Radical Arab nationalism was triumphant since it took over in the 1950s and 1960s in Egypt, Iraq, Algeria, Syria, Yemen, and Libya, until its confidence was shattered by military defeat in June 1967 at the hands of Israel. Since then it has been challenged directly by Islamism, which presented itself as both its heir and its adversary. The fall of Hosni Mubarak in Egypt in 2011, the collapse of Muammar Gaddafi's Libyan regime in 2011, and the more recent destruction of Syria illustrate the erosion of legitimacy of regimes that had promised economic modernization and social emancipation. To understand why radical Arab nationalism moved from triumph to decline in a matter of decades, we must study its beginnings and in a more general way return to the historic origins of the Arab states that set themselves up as monarchies and republics in consequence of their particular historical conditions. The disintegration of the Ottoman Empire brought about a form of protonationalism, which gave birth to conservative monarchies under the benevolent care of European powers in exchange for their support for anti-Ottoman policies. The urban elites of Syria and Lebanon were not, to begin with, hostile to the monarchical form of the Arab state to which they aspired. They supported the "Arab revolt" directed by Sharif Hussein in the hope that it would lead to a single Arab state encompassing the Fertile Crescent. But this dream was crushed by the colonial ambitions of Britain and France, and it has been betrayed by the new dynasties of Iraq and Jordan. These monarchies, as well as that of Saudi Arabia, came into being between 1920 and 1930; they were shaped to support the Europeans in their struggle against the Ottoman Empire. For reasons linked to their own conservative nature and their alliances with the colonial powers that protected them, they were a disappointment to the nationalists, who had borrowed their own concepts and methods from European liberal ideology.

This historical matrix is important if we are to understand the later evolution of the Arab world, which responded in different ways to contact with the all-conquering Europe of the nineteenth and twentieth centuries. While the monarchies were content to ensure the existence of formally independent Arab states, the nationalists proclaimed their will to reform society and catch up with the West, going so far as to adopt liberal values before moving away from them in defiance of Europe. Arab nationalism has a history of its own and its distant origins lie in the reaction to Bonaparte's expedition to Egypt in 1798, which was a severe shock to many among the elite, who were forced to acknowledge just how far ahead Europe

was in military, economic, and scientific terms. By a slow and sometimes contradictory process, liberal ideas penetrated the Arab world,
and eventually, in the second half of the nineteenth century, they
merged with a general rejection of the Ottoman Empire and then
evolved toward open hostility to the European powers following the
1916 Sykes–Picot Agreement. The struggle against colonial domin-
ion led to the installation of republics that were politically opposed
to the West. Paradoxically, they were closer to it in terms of ideology
than the conservative monarchies, which resembled the absolutist
model that had dominated Europe before the revolutions. From this
point of view, the republican elites, many of them military, were the
distant heirs of the liberal tendency of the late nineteenth century;
they had become radicalized by borrowing their ideological language from German idealism and their rhetoric of "Arab socialism"
from revolutionary Marxism. Gamal Abdel Nasser, Houari Boumediene, and Hafiz al-Assad were all closer to the Prussian or Soviet
models than that of the caliphate.

In fact, the Arab world created two types of state as a result of its
contact with the West: one based on the tradition represented by
monarchy, whose political interests chimed with those of the Western powers, and the other affirming its republican character and its
desire to end foreign domination in the region. The split between
these two competing projects led to extreme tensions in the 1960s
and 1970s (leading to bitter conflict between Egypt and Saudi Arabia
over Yemen, between Algeria and Morocco over the Western Sahara,
and between Iraq and Kuwait) and only settled down after the political weakening of the various republican regimes which, after the
military defeat by Israel in 1967, ceased to denounce the monarchies.
The monarchies were even asked for financial help with the rebuilding of the Egyptian and Syrian armies, when regional heads of state
met in Khartoum in 1968. Once the pan-Arabist project had been
dropped by the revolutionary colonels, the monarchies felt a greater

sense of security, which was further strengthened by Egypt's tilt toward the western camp after the death of Nasser. The rejection by Anwar Sadat, Nasser's successor, of Arabist rhetoric and the opening of the Egyptian economy to private capital flowing from Saudi Arabia and the Gulf Emirates as well as from the West heralded the failure of radical Arab nationalism. This was to be challenged, from the 1970s onward, by Islamism—an ideology that for years had been encouraged and used as a weapon by the monarchies. If the Islamists in Egypt and Algeria have gained in popularity since the deaths of Nasser and Boumediene, it is because they accused their successors of having enriched a minority by signing agreements with the International Monetary Fund (IMF). In the case of Egypt, there is the added denunciation of the peace treaty signed with Israel—which cost President Sadat his life.

Thus, the regimes of the republics, forced on the defensive and mired in economic failure, comprehensively lost their political battle with the monarchies. Moreover, the post-1973 oil price increases raised the latter to the level of major regional powers. At the time of the so-called Arab Spring uprisings, which began in Tunisia in December 2010, the monarchies gave their support to the rebellions— thereby taking their revenge upon regimes that had accused them a few years earlier of betraying the Arab peoples. In the long term, the regimes of the republics turned out to be more fragile than the monarchies where political opposition seemed less threatening. How may we explain this fragility of regimes that claimed to originate with the people and that had sworn to modernize their countries for the good of their underprivileged social classes? The July 1952 coup d'état in Egypt, carried out by the Free Officers, led to the seizure of power by military Arab nationalists in several other countries of the region. They had the look of a deep-seated movement of authoritarian modernization, which should have accelerated national construction and created the political and economic conditions for genuine social and cultural progress. Many academic studies have seen in them a form of Bonapartism, determined as they were to sweep away the archaic aspects of society and the shackles of dependency created by an economy based on the export of agricultural products and raw materials. With Nasser, Egypt undertook reforms that were just as bold and wide-ranging as those of Muhammed Ali, 150 years earlier, in an international environment that was far more favorable than that prevailing in the nineteenth century. So why did Nasser's political and economic program, which had the people's overwhelming support, fail to succeed and keep its promises? This question lies at the heart of this book, which attempts a critical analysis of radical Arab nationalism and of Islamism, the political ideology that opposes it. The hypothesis set forth here is that radical Arab nationalism, which gave birth to the republics, viewed modernization as a technical and administrative task on the premise that the state, controlled by military men, was the sole agent for change.

The analysis of the ideological texts of the different parties (the 1962 Egyptian charter, the Algerian national charter, the Baathist texts) and the policy speeches of Nasser, Boumediene, and Assad, all demonstrate a simplistic political philosophy reducible to a moral Manicheism that knows nothing of the cultural foundations of modernity or the sociological complexity of Arab societies and their contradictions. Radical Arab nationalism was promising justice from above at a time when the real challenge was to endow state power with electoral legitimacy in order that the elected bodies might reflect the various components of society. The complex social reality had been concealed by the myth of the people, a structuring concept of a utopian vision in which the collective exaltation of the group took precedence over human anthropology. This vision would have it that the people constitute a homogeneous entity with the idea that the unity of that entity is supposedly threatened by outside forces that have local support to call upon. To this effect, all social powers are neutralized so as to prevent resistance to the policies of the leader, who alone decides who will represent workers, farmers, young people, and various other socioprofessional groups. By rejecting any autonomy of economic, judicial, and trade union power, and by suppressing freedom of expression and freedom of the press, the military regime prevented society from developing its own regulatory mechanisms and its own authentic representatives. All private initiative was discouraged by the administration that sought to control every area of social activity, everywhere seeing enemies of the revolution that had to be neutralized. Society, in turn, adapted to this blanket control by gradually infiltrating the administration, the army, and other government institutions that became hotbeds of privilege and corruption. Accusing the market of promoting inequalities and dividing the people into rich and poor classes, the regime resorted to the model of a state-run economy whose purported mission was to share the national wealth on an equal basis. This enabled the use of the economy as a political resource to discourage all dissent when the state was the principal employer in the country, taking charge of social demands (employment, housing, health, education, transport, etc.) in return for allegiance to the leader—whose party decided who would represent the population in the country's institutions.

As the years went by, social demands steadily increased in step with population growth, making it impossible for the state to satisfy them. Oil-rich countries like Iraq, Algeria, and Libya were untroubled by deficits stemming from social expenditure and a generalized decline in productivity. But Egypt was forced to change its economic policy to extricate the state from bankruptcy in the mid-1970s, resorting to national- and foreign-derived private capital in the hope that an "opening of the door" (*infitah*) to the market economy would have the effect of creating employment. Fifteen years later the Egyptian example was followed by Algeria in the aftermath of the October 1988 riots, which brought an end to the state's monopoly over the economy. With exactly the same political personnel that was championing socialism, the regime set about implementing liberal economic reforms that favored speculation. As a result, speculation became the principal means of accumulating wealth. Populism, the ideological glue holding the regime together, was dealt a heavy blow by the ostentatious wealth of a new layer of society that came into being with the *infitah*. The contract around which the regime was built (social protection in exchange for political authoritarianism) was broken. The state renounced its social policies under pressure from the IMF while the population continued to be excluded from government institutions. Multiparty politics was technically allowed, but widespread electoral fraud gave a clear advantage to the former single party, which continued to hold its majorities in parliaments and assemblies. At the same time, relative freedom of expression emboldened Islamists to criticize the government and denounce the consequences of its economic and social policy, which gave them a popular base. As an ideological trend, Islamism has always been present in Muslim societies; what was new was the fact that, beginning in the 1970s, it became increasingly popular in the republics founded by radical Arab nationalism that indirectly gave birth to an equally radical opposition.

It is important to bear in mind the dialectical relationship between radical Arab nationalism and Islamism. The latter was inspired by the former's rhetoric and appropriated its populism to itself, denouncing the corruption of those in power, the social inequalities, and the decline in moral standards. Tackling the regime on its own ideological terrain, Islamism accused it of betraying the nation by forming alliances with the former colonial powers and of making agreements with the IMF, whose program had the effect of keeping the poorest classes of society in a state of semistarvation. In a way, Islamism sought to continue the struggle against the West that had taken place in the 1950s and 1960s and was subsequently abandoned by the republican regimes in the early 1990s.

It is no coincidence that the Islamist protest movement today is more popular and more threatening in the republics than in the monarchies, which have symbolic resources to counter it. Police repression against Islamist groups is just as harsh as in the republican regimes, but the monarchies have ideological and institutional frameworks that are more effective at eliminating the most violent extremists while integrating more moderate Islamists into the inner and outer mechanisms of the state. Based as they are on tradition and religious conservatism, the monarchies have always taught that believers must respect the authority of the king, who is the guardian of the social order willed by God. The monopoly exerted by the dynasties in terms of religious symbolism as related to legitimacy of the monarchies (Wahhabism in Saudi Arabia; sharifism in Morocco and Jordan) allows them to benefit from the support of the charismatic ulemas, both of the *zaouias* (religious centers built close to a grave of a saint) and of the brotherhoods that have followers in many sectors of the rural and urban population. Moreover, the monarchies have a religious institution—the Council of the Ulemas—that lays claim to the sole true interpretation of Islam, thereby disqualifying the Islamists on their own terrain. Sheikh Abdessalam Yassine, the representative of Morocco's extremist Islamist wing, was first placed in a psychiatric hospital and then placed under house arrest on the basis of a fatwa requested by King Hassan II from his Council of Ulemas. The same council exists in Saudi Arabia; its purpose is to disqualify all religious objection to the king's policies. The monarchies manage to co-opt moderate Islamists, but they are exposed to the minority of violent extremists who accuse them of furthering the interests of the West viewed as the implacable enemy of Islam. In Saudi Arabia these extremists carried out deadly attacks following the king's agreement to allow US troops into the country, which went on to invade Iraq and to liberate Kuwait in 1991. The dispute between the monarchy and al-Qaeda led by Osama bin Laden originated with the monarchy's decision to call in the US military to protect itself from Saddam Hussein. Yet it is not by ideological choice that the Saudi royal family maintains close relations with the United States; it is by political necessity, given the danger, in earlier times, posed by radical Arab nationalism and the current threat posed by Iran. The king has convincing arguments when he seeks the support of the Council of Ulemas, when the issue is the very survival of the monarchy of which they form a part. This was already the case in 1927, when Ibn Saud Abdulaziz, the founder of the kingdom, solicited the help of the British army to crush the revolt of the Ikhwan, the Wahhabi religious militia; in 1979, when elite troops of the French army neutralized extremists who had taken over the Grand mosque in Mecca; and finally in 1990, when an American military base was authorized on Saudi soil, with a view to liberating Kuwait.

The republics have to confront the Islamists on different terrain, and they appear to be less well armed ideologically for the fray. Claiming popular legitimacy, the military and civilian elites of the republics are suspicious of religious conservatism, which they accuse of exploiting economic and cultural underdevelopment. The republican ideology is more adapted to the factory and school than to the mosque; it also spreads the idea that the poverty of the people has political causes and is actively maintained by the West, which pillages the wealth of the Arabs with the help of local allies. Radical Arab nationalism has promised to break this cycle and place the state fully at the service of the people. However, as long as social inequalities persist, the elites will continue to lose credibility, thus giving the opportunity to the Islamists who take up the banner of a nationalist Utopia garnished with verses from the Qur'an. Ever since the mid-twentieth century, the Arab countries have been awaiting a change that will bring them progress and security. Yesterday it was the nationalists who promised to bring this about; today it is the Islamists.

PART I

Origins and Perspectives of Arab Nationalism

THE ARAB WORLD is a vast political entity that extends from Morocco to Iraq. For centuries it has had relationships of exchange and conflict with Europe. Prior to the seventeenth century, the military *rapport de force* between the two was more or less equal; the change in favor of Europe coincided with the gradual weakening of the Ottoman Empire. Napoleon Bonaparte's expedition to Egypt in 1798 demonstrated the military, scientific, and economic superiority of Europe. It opened the way to a political domination of the Arab countries and to the acculturation of a section of their elites, who became convinced that the best way of defending themselves was to imitate the Europeans, politically and culturally. The ideological arguments and controversies that began in the early nineteenth century and have continued to rage right up to our own time concern the form and content of this imitation, with special reference to Islam. For some, modernization is based on the implicit pattern of secularization; for others, it is accomplished with Islam as a religion linked to politics and to law. The Arab world is still wrestling with this question of Islam's place in society and the state at a time when many social practices have become secularized, as if consciousness was lagging behind the social and cultural transformations that have taken place in the last one hundred years. What is

11

lacking is the idea that religion is embedded in culture, implying that it is not an essence but a social construct that changes with time. This idea is foreign to medieval interpretation of Islam that impedes the aspiration to modernization, although this aspiration is shared by everyone. Despite the strong feeling of unity (*oumma*), the spread of nationalism has divided the populations of the region into separate and sometimes concurrent political entities. The condemnation by the ulemas of the *chou'oubia* (kind of ethnocentrism) has not prevented Islam either from accompanying nationalism or from giving it legitimacy. The desire to organize themselves as nation-states, and not as *umma* on the model of the caliphate, has proven stronger than the common cultural and religious heritage championed by the ulemas. The universalistic and transregional Islam of the ulemas and brotherhoods have yielded to "nationalist Islams" to such a point that religious holy days are celebrated on different days in Morocco, Algeria, and Egypt, demonstrating that the people have assimilated the culture of nationalism as a dialectical consequence of European domination and their rejection of it. There has also been a fragmentation of the geographical space occupied by Islam that has had no effect on its religious heritage, which steadfastly continues to reject secularization despite the sociological and cultural transformations society has undergone.

The struggle against colonialism mobilized the resources of identity, of which religion was one, leading to the ideological incoherence that might eventually prevent the postcolonial state from bringing peace in the political sphere. Nationalism succeeded in the first phase of creating a central power, but it failed in the second phase, which consisted in giving the governed a true sense that they were free. The liberation of the group does not necessarily mean the freedom of the individual. The former is the easy part because it unites everyone against foreign oppressors; the latter is the struggle of the individual against the group, and of the present against the past. To impose the institutional framework of a nation-state without giving the governed the civil rights that protect them from the arbitrary actions of their rulers is to prepare the ground for an authoritarian regime. Nationalism does not automatically create a nation if we understand by "nation" a political community at peace with itself. If it fails to win over local ethnocentricities, if it fails to endow political power with a public character, if it fails to secularize the law and take religion out of politics, the state will be authoritarian and brutal, headed straight for civil war. The Arab uprisings of 2011, with the extreme case of Syria, show the scale of the rift between governments and governed as well as the weakness of the fabric holding society together and the way it has been shredded by community, ethnic, and linguistic differences. The legacy of postcolonial nationalism in terms of national cohesion is nothing short of pitiful, as the violence of these rebellions shows all too clearly. It has proved incapable of transforming the social bond from "mechanical solidarity" founded on sentiment to an "organic solidarity" based on the social division and sharing of labor.[1]

The first part of this book reviews the historical framework of the rise of Arab nationalism in Egypt and the Middle East in its different moderate and radical variants.[2] After this, I shed light on the ideological limitations that have prevented Arab nationalism from building a rule of law. Finally, I show that the concept of nation is related to other concepts, such as citizenship, civil rights, sovereignty, and political liberty. A nation is not just a territory with a geographical frontier protected by soldiers; it is above all the space of a civil society that has separated religion from politics, secularized the law, and affirmed its autonomy in regard to the state, whose leaders are accountable to their electors within a peaceful system of electoral alternation.

Notes

1. For these two concepts of solidarity, see Emile Durkheim, *The Division of Labor in Society* (New York: Free Press, 1997).

PART I

2. On Arab nationalism, see Tibi Bassam, *Arab Nationalism: A Critical Inquiry*, edited and translated by Marion Farouk Sluglett and Peter Sluglett (New York: St. Martin's Press, 1981); Khalidi Rashid, ed., *The Origins of Arab Nationalism* (New York: Colombia University Press, 1991); and A. I. Dawisha, *Arab Nationalism in the 20th Century: From Triumph to Despair* (Princeton, NJ: Princeton University Press, 2016).

1

The Emergence and Development of Arab Nationalism

SINCE THE NINETEENTH CENTURY, any community that failed to organize itself into a nation-state risked occupation by foreign powers. The Westphalian order that had emerged in Europe two centuries earlier had spread all over the planet, imposing the concept of the nation-state; no population could escape it. Western Europe, with its overwhelming military and economic strength, was able to propagate its own form of political organization, the nation-state. The other regions of the planet had no alternative but to copy this model if they valued their existence as communities held together by bonds of culture, language, and history. It must be clearly understood that the non-European nationalisms that emerged following the colonial conquests, apart from a few messianic and millennialist movements, did not seek to revive the old political structures that had been swept aside by colonialism; instead, they expressed the desire to create a sovereign state endowed with a central power exercising, as much as possible, a monopoly on justice, violence, and education. This aspiration for political autonomy found expression either through adhesion to the liberal ideas of Europe or through attachment to a religious tradition. These two reactions to the European threat are illustrated by the experience of Egypt under Muhammed Ali (1769–1849) and of the Arabian Peninsula, where Wahhabism—after a few wrong turns—finally succeeded in establishing a centralized authority.

As in every other part of the world, the Arab peoples were caught up by a wave of nationalism in their fight against colonial domination. The emergence of nationalism in the Middle East and North Africa must be analyzed in the light of these facts, bearing in mind that local elites expressed either local patriotism (North Africa), hegemonic Pan-Arabism (Syria-Lebanon), or religion-based ethnocentrism (the Arabian Peninsula). The ideological differences between these experiments were the consequences of history and were unrelated to any supposedly immutable special characteristics. If the Egyptians opted for territorial nationalism, in contrast to the Syrians and Lebanese, who favored the doctrine of Pan-Arabism, it was because their respective relationships with the Ottoman Empire were not the same. The difference between the Egyptian experience and that of the Fertile Crescent derives from history and from the strategic perception of the adversary against which nationalist sentiment was pitted. In Egypt in the second half of the nineteenth century, the elites positioned themselves politically against the colonial ambitions of Great Britain by seeking help from the Ottoman Empire. By contrast, the Ottoman administration was perceived as the enemy, particularly by the nomad tribes of the Arabian Peninsula, where the influence of the city elites had barely penetrated a mostly Bedouin society. In the Middle East, the influence of European political ideas found a more favorable terrain in the major urban centers of Egypt, Syria, and Lebanon than in the peninsula. The nineteenth century was a period during which the Arabs, or at least the Arab elites, became aware of how far behind Europe they had fallen, and of Europe's consequent ambition to dominate them. To face the threat of a dominant and modern Europe, various forms of nationalism were present in the region: Wahhabism, born in the Arabian Peninsula in the mid-eighteenth century; the movement of

Rifa'a al-Tahtawi, which appeared in the wake of Muhammed Ali's reforms; and finally, the Pan-Arabism of Syrian-Lebanese Christian and Muslim intellectuals.

In the hinterland of the vast Arabian Peninsula, which was of zero strategic or economic interest to the European powers (apart from a few seaports in the area), the Al Saud family, after a string of defeats, had at last succeeded in eliminating its local opponents. Built as it was on the myth of defending the purity of Islam, the Al Saud project relied on Wahhabi religious rigor, whereby it succeeded in creating an absolute monarchy. Having grasped that the international *rapport de force* did not favor them, the Al Sauds renounced the dream of a new caliphate after conquering as many provinces as they possibly could. Instead, they created a political entity that was run as the private property of the Al Saud—after whom the country was named—while at the same time espousing the concept of Muslim universalism. The obvious contradiction between an appropriation of the state and the universalist symbolism of Islam was surmounted, several decades later, by the discovery of oil, the exploitation of which brought in sufficient funds to build up networks of clients rooted in urban and rural areas by distributing wealth in a way that would include the Saudi people in a circuit of consumption while excluding them from the running of the state.

The case of Egypt effectively sums up the opportunities missed by the Arab world in its quest for modernization. Having endured the course of liberal reform, very robust for the time, which was meted out by Muhammed Ali, Egypt had the nascent attributes of a nation-state. These were snuffed out by the British, whose interest lay in preserving their own strategic and economic interests as well as their influence, all of which were threatened in the region by their intimate rivals, the French. The hopes of Rifa'a al-Tahtawi seduced the Egyptian urban elite and nourished a liberal nationalism that sought to copy the Westminster model, wherein the king reigned but did not govern. This project aroused the hostility of the British themselves, who preferred an absolute monarchy in Egypt because they could control it; it was also doomed by the predominance of landowners in the Egyptian bourgeoisie. Fearing for their own interests, the landowners would not countenance any social change that might favor the rise of workers' or farmers' unions. As a result, liberal nationalism was obliged to turn its back on the majority of the population, of which it was afraid. Following the geopolitical upheavals caused by the First World War, Egypt formally became a sovereign state. The aristocratic elite, with liberal leanings in politics and conservative ones in social matters, supported the monarchic regime. In the 1920s and 1930s, the political game was so narrow that the same figures were constantly at office. The sterility of all this created a breeding ground for radical Arab nationalism, in particular after the creation of Israel in 1948. Four years later a coup d'état was implemented by "free officers" in July 1952, opening a new era in the Arab world.

Radical Arab nationalism was the expression of anger at European domination, which despised the native populations it controlled. It won a popular dimension by the solidarity with the Palestinian cause. The military expressed the people's frustration and brushed aside the governing elites, which they accused of being allied with foreign interests. They promised to catch up with the admired but hated West, perceived as an economic and military entity seeking to take control of the Arab countries. The organization of the army on the model of European armies nurtured the dream to catch up with Europe in a few decades. This dream underestimates the fact that the basis of European power was not military but intellectual and political.

Wahhabism as a Proto-Nationalism

In the academic literature devoted to nationalism, the Saudi Arabian experience is excluded, even though for all intents and purposes it represented the earliest attempt to construct a nation in the Arab world. From 1744 onward, the Al Saud family created a central power in the Arabian Peninsula that defied, at the time, the Ottoman caliphate, of which the peninsula was formally a part. Moreover, it sought to create an inherited monarchy like those that existed in medieval Europe, whose historians claim that they were at the origins of the European nation-states. In their opposition to the Ottomans accused of perverting Islam, the Al Sauds exploited ethnocentrist sentiment to rally the tribes of the peninsula, where a multitude of local powers were competing with each other, taking advantage of the strategic vastness of the desert. They formed alliances that enabled them to quell their adversaries in a tribal world where alliances were volatile and changed according to events and the evolution of the local balance of power. The advantage of the Saudi clan over their competitors was Wahhabism, which was useful to them in showing that they were the harbingers of a universalistic vision of Islam, defending the interests of all Muslims. The Al Sauds were able to exploit the opportunity gifted to them by the stern Wahhabi doctrine to overcome local tribal considerations and launch themselves into a political adventure whose declared goal was to impose the *true* Islam on all Muslims. They used their military strength to annex the maximum possible territory. The families of Al Saud and Sheik Muhammad 'Abd al-Wahhab strengthened their alliance by marriage from the start, in 1744, uniting to found a state whose religious bedrock was Wahhabism. In this alliance, politics was the senior partner, as later events were to show. The military strength of the one partner and the religious ideology of the other combined to create a coalition and a kingdom that bore the name of a family. The Al Sauds imposed themselves after an almost two-hundred-year competitive process, during which they were badly defeated twice in battle, once by the Ottomans (in 1818) and once by the Ibn Rashid tribe of the Shammar Mountains in 1870. A third

process of reconquest began in 1902, ending with the official proclamation of the founding of the kingdom, which was immediately
recognized by the foreign powers.

The political adventure began in the middle of the eighteenth century with a preacher, Muhammad 'Abd al-Wahhab, who dedicated
himself to purge Islam of the iniquitous innovations introduced by
the Ottomans and the Sufis. His message insisted on the oneness of
God and on a prohibition of all intercession between God and the
faithful. There was nothing original about this puritan movement in
Islam; thousands of other preachers had called for the same brand of
orthodoxy that was already a feature of classical Muslim theology at
the time of Ahmad ibn Hanbal. What clinched the success of
Muhammad 'Abd al-Wahhab was the military force of the Al Saud,
who carried many tribes with them in the mission to regenerate
Islam and fight those who would pervert it, especially the Ottomans.
From then on, Wahhabism became a puritanical doctrine with the
objective of fighting "miscreants and hypocrites." Its followers preferred to be known as "Al Mouahidoun": those who profess the oneness of God and who call for the unity of Muslims in this cause.[1]

The strength of Wahhabism lies in its ethnocentric appeal to re-
Arabize Islam, after its appropriation by Turks, Persians, Asians, and
the Berbers who have supposedly disfigured it. Wahhabism found
an echo among the Bedouin tribes who felt a duty to bring Arabness
back since the Prophet was himself a native of their peninsula. The
Al Saud family used Wahhabism in their political project to found a
central power that would affirm the autonomy of the peninsula
against the Ottomans. From the end of the eighteenth century, the
ambition of the Saudis was to supplant the sultan in Istanbul who,
anticipating the danger, called upon Muhammed Ali, viceroy of
Egypt, to go out and defeat them. The troops of Muhammed Ali
went to the peninsula in 1818, sacked the Saudi capital, and carried
off hundreds of prisoners in Istanbul where many of their leaders

had been beheaded on the orders of the Sultan. After the departure of the Egyptian troops, whose presence was incapable of maintaining Ottoman rule over the vast desert land, the power of Al Saud was reconstructed over a few years before collapsing again in a family quarrel over the succession. Defeated, the Saud family fled to Kuwait, where they settled. In 1902 a young Saudi, Abdulaziz, born in 1880, came back to the peninsula to fight for a new Saudi kingdom. He took up the project of uniting the tribes of the peninsula under the banner of Wahhabism. Coming from Kuwait, he attacked and took Riyadh in 1902. He proclaimed himself Emir of Nejd, his family's native land, and set about rebuilding the network of tribal alliances on which his ancestors had depended. He waged merciless war against his adversaries, notably the Al Rashids of Shammar. On the eve of the First World War, Abdulaziz, son of Abderrahmane Saud, showed that he had the statecraft to protect his own position as Emir of Nejd by taking advantage of the conflict between the British and the Ottoman Empire.

The alliance between Ibn Saud's warrior spirit and a puritan religious doctrine ensured the success of the Al Saud political enterprise, which, at the third attempt, had now achieved its objective of setting up a strong central authority that was feared within its borders and respected beyond them. This was largely thanks to those believers who willingly agreed to defend the true word of God, ready to sacrifice for the cause. Abdulaziz attracted a host of men from the nomad tribes and organized them into sedentary military units settled in local village garrisons. In this way he managed to weaken the tribal links of these fighters who pledged allegiance to Wahhabism. The Ikhwan—the name by which these military units were known— constituted a considerable strike force in a desert region that was hard for any regular army to control. The universality of Wahhabism, transcending tribal frontiers and championing Muslim unity, rolled back the warlike local ethnocentrism that had hitherto prevented the constitution of a central power. The Ikhwan did not answer to the Al Saud but to a religious ideal of which they themselves were the symbol. In Islam, political constructions are necessarily fragile because religious legitimacy finds its source in society itself and not at the pinnacle of an institution. Any individual who could claim noble ancestry—descent from the line of the Prophet or descent from a figure acknowledged as a saint—had a religious legitimacy that could also be used as grounds for political authority. The strength of Wahhabism was that it succeeded in delegitimizing these two potential sources of authority (sainthood and lineage), permitting the Al Saud to eliminate the sharifs of the Hejaz and the saints of the other regions of the peninsula. By simultaneously stifling Sharifian genealogy and Sufi sainthood, Wahhabism created a vacuum that the Al Saud occupied in the name of Muhammad 'Abd al-Wahhab's puritanism. Early resistance to the new Wahhabi order was swiftly and violently put down. The ferocity of the Ikhwan was unleashed on saint lineages, along with *razzias* (raids) on tribes and on cities that were unwilling to submit to the harsh Wahhabi doctrine. All this built up a serious reputation for the Ikhwan, who were feared for their methods and respected for their message.

Wahhabism was a powerful ideology of conquest, but it lacked the capacity to build a modern state on account of its aggressive proselytism, which was incompatible, naturally, with the Westphalian order imposed by Europe. As a warlike movement tending toward anarchy because of its tendency to attack any opinion that differed from its own, Wahhabism swore eternal loathing for the Shiites and Sufis; it was suspicious of city dwellers, whom it reproached with leading lives contrary to the teachings of the Qur'an. More importantly, because the armed soldier-believer could decide for himself where to draw the line between believers and infidels, he had a tendency to disobey whenever he considered the methods of his leader to be not in conformity with the law of God. Thus, the authority of the Al Saud began to be frequently called into question by the Ikhwan, who reproached the family with making agreements with foreign miscreants. In their loyalty to Muhammad 'Abd al-Wahhab, who taught that any knowledge having no basis in the Qur'an was flat heresy, the Ikhwan also concluded that technological innovations like cars, telephones, electricity, and the like were manifestations of the devil. On this question they directly opposed their military chief, Ibn Saud Abdulaziz, who, as a skilled politician, first tried to convince them of their error, and then fought them fiercely until they were neutralized. Their dogmatism and their ignorance of human reality and social necessity imperiled his political mission to build within the Arabian Peninsula a central power that would be strong within itself and independent of foreign powers alike.

More realistic than the Ikhwan, Ibn Saud had grasped the fact that scientific inventions and techniques were no threat to faith. He responded to their complaints, telling them to follow their own logic to its conclusion by putting aside their guns, which were the invention of "European miscreants." He ultimately destroyed them because he had a sense of the state that they conspicuously lacked. In 1929, after several months of negotiations, he led a military campaign against the Ikhwan, using heavy machine guns and airplanes supplied by the British and massacring several thousand. Before the start of this campaign he had tried and failed to make them see reason. In a speech delivered to the rebel chiefs in the fall of 1928 in Riyadh, he declared: "When I came to you, you were divided into rival clans and tribes, plundering one another and living by banditry. Your leaders encouraged your intrigues and flattered your pride. They perpetuated your quarrels, weakened your power, smothered and destroyed the virtues of your people. But I have made you all into a nation, in the fear of God."[2] After this violent episode, aggressive Wahhabism was quieted, and it became the monopoly of docile ulemas who embraced political realism and respected the foreign powers that ensured the survival of the dynasty.

The exceptional personality of Ibn Saud, a tenacious warrior and a remarkable strategist, enabled the Saudi state to succeed, thanks to his subtle manipulation of the foreign powers that were engaged in the region. He was used by the Ottomans against the British, but he also used the British to strengthen his own position. The economic sterility of the vast desert of the Arabian Peninsula, with no agriculture and no natural resources (except on the coast, which had strategic importance), was a major advantage for the Al Saud, whose authority over the interior was formally recognized both by the British and by the Ottomans. Ibn Saud wisely never threatened the strategic interests of Britain in Aden, Kuwait, and Qatar, although he did seek to extend his authority into parts of Syria and Iraq, which the Ikhwan attacked on several occasions. During the First World War, he was courted by both sides but preferred to remain neutral and await the outcome. When it came, he drove his rival Sharif Hussein from the Hejaz as soon as he was abandoned by the British, his former allies.

In the aftermath of the First World War, Britain and France recognized his legitimacy in the peninsula, which was of no interest to them apart from its position astride the sea route to India. With his keen sense of the balance of power, Abdulaziz had made Saudi Arabia the only Arab state to escape colonial domination. He had understood to the letter the meaning of the Westphalian order, signing the Jeddah Treaty with the British in 1927 and recognizing the Hashemites in Iraq after having fought them in the Hejaz and driven them out. He succeeded in creating a strong centralized government and in maintaining his autonomy vis-à-vis the foreign powers, which contained him in the greater part of the Arabian Peninsula. His life's project was the unification of that peninsula, including the gulf and Yemen coasts as well as the formation of an Arab caliphate that would include Syria and Iraq. The international balance of power prevented him from making this dream a reality, and he confined himself to controlling such space as his forces could take and hold, thus displaying a proper sense of reality. At home, he overwhelmed his traditional adversaries, the followers of Sharif Hussein and Ibn Rashid, using the fanaticism of the Ikhwan, whom he subsequently annihilated when they revealed their incompatibility with the *raison d'état*. Abroad, he manipulated the rivalries between foreign powers, capitalizing on his neutrality or support for them. By 1945, Saudi Arabia had become an irreversible political reality. The United Nations recognized it as a sovereign state that, with the coming of the cold war and the threat of radical Arab nationalism, placed itself under the protection of the United States, the world's most powerful nation, with its pressing need for hydrocarbons. After the upheavals in the region caused by the creation of the state of Israel and the nationalist fervor that ensued, the Saudi dynasty obeyed the logic of the Cold War by seeking the protection of the Western powers against regimes that had allied themselves with the Soviet Union and that had accused Saudi Arabia of betraying the interests and ideals of the Arab nation.

The Al Sauds were the precursors of Arab nationalism, creating a conservative brand of nationalism that has had no echo outside the peninsula. Nor has the religious intolerance of Wahhabism endeared itself to the urban elites of Syria and Iraq; its mistrust of Arab Christians and Jews and its rejection of the urban way of life has prevented it from benefiting from the support of any social group that aspires to an Islam—and a Christianity—that is tolerant and non-fanatical. These same groups had given a favorable reception to Sharif Hussein, supporting him in his project for an Arabian monarchy to supplant the Ottoman caliphate precisely because he did not hold with the active proselytism of the Wahhabis, his sworn enemies.

CHAPTER 1

WHAT IS WAHHABISM?

Wahhabism presents itself as a reformist movement. It preaches a return to the source to reestablish the puritanism of the *salafs* ("predecessors"), which has supposedly been twisted by "blameworthy innovations" like Sufi mysticism. This position is far from new, since it goes back to Ibn Taymiyyah (1263–1328), a noted adversary of Ibn 'Arabi (1165–1240). Wahhabism has revived an ancient debate within Muslim theology, declaring itself in favor of the position of Ibn Taymiyyah, a disciple of Ibn Hanbal (780–855). It echoes the austere living conditions of deserts and semi-arid regions, where men have little room to maneuver, given the relentless hostility of nature. To survive, a strong faith is a psychological resource that is indispensable to existence and generates huge energy for territorial conquest. Starting with the idea that life on earth is no more than a preparatory stage for eternal life, Wahhabism enjoins the faithful to devote themselves to the adoration of God; not to adapt their behavior to exterior reality, but rather to bring it into conformity with God's word. This concept would have it that all social or individual activity not linked to the vital necessities of biological reproduction is utterly futile and reprehensible. By submitting to God, the individual expresses a will to obey nature and draws on the power of God to achieve confidence and serenity in the face of life's mysteries.

Wahhabism preaches the following:

1. Sainthood is a heresy to Islam because Islam recognizes no intercessor between God and the believer. Unlike Catholicism, Islam rejects the idea of a clergy. Inasmuch as God alone is worthy of adoration, Islam accuses Sufis

of polytheism. This position is as old as Muslim theology itself, which, from Ibn Hanbal to Ibn Taymiyyah, has always rejected Sufi mysticism and retirement from the world. Islam condemns the monastic way of life, but its theologians have occasionally followed the teachings of Abū Hāmid al-Ghazali (1058–1111), who acknowledged that the spiritual and mystical dimension of Sufism was compatible with the Qur'an. Thus the Sufis were absolved from the accusation of *chirk* (associationism).

2. All knowledge that does not proceed from the Qur'an or the Sunna is miscreant (*kufr*). This requirement repeats the dogma of Hanbalism, which forbids all evolution of human thought. Thus, the faithful are condemned to repeat ad infinitum what the ancients averred. Muhammad 'Abd al-Wahhab contradicted this when he accepted reason as a source of knowledge, alongside the Qur'an and the Sunna. Reason is a human faculty that interprets the sacred texts according to the times and the cultural level of the faithful. Theologians use reason to make their case, but they have their own standards of reason. Ibn Hanbal made use of reason, and so did his adversaries.

3. Any denial that God's will (*qadr*) lies at the origin of all human acts is blasphemous heresy. This question has been debated by Muslim theologians since the birth of Islam. The two sides were Hanbalism, for which everything that occurs on earth is a consequence of God's will; and the *mu'tazilas*, for whom man bears a certain degree of responsibility for his own acts. Abu al-Hasan al-Ash'ari (874–936) built a doctrine based on a compromise between these two positions, whereby man's responsibility is a feature of the power of God. Muham-

mad 'Abd al-Wahhab returned to the original concept of Ibn Hanbal, rejecting al-Ash'ari's synthesis. It should be emphasized that this theme belongs to medieval theology and has lost all theoretical relevance in regard of the experiences of the everyday life.

Liberal Nationalism in Egypt

In the aftermath of Napoleon Bonaparte's expedition in 1798, Muhammed Ali, the pasha of Egypt, launched a campaign of reforms. The most spectacular of these was the sending of young Egyptians to be trained in France, England, and Germany for later service in the Egyptian army, administration, and educational organization. These reforms, to which the majority of the population remained completely indifferent, were supported by numerous urban families who encouraged their children to learn foreign languages, especially French. The elites of Cairo and Alexandria were attracted to the French language; among them was Rifa'a al-Tahtawi (1802–72), who returned to Egypt from a period of studies in France with a boundless admiration for French culture. He exhorted his compatriots to imitate the French model in its government and institutions with a view to putting an end to the political lethargy and weakness of Egypt. Tahtawi had a major influence on the Egyptian social elite of his time and ran a school dedicated to the translation of works by European authors (such as Montesquieu, Voltaire, François Fénélon, and others) with a preference for the style best suited to lay thought. He was, in fact, the inventor of the modern Arab language by virtue of having written and translated texts by foreign writers while simultaneously avoiding the emphatic rhetoric of religious discourse and its lyrical flights of rhythmic prose. Tahtawi was a patriot who dreamed that Egypt would evolve and draw even with France in wealth and knowledge. He wrote a book in which he explained the customs of French society, the self-fulfillment of men and women, and their love of art and literature.[3] His observations concerned every aspect of social life in the public arena, where, for him, a happy conviviality as reflected in the way the city was organized made the daily existence of Parisians, for example, an easy one. His fascination with French society, its customs, its way of life, and its political institutions was as evident as his desire for cultural changes in Egypt that would equal the model of French civilization. He wanted to show his compatriots that a country is only strong when its inhabitants are free and protected by the rule of law. But he only saw one side of French society, that of the upwardly mobile bourgeoisie living in the more affluent quarters of Paris. Nowhere in his books does he mention the workers and peasants whose harsh conditions of life formed a subject matter of nineteenth-century French literature.

The idealization of the French did not smother his love of his own country, which in his eyes had remained completely inert since the time of the pharaohs. Espousing liberal ideas after reading Montesquieu and Voltaire, he expressed his admiration for the nation-state and its political institutions, founded as they were on the basis of civic culture. Tahtawi is seen as the father of Egyptian nationalism for having introduced the word "*watan*" (nation) into the political lexicon, which later became a rallying cry. *Watan* meant not the Muslim *umma* but the Egypt of the villages along the banks of the Nile. The urban elites who backed his project had a different perception of religion and were ideologically prepared to express a national awareness similar to the one that had emerged in Europe. From this standpoint, Tahtawi was a vector of acculturation who touched the educated elite, a social minority that had become patriotic in the abstract, in the conviction that religious universalism could not create a nation with a flag and territorial frontiers. Tahtawi detached himself from the religious attitude that considers other faiths inferior, even if he showed respect for Islam. During his time in France Tahtawi was attracted by a brand of religious tolerance, but he failed to grasp that the liberal ideas that he championed were in direct contradiction to the symbolic order that otherwise gave meaning to the lives of Egyptians. The reforms he dreamed of contradicted the interpretation of Islam propounded by the ulemas of Al-Azhar and the Sufi saints. Tahtawi was an elitist in an Egypt where the majority of the population was attached to the traditional Islam of past centuries; ordinary Egyptians saw themselves as members of the *umma*, which included all Muslims. Religious solidarity structured the perception of a political order based on lineage and village on the one hand, and on the other the *umma*, of which the caliph in Istanbul was the incarnation. Europeans were perceived as miscreants plotting against Islam, not as foreigners threatening the interests of Egypt. The Egyptian peasant farmer was steeped in a religious culture that supplied the framework for a coherent social reality. For him, Islam was not so much a set of ritual practices as a way of life that gave meaning to his existence. Despite his religious belief, not unexpectedly, Tahtawi provoked the opposition of conservatives who were loyal to the ancient Islamic tradition. The changes he wanted aroused fears that Islam might be marginalized by an elite that was open to Western culture, implying the blanket secularization of society—which the ulemas of Al-Azhar rejected out of hand.

Paradoxically, his project was not held in check by the conservative forces of Al-Azhar alone; it was the ulemas of Al-Nahda, appealing to the modernization of society, who strangled it by proposing a synthesis between attachment to tradition and the urban elite's aspiration to modernity. The ulemas of Al-Nahda favored a third way between the rigid doctrines of Wahhabism and Tahtawi's modernization, accepting the latter's nationalism but rejecting its liberal substance. They reconciled nationalism with Islam while opposing the secularization of society and of politics. For them, secularization in Europe was justified because of Christianity's intolerance in opposing social progress and scientific discovery, but in Muslim societies they reckoned secularization to be pointless since holy writ recommended the use of reason to uncover the secrets of the natural world created by God. The Egyptian nationalists had accepted this perspective of Al-Nahda, with its nod both to Tahtawi and to Mohammed Abdu. It was as if nationalism had to pay a price for renouncing the secularization of thought, to be accepted by wider public opinion.

Thus, an apology of Islam was necessary, one that would reaffirm with the ulemas of Al-Nahda that Muslim societies had no need to confine their religion to the private sphere, as Europeans did. This was because Islam was "a religion of tolerance, open to science and progress." For the ulemas of Al-Nahda, scientific and technological progress such as railways and steam engines were not the work of the devil. On the contrary, they said, the Europeans had created them by the use of reason, given to man by God so that he could understand and master nature. In the last thirty years of the nineteenth century, it was this consensual message that broke through and was embraced by both Muslims and Christian nationalists in the Arab world. Al-Nahda succeeded in containing Wahhabism, which failed to make inroads among the urban classes of the Middle East, but it also rolled back the modernist project of liberal nationalists like Tahtawi that had followed on from Muhammed Ali's earlier reforms. The drive for modernization had been absorbed by Al-Nahda, and this fact had an important effect on the religious and secular elites of the time. Mohammed Abdu became a consensual intellectual figure who had contrived to spare both Egypt and the rest of the Arab world from an open confrontation between conservatives and modernists; given that, with a few exceptions, both went along with him. While legitimizing nationalism, he had renewed the bond with Islam, which he mobilized as a resource of Arab identity to resist European domination. This operation was made easier by the fact that the would-be dominators were non-Muslims. Had the British and the French been Muslims, the history of the region would probably have been totally different. Fluctuating between territorial nationalism and the universalism of the *umma*, Al-Nahda had no quarrel with the Ottomans—even though Jamal al-Din al-Afghani had condemned the methods of the Caliph Abdulhamid, which had caused him much trouble in Istanbul. Without being a Pan-Islamic movement, Al-Nahda called for Muslim solidarity to resist the colonial ambitions of the European powers. The elitist liberalism of the nineteenth century did not ask for religious reform as long as the Nahda contributed to the birth of nationalism. Liberalism needed Islam to convey the nationalist ideal among the middle classes and beyond. Liberal movement was more concerned by British domination than the need of religious reform. Probably in the mind of many nationalist Egyptians, this task had to be postponed and would be addressed after full independence. They solicited the support of the Ottoman caliph to limit the ambitions of Great Britain, even though the sultan headed a state that did not endorse the separation of church and state. They themselves saw Islam as a political resource of which they could make use in their national struggle. Without roots in the heartlands of Egypt, the nationalist party was not strong enough to stand up to the king, let alone the British colonial governors, as Arabi Pasha's failure to seize power showed very clearly. Arabi Pasha's putsch led to Egypt's loss of independence in 1882 and was not followed by a general uprising of the population, which was as yet unimpressed by nationalist ideas. With no popular support, the nationalists appealed to the other powers competing with Britain for influence, playing them against each other. They turned to France but were abruptly disillusioned when Paris agreed to allow London to place Egypt under its tutelage in exchange for French control over Morocco.

Tahtawi's brand of nationalism, which was continued by Mustafa Kamil (1874–1908, the founder of the Nationalist Egyptian Party) and later by Saad Zaghloul, was permanently confined to urban elites, despite the religious legitimacy given to it by Al-Nahda. It had rallied to its cause the great landowners who opposed the British but who strongly resisted the idea of emancipating the fellahin they were exploiting. The landowners who lived in Cairo or Alexandria and who were generally hostile to any social change were a significant handicap to national awareness, which urgently needed social mobility and cultural changes. The bipolar structure of society prevented the nationalism of the elites from reaching the huge majority of the population, who lived in feudally regulated villages where equality was completely unknown. For ordinary villagers, whose main preoccupation was to cope with the harsh conditions of daily existence, politics was the business of the landlords, on whom they were economically dependent. The British played an active role in maintaining the feudal status quo by discouraging industrial manufacture; they did this to head off any potential competition with their own manufactured goods exported to their colonies. Instead, they encouraged Egypt to specialize in the production of cotton along the banks of the Nile, thus winning allies among the landlords torn between the prospect of independence for their country and their own immediate financial interest. By opposing the creation of a wealth-creating capitalist market in Egypt, Britain impeded the rise of a national middle class that could potentially threaten their own political and economic interests. It condemned Egyptian nationalism to a period of political sterility from 1920 to 1940, despite the nation's accession to independence in 1922. Successive Egyptian governments were led by politicians who embraced a parliamentary regime dominated by representatives of the landlords. The elections, manipulated by the urban and rural elites, excluded the overwhelming mass of the population. Electoral alternation was taking place within the Wafd Party by political professionals who were more interested in enriching themselves than in the emancipation of exploited fellahin. The sterility of this political game, which continued for three decades, created all the necessary conditions for authoritarian populism when the army seized power in the 1950s.

Tahtawi and the elite he influenced underestimated the social transformations that, in Europe, had accompanied or preceded the formation of the nation-state in cultural and economic terms. Carried along as it was by writers and intellectuals, nationalism was not even supported by an economically active, politically autonomous social class. Between 1880 and 1930, Egypt produced such great liberal intellectuals as Qasim Amin, Lutfi Sayyid, Ali Abderrazak, Taha Hussein, and others. But having no support from a national middle class, for whom they might have been the ideological vanguard, they were unable to influence the course of history and were forgotten within one or two generations. Without strong social forces to underpin it, nationalism remains an idealistic aspiration lacking the political means to realize its true goal: a modern state. In a way, Tahtawi, Kamill, and Zaghloul represented bourgeois society, in the European sense of the term, at a time when there was no such thing as a national bourgeoisie in the land of Egypt.

From Liberal Arabism to Radical Arab Nationalism

Historical Syria, known as Bled Echam, was made up of present-day Syria, Lebanon, and historical Palestine. It was the cradle of Arabism that evolved in Syrian intellectual milieu aspiring to an Arab nation-state freed from Ottoman tutelage. These milieus learned about the notions of citizenship, civic rights, and freedom of expression from religious missions (French, British, American, and Russian). These missions were omnipresent in the Middle East from the beginning of the nineteenth century, developing confessional school systems in conformity with the European countries' policy of protecting religious minorities. Attracted as it was by European liberalism, this movement of homegrown nationalists was not at the beginning hostile to the sultan of Istanbul, despite the serious aim of the European powers to weaken the Ottoman Empire by imposing restrictions on its non-Muslim subjects. Butros el Bustani began expressing a non-confessional Syrian patriotism in the 1860s, viewing Syria itself as a part of the Ottoman Empire, which he dreamed might be reorganized on the American federal model. Shocked by the 1860 massacre of Christians, Bustani called for an "Arab Fatherland" within historical Syria that would strengthen the bonds of solidarity between Arab Muslims, Christians, and Jews. Bustani had only limited influence in his lifetime, and a few years later other intellectuals in the region were to develop his ideas, although with an anti-Ottoman tilt. One of these, Najib Azoury, a Christian from the mountains of Lebanon, went so far as to suggest separating the caliphate from the Ottomans and bestowing it on a descendant of the Prophet. This Arab caliphate, whose seat would be Mecca, would be the symbol of the unity of the Muslim *umma* and would have a religious function, giving its blessing to a political leader who would rule an Arab fatherland extending from the Suez Canal to the Persian Gulf, including the Arabian Peninsula. The capital of this empire would be Damascus, the former centerpiece of the brilliant Omayyad civilization. The fact that here was a Christian who wanted an Arab caliphate—probably along the lines of Roman Catholicism—reveals the sentiment of exaltation of Arabness among Christians. They were anxious about the loss of authority of the *millets*, which used to ensure the application of the rights of the respective religions. The reforms of the nineteenth century (Tanzimat) led to the end of the *millets*, to the confusion of the minorities of Arab Christians and Jews. For these non-Muslims who were nonetheless fiercely Arab, Pan-Arabism was an alternative that allowed them to remain faithful to themselves. Nevertheless, they were defending the liberal ideas they had absorbed from their education in the mission schools.

By the end of the nineteenth century, anti-Ottoman sentiment among nationalists had grown formidably on account of Istanbul's determination to impose the Turkish language on its provinces, to the detriment of Arabic. Pan-Arab nationalism also developed in parallel with the nationalism of the Young Turks of the CUP (Committee of Union and Progress), who sought to make themselves distinct from the Ottomans by founding a Turkish nation backed by *turanism.* The rejection of Muslim-Arabness by the Young Turks confirmed the Arab nationalists in the idea that the Ottomans used Islam to devalue the notion of Arabness, to which they were foreign. They claimed that the Turks, originally a nomad people from Central Asia, had played no role whatever in the brilliant Muslim-Arab civilization and had merely taken military advantage of its decline to seize the caliphate, whereas they had no legitimate right to usurp that noble function, which properly belonged to the Arabs. The European countries encouraged this notion of Arabness with a view to promoting their own colonial ambitions on the continent, viewing the Ottoman Empire as an obstacle to their own eastward expansion.

At the outbreak of the First World War, in which the Ottoman Empire took part as an ally of Germany, the demands of the nationalist Arabs were backed by the British and the French. The Ottomans saw this as an act of betrayal and punished it with savage repression, thus widening the gulf between the two camps even further. Nevertheless, the arguments of the European-educated nationalists, whether they were Muslim or Christian, went unheeded by the rural masses—that is, the majority of the population who were more receptive to the ulemas and imams of the mosques favorable to solidarity with the Ottomans. The mass of Muslims only changed their minds about the Ottomans when urged to do so by Sharif Hussein, who was followed in his quality as guardian of the Holy Places of Islam and descendant of the tribe of Hashem, to which the Prophet himself had belonged. It was as if, in the Arab world, the mobilization of the masses had to be accomplished by way of Islam and the sacred Qur'an. Sharif Hussein also appealed to Arab ethnocentricism, just like the urban Arab nationalists did, but his appeal made explicit reference to jihad, holy war, with the idea that the Ottomans had strayed from the true way of the Prophet. This won Hussein the support of the Bedouin tribes and the rural population. The anti-Ottoman urban elites now saw an undreamt-of opportunity to create the Arab state they longed for, hence their enthusiasm for Sharif Hussein, who saw himself as caliph, at the head of a political entity that would replace the Ottoman Empire.

Better still, the British promised to help this happen. The rejection of the Turks by the nationalists led them to support the Arab Revolt of 1916, providing the rebels with money and weapons. This European assistance did not worry the nationalists, who were ready to use any means to see their dream realized. To fight the Muslim Turks in alliance with the Christian British and French demonstrated quite clearly that, as far as they were concerned, Islam was not a political marker. The nationalists were unconcerned about the ideological differences between their vision of a secularized world and that of Sharif Hussein, who was a tribal leader deeply attached to religious legitimacy. Blinded by their anti-Ottoman sentiments, they may have thought that an independent Arab monarchy was bound to evolve toward the constitutional, parliamentary model.

After the defeat of the Turks, to which Hussein felt he had contributed very substantially, Hussein entered Damascus at the head of his troops in April 1920. He duly proclaimed the establishment of an Arab kingdom extending from the Gulf to Sinai, including the Arabian Peninsula. But the European powers went back on their promises, signing the Sykes–Picot Agreement, which revealed their implacable hostility to the project of a unified Arab kingdom. The British and French had secretly agreed upon the partition of the territories of the Ottoman Empire. When French troops marched to Damascus from Lebanon in 1920 to drive out the ephemeral King Hussein, the nationalists felt utterly betrayed by their former allies. Sharif Hussein retired to the Hejaz, of which he had been the emir before his adventure of 1916. After the abolition of the caliphate by Mustafa Kemal in 1924, Hussein called a conference in which the delegates of several Muslim countries took part; all recognized him as the new caliph and as the symbol of the unity of the Islamic *umma*. Within a few months, however, Hussein was driven out of the Hejaz by the Wahhabis and took refuge in Iraq under the protection of the British—who, to console him, created two monarchies for his sons, one in Iraq itself and the other in Transjordan. Thereafter the Hashemites remained the allies of their British protectors, definitively repudiating the Pan-Arab project and accepting the Sykes–Picot Agreement. Their immediate political interests had prevailed over the Pan-Arab dream they had incarnated for a few years.

The wanderings of Sharif Hussein, who was so comprehensively manipulated in the battle against the Ottomans, had a considerable influence on the ideological orientations of Arab nationalist thought, which now moved away from liberal ideals of France and Britain to espouse a culturalist populism that was closer to that of Germany. By the end of the 1920s Arabism had abandoned the liberal ideology to which it had adhered in the nineteenth century, in favor of a cultural model inspired by Pan-German ideas and a populism that exalted the virtues of the Arab people.

Between the two world wars, a climate of suspicion and hostility toward Europe prevailed among the Muslim and Christian nationalists who aspired to an Arab nation in which the confessional division would be abolished. The Sykes–Picot Agreement and the promises made to the Jews of Europe for their installation in Palestine were an appalling shock to the groups that had allied themselves with the British against the Ottomans.

These, then, were the historical circumstances that fashioned a new Arabist ideology that was expanded and deepened by the writings of Sati al-Husri (1880–1968), inspired by Johann Gottlieb Fichte and Johann Gottfried von Herder. Sati al-Husri was a former high official civil servant of the Ottoman Empire; he joined Sharif Hussein in 1916 and thereafter worked for his son in Iraq until 1941, at which time he was involved in a conspiracy against British interests and had to flee to Egypt. There he established a comparison between Pan-Germanism and Pan-Arabism, which he believed had many aspects in common. Rejecting the French concept of the nation and the cosmopolitanism of the European Enlightenment, al-Husri was also suspicious of communist internationalism. As a consequence, he developed his own "culturalist" vision of the nation, which appeared to him like an organic corpus held together by language and the sense of a shared past. Having studied the history of nineteenth-century Germany and Italy, he dreamed of an Arab Otto von Bismarck or Arab Giuseppe Garibaldi who would reunite the Mashreq and the Maghreb around what was for him the Prussia (or the Piedmont) of the Arab world—namely, Egypt. Publishing books and giving conferences in Cairo, he rallied to his Arabist cause a number of Egyptian writers who were attracted by the idea that their country had a historic role to play in the destiny of the Arab world. His views were taken up by nationalist intellectuals and militants, among them Zaki al-Arsuzi (1899–1967) and Michel Aflaq (1910–89); these idealized the Arab language and militated for a united Arab nation driven by a mystical resurrection (the word *ba'ath* means "resurrection") to accomplish its eternal mission. From the Baathist standpoint, the nation is not a sociological entity but a linguistic collectivity based on a fervent discourse exalting an Arabness, of which Islam is the formative essence. The Baath militants had no critical distance in terms of the conservative interpretation of Islam perceived as truly based on revolutionary virtues. Aflaq, the Christian cofounder of the Baath Party, was able to write in 1947 that Islam was a religion of social justice and the soul of the Arab people. It was the exact opposite of what the nineteenth- and early twentieth-century Western religious missions, serving the interests of their respective countries, had taught.

Thus, the ideology of the Baath Party, shaped in the 1930s by the writings of Zaki al-Arsuzi and the activism of Michel Aflaq and Salah al-Bitar, transcended confessional frontiers with its anti-Western ideas and its mythical ideal of the Arabic language. With this mutation, Pan-Arabism was able to turn its back on the monarchical parenthesis of Sharif Hussein while praising moral values of Islam.

The Second World War favored the propagation of nationalism among a middle class that was on the rise due to a relative broadening of education, along with economic and social change. By the close of the 1940s the various Arab armies had assimilated a generation of officers who strongly resented old-style professional politicians with links to landlords and other powerful figures. The nationalist discourse, which had become more ideologically coherent with Sati al-Husri's intellectual contribution, was very attractive to younger officers, embracing the mission of affirming their countries' independence and modernizing their societies and economies. The Baath Party began to infiltrate the armies of Syria and Iraq, setting up secret cells. A dynamic of direct army involvement in politics was evinced by the first coup d'état in Syria and accelerated by the creation of Israel in 1948. An era of charismatic young officers haranguing enthusiastic crowds had begun, giving nationalism a popular base that it had never had before. The Arab nation, also called the *umma*, became a quasi-religious ideal riding a wave of popular fervor.

The geopolitical upheavals in the region that followed the Second World War created a state of euphoria in the Arab world that was to last until 1967. The golden age of Arabism was between 1940 and 1960, at which time it had immense potential for popular mobilization. In 1952 the Egyptian monarchy was overthrown by a group of officers led by Col. Gamal Abdel Nasser, hero of the crowds from Baghdad to Casablanca—and, indeed, brought into being the stereotype of what we still call the Arab street. In the 1950s Nasser was a hero to whole populations whose hopes he was able to articulate. The diplomatic fiasco that followed the 1956 triple aggression of the British, the French, and the Israelis made Nasser the first Arab figure to successfully defy Western domination. He declared himself ready to liberate Palestine, unite the Arab world, and set it on the road to full emancipation and modernization. Carried forward by the unstoppable dynamic of decolonization and taking advantage of the Cold War, which allowed him to tap into the diplomatic and military resources of socialist Eastern Europe, for a decade Nasser embodied a power that for the first time in more than a century had rolled back colonialism.

The Nasser epoch shifted the Arab center of gravity from Damascus to Cairo. Nasser transformed Egyptian nationalism into Pan-Arabism, a novelty that both delighted and irritated the leaders of the Baath who felt robbed of their ideology. Indeed, Nasser had pushed them into the background at the moment when their dream seemed about to come true. But this was no time for distractions, and the masses now expected concrete actions to unite Egypt and Syria, in the form of the United Arab Republic, which would be joined by the other countries of the region as an established state. One month after this proclamation, in February 1958, the "Arab street" was already restive in Jordan and Lebanon, demanding that their respective governments join the United Arab Republic. In July 1958 the Iraqi monarchy crumbled in the face of a popular uprising and was overthrown by the army.[4] After a short period of chaos, the Baathists took over in Baghdad and Damascus through military coups—or rather, appeared to take power, for in reality the generals merely used the symbolic power of the Baath to set up authoritarian regimes.

Since the fall of the Hashemite dynasty in Iraq, the monarchies had felt directly threatened by neighboring republics. They also mistrusted their own armies, whose officers were sympathetic to Nasser's call to overthrow every regime that had allied itself with the "Western imperialists." Thus, in the wake of the Cold War, a bitter rivalry emerged in the region between republics embracing anti-Western nationalism and monarchies cleaving to religious tradition and legitimacy. The monarchies were forced to seek support from the Western powers and to become indispensable Western allies in a region blessed with more than 60 percent of the world's oil reserves. Meanwhile, at the other end of the Arab world, in North Africa, decolonization was proceeding by violent stages in Morocco and Tunisia, which won their independence in 1956, while in Algeria a bloody liberation war started in November 1954. The North Africans were encouraged by the Arab countries, which gave them symbolic and diplomatic support.

By the 1960s all the Arab countries, with the exception of Qatar, were formally independent and run either by presidents who had seized power by military coup d'état or by kings and emirs belonging to family dynasties. The revolutionary nationalism of the republican regimes, which had previously carried all before it, was checked by the military defeat of June 1967, which exposed the weaknesses of governments hobbled by excessive centralization, underperforming economic sectors, and incompetent, corrupt state employees. The monarchies exploited this situation to re-legitimize themselves in the eyes of Arab public opinion appalled by the scale of the military disaster of 1967.

They contributed financial aid to rebuild the Syrian, Egyptian, and Jordanian armies. Col. Muammar Gaddafi's 1969 coup d'état, which deposed King Senussi of Libya, was anachronistic from this point of view. However, it was not until the war of October 1973 against Israel that hostility between the republics and the monarchies began to ebb, the monarchies having financed the Egyptian army's liberation of the Sinai Peninsula. The rise in the price of oil that followed this war gave even more influence to the monarchies that became fabulously wealthy within the space of a few years. By the 1970s radical Arab nationalism had lost its battle both with the monarchies and with the West. It had comprehensively failed to keep its promise to modernize society, develop the economy, and put an end to underdevelopment.

Notes

1. A similar doctrine had appeared in the Maghreb several centuries earlier, under the direction of Ibn Toumert, who founded in 1121 an immense Almohad Empire covering the whole of North Africa and the greater part of Spain.

2. Quoted in Yves Besson, *Ibn Sa'ud, roi bédouin: La naissance du royaume d'Arabie Saoudite* (Lausanne: Éditions des Trois continents, 1980), 1.

3. Rifa'a Mohammed al-Tahtawi, *L'or de Paris: Relations de voyage 1826–1831*, traduit de l'arabe par Anouar Louca (Paris: Sindbad, 1988).

4. Forty-two years after the Arab Revolt of 1916, the nationalists had finally avenged themselves on the Hashemites, who had betrayed them by accepting the Sykes–Picot Agreement.

2

The Ideological Limitations of Radical Arab Nationalism

RADICAL ARAB NATIONALISTS took over in several Arab countries in the 1950s and 1960s by promising the masses that they would catch up with the West, develop the economy, and liberate Palestine. Two decades later none of these promises had been kept, and the countries are still unable to generate sufficient wealth to supply the people's needs. It is useful at this point to analyze the failure of radical nationalism—above all, in countries like Algeria and Iraq, endowed with wealth coming from oil.

The hypothesis in this book is that the failure finds its origins in the nature of the state power in which the executive branch could not tolerate the autonomy of the legislative and judiciary branches. The regime fought any kind of grassroots organizations or intermediate bodies—parties, trade unions, associations—and the press was reduced to total obedience, parroting the line of the leader, who would brook no contradiction. The nation had to be purged of all political conflict with the utopian aim of depoliticizing society in order to supposedly strengthen its cohesion and unity. Society had to be united behind the sole idea of national unity supposedly threatened by the divergent interests of individuals and social groups. This idealism inspired economic policies that spurned the elementary laws of political economy to affirm the superiority of the state administration. The objective was to create a nonconflictual society and a merchant sector that would rise above the respective interests of those participating in the economy for the supposed benefit of all. The discourse was dependent on the notion of "the people," as opposed to "society," and it was generally hostile to the market, which was accused of harming the original unity of the people. The rationale of the system as a whole was to lock all trading activity inside the state's sphere of influence, thus begetting a controlled economy that was expected to satisfy the people's needs in terms of jobs, housing, health, education, and transportation. The overall objective was to create a system for producing and sharing wealth, which would in turn ensure social justice. For all this to happen, the state had to control the economy, and, in doing so, it had to promise to satisfy the social necessities of the population, especially the poorest.

President Gamal Abdel Nasser of Egypt put this model to the vote in 1962, and it was adopted by referendum with 99 percent approval. His guiding text, called the National Action Charter, contained an implicit contract between the people and the state: the state would cover the essential needs of the people, who in exchange would forfeit their civic rights, particularly the right to freely elect their own representatives. In 1976 Algerian president Houari Boumediene adopted a similar text—also called a national charter—to give himself a popular legitimacy that would dismiss the legitimacy of electoral democracy. In Syria, Iraq, and Libya, the same political dynamic was at work, stirring up the people with fine words while preventing by law the emergence of a civil society independent of the state power.

The ideological limitations of radical Arab nationalism are discernible on three levels. First, it ignores the international system of pricing whose rationale and constraints are unavoidable. Second, it refuses any kind of compromise with the private economic sector and the worker's unions. Third, it underestimates the cultural aspects of development perceived as a technical matter.

Radical Arab Nationalism against the Market Economy

Nasser's Egypt, Boumediene's Algeria, Saddam Hussein's Iraq, and Hafiz al-Assad's Syria invested several hundred billion dollars in the creation of modern industrial sectors in order to stimulate their national economies to development and growth. This effort was accomplished within the framework of state-owned economy rejecting out of hand the pricing systems of an international market that they suspected of hampering national development. The private economic sector was held in check in the expectation of its extinction or absorption by the public sector. Aside from its basic attributions such as printing money and exercising a monopoly on violence, the state had to provide employment and satisfy the social requirements of the people. It had to find a way of substituting itself for free market forces to protect the poor. For government leaders, the option of a controlled economy was expected to favor the accumulation of wealth that would then be apportioned more justly by a state that proclaimed itself to be on the side of the poor.

This belief was shared by the masses, who expected the state to supply their every need in matters of work, health, education, and so on. There was very little determined opposition to the state's takeover of the economy. A consensus emerged: the generous state would stand against the private interests of any social group that was being enriched by the free market. In reality, the option of an administered price system was the only option available because the political logic of the populist Arab regimes is incompatible with a situation where the social groups can organize themselves in order to defend their own specific interests. The market includes different and opposite classes in the production and sharing of wealth, and these classes clash over the price of goods as well as over the differing interests of employers' unions, workers' unions, and the associations of various professions whose purpose is to defend their members. In this way the market unleashes a dynamic of conflict settled in the framework of the rule of law and democracy. Jürgen Habermas saw it when he observed that the rule of law corresponds to the rules of the market to the extent that it is built on institutional counterweight to the executive power.[1]

The state-owned economic sector was set up to allow the leaders to use the economy as a tool for securing political obedience. The objective was to make every individual an employee of the boss-state, which could then discourage all political dissent with the threat of redundancy. Socialism was proclaimed as the justification for this model since it could legitimize the single-party system and the privatization of power. It gave an ideological justification to forbid autonomous employers' associations and free workers' unions. This ideological orientation had the favor of Arab communists, who dreamed of a classless society that would leave capitalism behind forever. They called this "the way of non-capitalist development."[2] What Nasser, Assad, and Boumediene liked about socialism—the philosophical basis of which they entirely rejected—was the single-party system that justified their appropriation of power and the installation of a state-run economy. They adhered to socialism as long as it provided an ideological framework to control society and to avoid the rule of law. Under a so-called socialist regime, civil society is prevented from forming, and, notably, employers and workers are prevented from claiming any kind of empowerment to defend their interest. It should be emphasized that Arab socialism, hostile as it was to Marxist political philosophy, was not seen as an overhaul of capitalism's contradictions; instead, it was perceived by Arab leaders as a means of monopolizing power forever in the state apparatus and institutions.

In this way a broad public economic sector was built in order to create more wealth for the benefit of the people. Alas, within a short period it turned into a burden for the state budget, which had to finance its deficits. Waste, bad management, predation, and corruption became so rampant that they contributed to the failure of economic policies originally designed to create wealth. It is not the public nature of the sector that is the problem; rather, the problem is the absence of an independent judiciary. A public sector is an absolute necessity in underdeveloped countries where private capital is drawn to speculation and very seldom invested in industrial projects. However, a public sector is only efficient or profitable when the judiciary system is able to protect it from waste and corruption. Only an independent judiciary could have prevented the embezzlement and waste upon state enterprises that were plundered by networks of clients expressly organized to steal the maximum from a state unable to protect public property from the greed of its own agents. There is a difference between a public sector that produces wealth in the shade of a competitive system and an indebted public sector subsidized by the state budget and by the loss of purchasing power of the consumers. An economic sector in deficit is not public because it does not serve the public interest. It serves the interest of a regime that needs to redistribute wealth around a client network that in turn serves the regime as a go-between and a social base. The price is very high, both for the collectivity and for the buying power of fixed revenues. The injection of huge amount of currency without creation of corresponding value disturbs the relative equilibrium within the price system and impoverishes the poorest even further by prompting a transfer of value from which speculators will profit and amass gigantic fortunes. If the rules of the market are ignored for political reasons, the price system avenges itself in a way that is worse than the market inequalities. This is the real cause of economic dysfunction and the pauperization of the majority of the population.

The relevant contradiction in economics is not the one that brings the public and private sector into conflict but the one that makes the distinction between profit, which is a creation of value, and rent, as a transfer of value already created.[3] In an underdeveloped economy, the antagonism is between unearned income and the kind of real added value that can broaden a country's economic base.

In order to meet the state's huge needs for currency, the banking system has to obey administrative injunctions regardless of the volume of wealth created. The independence of the central bank issuing the money supply is suppressed in order to print enough money for the governments' requirements. The quantity of currency in circulation does not reflect the economic needs of the market but of political necessities of the regime. The government effectively arrogates to itself the right to fix the parity of the local currency without reference to such constraints as the external balance of payments or the productive capacity of the economy. In this way it makes up for budget deficits and chronic debt by skimming off the buying power of fixed income. The exchange rate of any local currency with foreign currencies is a variable that determines the purchasing power of wages and the levels of consumption of imported food products. By injecting huge sums of money into the economy without any corresponding physical productivity, the state again shakes up the price system that sets the relation between wages and cost of living. Wage levels are too low, so many young people forsake agriculture and seek other opportunities in the informal sectors of the cities. A fall in real wages is engineered by manipulating the exchange rate, by which the state procures supplementary revenues for itself in local currency. The generosity of populism is praiseworthy indeed, but its results have proven contrary to its goals, limiting the productive capacities of the economy and creating colossal private fortunes. All this impoverishes the middle class and increases poverty.

To preempt hunger riots, the state establishes subsidies for essential products. The populist leaders believed that they could make corrections to the market rules by administrative coercion. By doing this, they freed themselves from any political constraints requiring them to submit to the economic criteria of international competition. For example, autonomous professional associations and free unions would never have accepted the large-scale manipulation of local currency that heavily diminished the purchasing power of salaries. The market is not a technical mechanism; it is a social system regulated by a balance of power that favors the creation of wealth consistent with a legal framework that gives everyone involved the possibility of defending his own interests. An effective political policy with a historical perspective is one that prepares the national economy to compete in the international arena with a view to exporting commodities produced locally. We should remember that the products of different national civil societies are bought and sold in the marketplace of the world economy. What do the Arab nations produce today for the international economy? Their wealth derives principally from raw materials, tourism, money earned abroad by their own emigrant workers, and, for certain countries like Egypt, international aid.

Radical Arab nationalism sought to embed the economic dynamic within a political-administrative framework that would ensure equality among consumers. This utopia is opposed, in consequence, to the emergence of a civil society that could later claim the autonomy of the economic sphere. Radical Arab nationalism cannot deal with economy without using it as a political resource. The utopia consisted of building a modern economy with the latest machines and technology outside the rationale of the marketplace. It is a fetishist approach of economy that ignores that production and repartition obey rules of their own. The most sophisticated technology in the world cannot create a modern economy by itself. The machine is the technological

51

aspect of a social organism in which labor and capital reach a compromise under the pressure imposed by the international price system. The level of marginal productivity of capital and that of the rate of exploitation of work are linked to wage rates and are in tune with the wage rates of international competition. Profitability is therefore not something inherent to the machine but to the social organism itself. As part of the technical support mechanism of a social relationship, the machine draws its efficiency from a political-judicial framework known as the rule of law. The modern economy consists of an ensemble of production techniques working within a judicial framework that protects its capacity to compete. The techniques of production would lose all their efficiency if they were cut off from their judicial framework, and this signifies that the technical elements of the market are not in themselves productive. A machine in France or Japan does not have the same marginal productivity that it has in Algeria or Egypt for the simple reason that the use of the machine is consistent with the entire social system—not only in its economic aspects but also in its political and juridical ones. The productivity of the machine is linked to the levels of intensity of the work carried out by workers. It is also tied to the rate of exploitation of work that, in the West, is set by the *rapport de force* that exists between unions and employers. Deprived of free unions, public sector workers in the Arab countries fall back on passive resistance, which translates into the underuse and the reduced productivity of their machinery. It is no paradox to state that without free unionism, the return on capital achieved by machines will never match that achieved by international (i.e., foreign) competitors.

The same can be said of capital itself. Ten million dollars is viewed merely as a sum of money in Algeria, whereas in Great Britain or Sweden it is viewed as capital with the power to create further commercial value. In the public sector in Algeria, such an amount of money will be quickly wasted. The colossal revenues proceeding from the export of hydrocarbons in countries like Libya, Algeria, and Iraq do not have the same commercial value or the same financial potential for gain as they would have in France or the United States because they do not have the same legal protection against arbitrary confiscation, waste, and corruption. The construction of one mile of freeway in Algeria or Saudi Arabia today costs those countries considerably more than it would in Switzerland or Norway. Algerian generals and Saudi princes routinely take large sums for themselves from every investment the state makes, just as the feudal lords of Europe did in the Middle Ages.[4] This unearned income raises the prices of products and diminishes competition with competitors abroad. Money is only capital within the framework of a marketplace regulated by the rule of law. Otherwise it is just wealth designed to be destroyed in consumption and waste. That is, the market is a process regulated by a twofold balance of power: between the state power and civil society and between the workers and the owners of business under the pressure of the international competition. Economism supposes that the market economy rests only on machinery while it is actually the result of conflicting interests. A market economy needs to be built from the bottom inside society and not from the top. If economy is embedded within society top, it creates wealth; if it is under the control of the state, it entails deficits. It explains the economic failures of Arab countries in which political rationality takes precedence over economic rationality.

In a rentier economy, the wealth is not created locally and the state budget does not rely on local taxes. The state finances do not depend on society; on the contrary, society depends economically on the state. This means that Arab economies are in pre-Ricardian stage in which the concepts of economics (profit, wages, interest rate, labor theory, marginal cost, price system, and so on) have little relevance. The local economy is better understood with a physiocratic model in which the rent, as defined by Ricardo, is the main income. The object of political economy is the mechanism of the creation of value accumulated and distributed through a price system obeying its own logic, as indicated by Léon Walras. Of course, there exist in Arab countries goods that are produced, but this trading activity belongs to the sphere of economic anthropology rather than that of economics. To put it another way, the logic that dominates the sphere of goods and services reflects a pre-Ricardian physiocratic theory. The goal of political economy pertains to the value produced within the framework of a market that submits production to competition by way of a system of prices designed to allocate rare resources. Driven by the dynamic of competition, the Walrassian price system adjusts supply to demand by following the trend toward lower marginal productivity of production factors.[5] In the state-owned economy of many Arab countries, there is no competition due to the sheer weight of the state's economic sector; moreover, the state is the principal entrepreneur with the particularity that it is locally subject to no financial constraints whatsoever. It can remain aloof from the latter because of the exportation of raw materials or oil. Without financial constraints and with no shortage of currency, it has no need to rationalize work processes like the international competitors. The income from oil exports, tourism, and/or money sent from abroad by emigrant workers, international aid, and the manipulation of local exchange rates allow the entrepreneur state to defy economic rationality. The populist model bears a major contradiction: the sphere of production and exchange, which normally pertains to the private sector, is made public while the sphere of the state, which is normally a public concern, is privatized by a narrow circle of leaders. Arab socialist experiences have all failed because they were all undermined by this fatal contradiction. These regimes set out to build a public economy, whereas government is outside of public control. This incoherence was lethal because it enfeebled an economic activity that was more and more regulated by the logic of a rentier-state.

Hence the stagnation and impoverishment of populations whose needs in terms of housing, health, education, transport, and so on were steadily less satisfied as time went on.

The populist economic model of the 1950s and 1960s reached its limit in Egypt in the 1970s and in Algeria in the 1980s. Egypt tried to salvage its sinking economy by appealing for private investment because it has no major exterior income. This new policy, inaugurated by Anwar Sadat, Nasser's successor, had the long-range objective of reestablishing the original rules of the open market. The reform was accompanied by a political change, which brought an end to the single-party system. Sadat broke with the ideological options contained in the National Action Charter of 1962, which was replaced in 1974 by the October Charter; this called into question the social contract by which people give up the right to elect freely their representatives to gain in return social rights. Under Sadat's regime, Egyptians were in theory permitted to elect opposition members of parliament, and the state ceased to meet their social expectations. Algeria took the same path of reform in the mid-1980s, when it came under pressure from a substantial drop in the world oil price. The single-party system was abolished in 1989, and private capital investment was solicited to finance activities that had previously been state monopolies. In both countries, parties were formed, privately run newspapers sprang up, and the freedom to criticize the government was recognized, but there was no move to install a different regime, as there had been in Latin America and Eastern Europe. It was as if economic reforms and political changes had been set in motion by the leaders only to strengthen the existing regime, which blatantly rigged elections to ensure a permanent parliamentary majority for itself. By taking the path of reform and then refusing to allow any political transition, the Egyptian and Algerian regimes lost their coherence: they are neither populist nor democratic. In fact, they have the flaws of both systems as far as populations have no way of choosing their own representatives and the state can no longer meet their social needs. Economically, the reforms spawned a form of private speculative capital that grew up in the shadow of the old client networks sponsored by high state officials, both civilian and military. The appeal for private capital favored the emergence of colossal fortunes held by individuals who formed a kind of monetary bourgeoisie perfectly adapted to the ideological incoherence of the Egyptian and Algerian regimes. With its exclusive links to speculators and financial predators, this bourgeoisie had no democratic inclination whatsoever and even less desire to break with a regime that allowed it to reproduce and grow ever stronger. Sensing that the competition of an open market would annihilate the rent-seeking mechanism that is the source of its wealth, this new class even opposed the liberalization of economic activities, a policy that prevented the broadening of access to business. To start a private economic activity, one needs the support of a high-ranking officer or civil servant to join the accumulation club. So, Egypt and Algeria underwent a period of speculative capitalism, held in place by a wealthy bourgeoisie that was fiercely antiliberal and antidemocratic. It is no surprise that this bourgeoisie was horrified by the Arab Spring of 2011 and supported the coups d'état in Algeria and Egypt that followed on the heels of free elections.

POLITICAL ECONOMY AS A SOCIAL AND HISTORICAL SCIENCE

Political economy is a social science and as such has a historical underpinning. It is the study of the empirical process of value creation through labor as measured by the concepts of wages, profit, interest rates, and so on. These concepts revolve around the problem of the measurement of value created by the social mechanisms that prompted the emergence of the

European bourgeoisie in the eighteenth century. The fundamental concepts of political economy were worked out by Adam Smith and David Ricardo to manage the distribution of wealth based on the *rapports de force* within the merchant sphere. Karl Marx's critique showed that this distribution was unjust to the true creators of value, who were held back by low wages, but the neoclassical reaction to his ideas was to recast the theory of Smith and Ricardo and refuse that labor would be the sole source of value but merely a factor of production among other factors, subject to the law of marginal return. The main hypothesis of the neoclassical theory—the blueprint of a pure and perfect free market economy—liberates an underlying dynamic of diminishing wages and diminishing profits. In the theoretical and unreal neoclassical world, should there ever be a pure and perfect free market economy, wages and profits would both stand forever at zero.

This approach, which dominated economic thinking between 1870 and 1930, contributed heavily to the 1929 crash, which robbed it of legitimacy and paved the way for the Keynesian economics that accompanied the welfare state ideal in Europe until the 1970s. The decline of the welfare state and the coming of globalization revived the idea of the neoclassical theory as a basis for a new liberalism. This doctrine was enshrined in the Washington Consensus on economic reform achieved by the International Monetary Fund, the World Bank, the World Trade Organization, and the US Treasury, abetted by the think tanks that served as laboratories for their ideas. Basically, it recommended dismantling the tariff system and freeing competition to take advantage of the low wage levels in developing countries. The calculation was that, following the full development of capital on an international scale, jobs would become harder to find and wages would rise in the countries of the southern hemisphere until they matched the wages of the countries of the north.

The neoliberal theory of the Washington Consensus "corrected" the neoclassical theory, just as the neoclassical theory "corrected" Ricardo's and Smith's work. Its mistake was to commodify or reify the concepts and isolate them from their sociological and historical context. The error was also conceptual since it generalized the laws of the market to nonmarket goods such as health, security, education, communications, and so on, which are indispensable to economic development. These nonmarket goods constitute what the early-twentieth-century English economist Alfred Marshall called "external economies": they do not create wealth, but without them wealth cannot be created. This approach of the market consists of measuring all goods against the yardstick of marginal productivity, including the health and security services. The objective of the neoliberal utopia is to submit all aspects of social existence to market forces, including the domestic sphere, in which fathers, mothers, and children would obey an economic rationale in all their relationships. This dehumanization, as Karl Polanyi would say, expresses a basic ignorance of the market—which is a rational organization for the production and exchange of goods distributed through a pricing system regulated by wages and profit margins. If the neoliberal utopia denied the historic character of the market, the statist utopia outright rejected its laws. An illustration of this is the experience of the Soviet Union, which attempted to build a modern productive economy independent of market forces. Third world populism, of which radical Arab nationalism is one version, is also hostile to the free market, which is accused of functioning in favor of the rich. There are two extreme positions, neoliberal and populist. The former underestimates the historic character of the market while the latter seeks to substitute state administration for it. Nowhere in the world is there a genuinely free market because its forces are so powerful that they threaten to blow society apart. It has to be regulated to prevent monopolies from skewing the effects of competition and holding consumers hostage.

The rule of law is indispensable to any society organized in the form of a market, both to protect its most human aspects and to preserve nonmarket products from the logic of the marketplace. This was the teaching of Karl Polanyi, who saw in the advent of the market the greatest change in the history of mankind. But the necessary regulation of the market does not signify its negation or some kind of utopian substitution for it by a government-controlled economy. If the government overmanipulates prices, the market takes its revenge on the consumers who have the lowest purchasing power by generating a rent-seeking mechanism. When the government attempts to control it, the market doubles back on itself and generates a black market, where the prices reflect "true" value. The regulatory system for prices expresses a level of capital viability and a degree of productivity in the labor force under conditions of international competition because the price system we have now is not national but global. A car, a pound of meat, or a ton of cement have the same real value in Paris as they do in Cairo. The artificial parities between nonconvertible local currencies, along with state subsidies, inhibit integration into the international price system.

There exists a dialectic relation between the categories of society, market, and state well analyzed by Karl Polanyi in his major work *The Great Transformation*, about England in the late eighteenth century, where land and labor force had become commodities within the context of a nascent capitalism in the grip of an implacable pricing system. Using historical data, Polanyi explained that, while the market is now ineluctable and no human collectivity can escape it, it also has the capacity to destroy the human substance of social existence if there is no rule of law to circumscribe its blind destructive power. The Marxists were obviously the first to grasp this, but only a few of them, such as the Russian Yevgeni Preobrajensky, understood that it had to be circumvented, not tackled head on. Léon Walras' work on the prices of the market could have written, echoing David Hume: "We control the price system by obeying it."

Populism against Society

Populism is hardly specific to Arab countries. It first appeared in Russia in the late nineteenth century, with populists denouncing the evil effect of capitalism on the peasant population, and in the United States at around the same time, when farmers found their livelihoods threatened by agricultural machines. In Latin America, populism expressed the peasants' demand for justice when they were exploited by wealthy landowners allied with the interests of American companies. Populism, in fact, is an ideology that has spread wherever there are traditional societies dislocated by a late-arriving capitalism that obstructs economic development. The social groups and individuals that are the victims of such capitalism cultivate values that idealize the people in general and the farming population in particular, an attitude that favors the emergence of authoritarian ideologies represented by messianic leaders who promise to defend the weak and reestablish justice. Italy in the 1920s and 1930s, Latin America in the first half of the twentieth century, and certain Arab countries from the 1950s to the 1970s all produced national variants of populism.

Influenced at the beginning by liberal values, Arab nationalism grew radicalized in the 1930s and 1940s and became popular when it resorted to the populist perception of Western domination. The texts of Sati al-Husri (1880–1967), Zaki al-Arsuzi (1899–1968), and Michel Aflaq (1910–89), and later of the Baath Party, the National Liberation Front (Front de Libération Nationale), and the speeches of Nasser, all express an enchanted vision of politics in which the people, the guardians of the noblest traditions of the country's past, reject injustice and claim their right to participate in the modernity from which they have been excluded by malicious foreigners. This ideology indicates that Arab society is no longer traditional, but it is not economically and culturally modern either. The economy of self-sufficiency has been destroyed by currency exchange, community solidarity has been dissipated by diverging individual interests, and the bonds of allegiance to tribe and religious brotherhood have been weakened. Populism promises to rescue a social cohesion that is under threat from the economic and sociological changes that have been taking place since the mid-nineteenth century. It seeks an answer to this identity crisis by mobilizing individuals and social groups that are merged willy-nilly into a broad ensemble that it perceives as an entity called "The People." These are the cornerstone characteristics of radical Arab nationalism, which is a synthesis of modernist aspirations and utopian expectations. It attempts to build a homogenized modern nation by a line of reasoning that insists on the cohesion and unity of the national group while remaining ominously silent about the individual's rights. This synthesis successfully led the struggle against colonial domination that was seeking to take advantage of the region.

Nationalism in its radical form in Egypt, Algeria, and Syria was a response to British and French domination and their disdain for native peoples. Radical Arab regimes formed to defend the national group, a supra-organic entity in which individuals have duties but no rights. Sublimated by this line, the national collectivity is supposedly represented by a leader who alone is authorized to speak in its name. Any individual could be arrested or imprisoned without trial if accused of conspiring against the people or its leader. Colonel Nasser's regime was the prototype of this system, which was abstractly kind to the people but very cruel to any person who expressed doubt or criticism. Nasser, a nationalist and authoritarian leader, dreamed of an industrialized Egypt that he would run with no institutional counterweight. He had a vague idea of modernity, subscribing to a kind of syncretism between medieval culture and material modernity. He liked importing the latest industrial technology from the West, but he hated public freedoms and the laws by which civil society poses limitation to the executive power. He did not grasp that the working process of industry requires that a civil society be put in place; he was viscerally opposed to such a society because he could not abide the idea that Egyptians might compete openly for goods, services, or political power. His project was a blend of utopian traditionalism, exclusive nationalism, romantic socialism, and anthropological naivety. He understood the concept of cultural revolution as the return to a mythic Egyptian identity supposedly destroyed by Western influences. Nasser was a sincere political leader, but his project, just like those of Boumediene and Assad, was doomed to failure. Within a decade, he contrived to annihilate the Egyptian bourgeoisie and, with it, the areas of freedom of expression in which had flourished an intellectual and artistic life that was unique in the Arab world for its vitality and quality. What Nasser loathed most was political squabbling between Egyptians; he dreamed of a unanimity ensured by a state under the tutelage of the army, and of a modern economic sector run by the administration. His dream was to create an ideal state—generous, nourishing, protective, prosperous, and managed by competent, honorable, and dedicated civil servants. This project demanded that each state employee place himself at the service of people whose needs should be met by the state. This state employee would be answerable not to the governed but to his superiors, who would necessarily evaluate him on his capacity to obey them, rather than on his competence. Thus, the Nasser regime sought to build an ideal administration run by good and disinterested functionaries at the service of a people "united like the fingers of a hand." The leaders identify with the people as if the people were wielding power. From this standpoint, they refuse any institutional constraint that would curb the implementation of their program. The rejection of politics and its conflictual nature was the salient characteristic of the populist project. It simply denied the existence of plurality; there was no need, after all, to institutionalize something that did not exist. Populism, however, did not prevent political conflicts; on the contrary, these took place regularly at the top of the state apparatus, with plots and coups d'état. The populist project wanted no part of civil society, with its disagreements and divergent individual or group interests, preferring to see the nation as a homogenous entity whose army would be its vanguard.

In Egypt the chief theorist of this approach was the journalist Mohamed Hassanein Heikal, who, in his editorials, proclaimed what the national interest was and what an intellectual should be, forever hammering home the idea that the army's role was revolutionary. For Heikal, the army was the vanguard of the people, and its mission was to defend the country against foreigners and their homegrown allies. So it was natural that the political chiefs should be soldiers ready to sacrifice themselves for the nation. The military co-opted civil elites to run the administration and modernize the nation while preventing all political dissent. A specialized corps within the army was formed to track down opponents accused of seeking to divide the people. The populist regime placed the economy under state control and did the same to society, which was forbidden to put forward its own representatives independent of the regime. Society was sucked into the machinery of state organizations, which prevented any kind of civil society from taking shape. The theory was that every citizen would be a state employee, living on an income that could be withdrawn if ever he or she questioned the government policy. This utopia of a nonconflictual society cut the state off from its social roots and—paradoxically—turned it into an entity hostile to the people at large. The people responded by developing two attitudes of their own: the first, apathy; the second, rebellion. Their total lack of interest in the res publica was punctuated by recurrent rioting throughout the country, signifying that society was not in step with its state and was settling irrecoverably back into a *siba* (Arabic term meaning stateless) culture from an earlier time. Populism cut the administration off from the population and led it into a morass of corruption.

Using several different ideological pretexts, the regime mobilized all its resources to remain unshackled by society. If any individual or group manifested its discontent or held the leader accountable for the management of public property, this was viewed as ingratitude and lack of confidence in a man who is above suspicion. Niccolò Machiavelli would have said that the Arab leaders had found an appropriate way to force acceptance of absolute power: All public freedom is suspended so that the leader might not be hindered in the execution of his revolutionary mission, which is supposedly generous and impartial. But however generous he may be, the prince invariably has an overriding interest of his own, which is to remain in office and elude popular control. The science of power, which was conceived by Machiavelli and Thomas Hobbes, teaches that man is naturally drawn to power and the honors that come with it, showing "a general inclination, a perpetual and relentless desire of power after power, that ceases only in death."[6] If Machiavelli and Hobbes are right, no prince will ever voluntarily give up the smallest particle of his power.

As a political ideology, populism is consistent with the expectations of the people and of their collective representation. Yet the prince never depends on coercion alone to impose his authority. He needs to legitimize it with an ideology that people can obey and freely acknowledge. Without "false consciousness," says Marx, the mechanism of legitimacy cannot function and force is never enough to keep a government in power forever. This means that populism is not the Machiavellian invention of power-hungry tyrants. It corresponds to a cultural view of politics that is shared by many social groups. It has historic relevance and is a de facto mobilization resource used by candidates for office. This approach anchors politics in society and history, and not in the psychology of individuals. If Nasser, Boumediene, and Assad took over in their countries, it was because populism corresponded to the social expectations of the majority of the population, which was appalled by the inequalities created by the market and by the new mechanisms of social mobility. Alert as it was to all this, radical Arab nationalism became a political force rooted in the population promising to fulfill the expectations of the larger number of the population. The reluctance of populism to speak of "society," preferring the notion of "the people," goes back to the idea that society is a breeding ground for competition for wealth and honors; it is also seen as a vehicle for refractory social demands like union freedoms, fair pay, and reasonable purchasing power. Society, from the populist standpoint, is a hotbed of social inequality and the lust for gain that satisfies the egotism of the powerful. The disorder reigning in society generates the kind of political tumult dreaded by populism, which prefers the serenity of a people united behind the leader. There are no individuals among "the people," a homogenous and compact entity with no need for any rule of law. "The people" are content with little, and that is their strength; they are unaffected by egotistical self-interest, and they are capable of great sacrifices in defense of their unity and their identity. "The people" are silent, even when they are suffering, whereas society is vindictive, full of clamor, even when it lacks for nothing.

From their earliest days, Arab populist regimes took this imaginary "people" as its social basis, rather than "society." The populist project consisted in building a state of the people to eliminate the conflictual character of a materialistic society, whose goal was merely well-being. Like Nasser, Boumediene reproached society with conspicuous consumption.[7] The concept of the people, arising from resistance to colonial domination, was carried over and politically exploited so it could be substituted for a reality that populism disliked: society. If these Arab countries failed in their fierce determination to modernize, it was because all their development policies were designed to satisfy the aspirations of an imaginary people and not to a real and conflictual society that was thought to be too materialistic by the populist ideology.

Nourished by populism as it was, Arab nationalism seems to have been mesmerized by the state power posited as an end in itself, neglecting individual's civic rights. The state power was sublimated because it was perceived as the idealized political expression of the people from the moment it was under the control of the nationalists. However, sooner or later, society gets the upper hand on populist utopia since the people can only exist within society, sociologically distributed among groups whose interests are divergent. As a compact entity expressing a single will, as one man might, the people is a utopian or imaginary construct serving leaders who claim to be the people's incarnation. Because they assume that they are the people's incarnation, there is no need to be accountable to any institution.

The notions of "people" and "society" must also be analyzed within the frameworks of sociology and political philosophy. How can we define "the people"? It is a collection of individuals united against potential adversaries and sharing a common history. Individuals form themselves into a people when they are threatened by danger from the outside, when a foreign power attacks them. The concept of people is a state of mind that grips individuals when they perceive that the existence of the community they form is oppressed or threatened. In this situation individuals set aside their personal interests and dedicate themselves to the defense of the community. This becomes a mobilization around symbols that feed a kind of collective ecstasy and a spirit of sacrifice. Heroes emerge who become ordinary individuals again once the danger is past and the enemy defeated. The people dissolve again into a collection of individuals with divergent and contradictory interests when the peril from outside goes away.[8] In wartime the notion of the people is revolutionary, but in time of peace it is used by authoritarian governments to justify repression and arbitrary rule. In the West the notion of the people is used by extreme right-wing parties as a criterion of belonging to the national community and is also a sentiment that emerges in times of deep crisis. Populism is no more than an ideology that allows political leaders to claim to be the people and to put under the carpet political and social inequalities.

Thus, "people" and "society" are categories whose ideological and historical contents are totally at odds. The former is warlike and appeals to the sense of kinship, spirit of sacrifice, and ecstasy. The latter is worldly and dominated by selfish traders driven by the logic of interests, "the icy water of egoistic calculation," as Marx put it.[9] Social life in such a society is only possible under the rule of law. This radical difference between the two categories explains why populist ideology prefers to escape the harsh reality of society. It also explains why populist Arab regimes turned their backs on constitutional law, since it is a fact that the notion of the "people" is not recognized or used therein. Populist political system and its political culture are based on a notion that is not relevant to constitutional law.[10] So "the people" is neither a sociological reality nor a juridical category in public law: it is an ideological representation appearing at certain times in the history of a society that can be defined as a collection of individuals claiming a shared identity and having particular aspirations. The antagonisms between the members of society run so deep that it is only possible for them to coexist if they are protected by the rule of law in a public arena characterized by competition for material and symbolic goods. Daily life would be hellish in society if individuals were not subject to laws guaranteed by the government. This is not just a theoretical premise; it is a conclusion reached by citizens themselves when they must go through hardship to get what they need in daily life.

The Arab countries borrowed the idea of nationalism from Europe in reaction to European domination, organizing themselves into nation-states with centralized political powers. They managed to install an administrative organization but failed to import the institutional counterweights that protect the citizens from authoritarian rule. The nation-state spelled the destruction of all local powers and structures such as village authorities, *archs* (tribes), religious brotherhoods, and so on. In the absence of intermediate bodies, as Alexis de Tocqueville pointed out so well, the nation-state becomes a tentacular administrative machine confronting a myriad of disorganized individuals who have the feeling they are not heard by an inhuman bureaucracy that would function for itself alone. Under the Ottoman Empire, the individual had no relationship with the central power and did not depend on it to ensure his safety or to travel or to feed himself. He had no need to declare the birth of a son or the death of a grandfather; he required no special permission from the sultan to make his pilgrimage to Mecca. Today the citizen depends on the state in every sphere of his daily existence.[11] And yet this citizen is not heard in the elected bodies since the elections are rigged.

Once the conditions of self-sufficiency have been destroyed, individuals turn for their subsistence outside the domestic sphere in a situation of scarcity since the commodities are supplied by the market. As an interface between the domestic sphere and the market, the state administration undergoes pressure from formidable networks stemming from the state itself. A high-ranking civil servant has a strategic position in the economy of the rentier-state. This explains the corruption that exists at every level of the Arab state as well as the brutality and jealousy of daily relationships when people are fully aware that a neighbor or a colleague at work has taken a share that is not his due. Corruption is not exclusive to Arab culture—far from it; it is a natural tendency in any society, curbed to some extent in political systems with independent judiciary and free press. Meanwhile, the poorest people—who are dependent on the state because they are dependent on the prices of imported food products—dream of a just prince who will curb everyone's freedom so that everyone can receive a fair share of things. The popularity of the Islamists comes from this dream of fair distribution of wealth in a situation where the state administration has been committed to meet the social needs.

In the past the central power existed through its symbolic attributes and manifested itself by levying taxes, at which time everyone found himself at the mercy of the sultan's army. Like all premodern power structures, the sultan was authoritarian and predatory. Groups protected themselves from the violence of the *beylik* (local Ottoman administration) by falling back on tribal solidarity, which in certain cases was a declared *siba*.[12] The colonial state, which was built on racism and violence, perpetuated the predatory logic of the *beylik*. In Algeria, the colonial state took in large-scale lands from rural populations who were condemned to famine and exodus. The history of the Arab countries does not feature the state as an organ emanating from the collectivity, and whether the government was Ottoman or

European, it was ever an oppressive apparatus, foreign to the social groupings it dominated, for whom it was simply a threat. Wishing to have done with this threat, the nationalist movements set out to build a state whose source was the people and that above all served the people. The populist Arab regimes founded their legitimacy on the promise to achieve the ideal of a national movement driven by a modern nation governed by a just and humane state. Rulers and ruled would be in step: hence the popularity of the populist leader, who personified the country's longing to develop and industrialize at last.

SOCIAL DIFFERENTIATION AS AN INELUCTABLE TREND

Social differentiation is a basic theme of classical sociology (Ferdinand Tönnies, Emile Durkheim, Max Weber, and others), which insists on the autonomy of fields obeying their own logic. When politics frees itself from military and religious forces, and when economics frees itself from politics, each obeys its own rules. Modernity is the process of subjectivization and separation of the differing social logics to which, in a contradictory way, radical Arab nationalism has been resolutely opposed for the last half century. The differentiation of social practices has resulted, among other things, in an academic division of the various disciplines so that each has had its own field of study: economics, sociology, political science, and so on. Remember that the empirical goal of social sciences is a total sociological reality that we, as scholars, separate for methodological purposes into sociology, economics, psychology, and so on. In circumstances like those of the Arab countries, in which social differentiation is under way, economics, sociology, and political science do not have specific research objects of their own.

To this end, economic anthropology (for the sphere of goods and services) and political anthropology (for relationships of authority) are methodologically better equipped for approach of social life in Arab countries. Academic works on developing countries tend to ignore this methodological specificity and approach them in using the same concepts to study Western societies. The difference is at any rate cultural; it is historical. Many Western scholars who do not give importance to this epistemological difficulty lean to the conclusion of cultural backwardness or even lack of rationality, without suspecting that their methodology is flawed. Political science, for instance, is dedicated to the study of Western states with a secularized political culture. In Arab countries, the transition from communities to society is still under way. Radical Arab nationalism has actually hindered this process instead of accelerating it.

We must further emphasize the notion of a society that is an articulation of contradictory interests that may only be rendered compatible by the rule of law and by the capacity of each participant to defend his rights under the law. Social scientists, from Adam Smith to Karl Polanyi by way of Ferdinand Tönnies, have agreed that society is the creation of the market and that social peace is consubstantial with Immanuel Kant's idea of the rule of law. Kant discusses what he calls "insociable sociability," meaning that individuals are asocial.[13] They can only form societies through the law and through institutionalized authority. This means that society is not a natural grouping of human beings; instead, it is a historical construction within which political, ideological, and economic factors take their share. Economically, a society depends on the wealth it creates through labor; politically, it becomes aware that it is the source of both law and political power.

From this point of view, the Arab countries are not societies according to the sociological meaning of the word. Economically, they are not developed, and they rely on exportation of raw materials (gift of mother nature) or international aid. Politically, they have never contrived to endow power with the public character it has in modern societies.

Economism as a Response to Cultural Crisis

During the debates organized by the Nasser regime in the late 1950s aiming to gain the support of Egyptian intellectuals, Hussein Fawzi drew the attention to an issue that lay at the heart of the contradictions affecting the development of Arab societies, particularly the question of culture. "Until now," he declared, "only the material forms of civilization have prevailed neglecting the mental and emotional state of the Nile Valley regions."[14] By mental and emotional state, Fawzi meant culture in its broader aspect, understood as an intellectual approach by which society organizes itself and by which the individual apprehends the reality surrounding him. Culture as a view of the world is a fundamental issue because it confers a meaning to the values of individuals and gives legitimacy to their social and political arrangements. To suppose that it is a passive reflection of material conditions is to deny that man is a historic agent who creates the social conditions of his existence. This question, vital though it is, was rejected by the populist regimes with the idea that the eradication of poverty by industrial development would automatically produce the required cultural changes since it was understood that schools would be available for all children and would end illiteracy. But the problem of what else would be taught in those schools and the worldview they would impress on the younger generation was never explicitly addressed. The all-encompassing focus on economic matters spared everyone to think about the content of culture taught at school because it was assumed that the modification of material structures would automatically imply a rebirth of the past culture that the current state of ignorance had supposedly obscured. This ideological view tasks the state with reviving the cultural heritage that society may have forgotten because of foreign domination. Hence the contradiction inherent to authoritarian populism: on the one hand, it seeks to modernize the economy; on the other, it has no cultural policy on which to base that modernization.

Arab societies have been deconstructed by the capitalist economy that began a process of destruction of the traditional social framework followed by rural exodus and urbanization. In Europe, Marx has called this process "the primitive accumulation of capital," in *The Capital* (book 1, section eight) with the difference that it was not brought to its conclusion in Arab societies. The old order was merely destroyed with no new one introduced in its place. Radical Arab nationalism undertook to complete the process begun by the European powers, which had refused to modernize their colonies and semicolonies. In rejecting foreign domination, the Arab peoples aspired to create a nation of their own, which was a concept both political and cultural. The nation, a European political invention, is the ideological and cultural representation of a human collectivity, organized as a state that functions based on generally broad political participation by all concerned. The categories of nation, state, civil society, and market share a historical content upon which modernity in Europe was built. They are vehicles of a cultural view of the world that has broken with the intellectual heritage of the past. The lesson to draw is that there is no development or modern economy without a genuine civil society. Civil society is not an organic entity with a collective soul and a transcendent center; instead, it is a collection of individuals possessing rights that are protected by the rule of law that originates within society itself. With René Descartes, Baruch Spinoza, and Kant, the Europeans made a clean break with the medieval philosophy that they shared at that time with the Arabs. With these thinkers, Europe and the Arab world ceased to be historically in step. The gap between the West and the Arab world is first of all intellectual. Radical Arab nationalism was mistaken in putting forward economic development. There is no development without the empowerment of citizens forming a civil society.

These historical-theoretical elements must be borne in mind if we are to make comparisons between the two experiments. From this standpoint, civil society is a purely Western historical phenomenon. It is a form of social organization characterized by its institutionalization of power and juridicization of social relations, by its way of creating wealth through a system of prices regulated by competition, and by a view of the world that structures social links around the individual as historic agent, as conscience, and as subject of law. The major science of civil society is, from this point of view, political economy that is no more than the rational conceptualization of the ebb and flow of material wealth. Political economy is founded on two ideas: one was formulated by Adam Smith, who showed that labor is the sole source of wealth, and the other one by David Ricardo, who explained that the rent, linked to scarcity, is morally illegitimate. These twin concepts of the central issue of political economy form the backbone of a state. Nation, state, market, and civil society are features of the same historic reality. Smith's and Ricardo's political economy is the blueprint of civil society organized politically as a rule of law, economically as a market, and culturally as a nation. This complex—rule of law, market, nation—appearing for the first time in the West was to dominate the planet by imposing the criteria and norms that resulted in the development of the North and the underdevelopment of the South.

The Arab world has missed out on three revolutions that changed the course of human history and led directly to the present globalization. The first was the Enlightenment, or intellectual revolution, of the seventeenth and eighteenth centuries. The second was the nineteenth-century Industrial Revolution, for which the Enlightenment had prepared the ground. The third was the technological and scientific revolution of the 1960s and 1970s. The Industrial Revolution and the material civilization did not come about as a natural evolution; they were the result of social and intellectual transformations that Arab populism totally underestimated when it went into ecstasies over the industrial and technical side of the change; it ignored the cultural and political background from which economic development had emerged.

Of course, there were the attempts at social and intellectual reform made by Al-Nahda in the final third of the nineteenth century, with Jamal al-Din al-Afghani and Mohammed Abdu. But the thinkers of this movement did not have the audacity to dismantle the old Muslim theology inherited from the past. Al-Nahda neither renewed nor criticized the old theology that continued to structure the Muslim culture. Al-Nahda had authorized the faithful to master the natural sciences (physics, biology, chemistry, and so on), but it did not prepare them to embrace social sciences and humanities such as political economy, anthropology, sociology, and history. There were a few attempts to do this, quickly stifled in their infancy, like that of Sheik Ali Abderrazak, a disciple of Mohammed Abdu, who was condemned by Al-Azhar. The ideologists of nationalism adhered to the teachings of Al-Nahda, which advocated European-style science and technology while rejecting the secularization of social thought. Michel Aflaq, one of the founders of the Baath Party, spoke of the Prophet Mohammed as the first Arab nationalist, whose mission was to reestablish justice on earth and enlighten the rest of humanity. When it took over the state, radical Arab nationalism asked the

75

ulemas to support socialism and teach that it was compatible with Islam.[15] This posture gave them the authority to condemn all secularized social thinking that did not conform to the old religious tradition, but it did not help to construct a body of thinking about the problems caused by the fact that Muslim society had fallen so far behind. On the contrary, it made the situation worse by giving political legitimacy to religious discourse and by preventing religious thought from forging a brand of Muslim theology that would rest on a modern metaphysical base. Hence, the Arab regimes depended on technocrats and ulemas while clamping down on intellectuals and driving them into exile. Consequently, engineers and clerics cohabited in the same social sphere and from time to time might be one and the same person. Nasr Abou Zeid pointed out this glaring contradiction, but well before him, in the 1960s, Abdallah Laroui had put together a typology of the intellectual in the Muslim world, particularly distinguishing the religious cleric from the technocrat.[16] There was effectively a division of the epistemological field between areas pertaining to identities defined by language and religion, on the one hand, and areas linked to the morphological and material aspect of society that were subcontracted to engineers, physicists, and medical doctors, on the other hand. The revolutionary Arab nationalism of the 1950s and 1960s accommodated itself to this dichotomy that later had immense ideological and political repercussions. Thinkers who had tried to criticize tradition were excluded from the school syllabus; children were taught a mythified and idealized version of the past, with no critical consciousness whatsoever—hence the impression of an Islam that had navigated for centuries through a historical vacuum. The narrative remains that the perfection of the Prophet's generation resulted in territorial conquests and a brilliant civilization, after which it was infiltrated by foreign influences that led to decline and Western domination. Mass education continued to shape a younger generation with medieval scholastic concepts that went hand in hand with positivism in natural sciences. The discourse on the representation of the self, going back to *al-açala* (identity inherited from the past) is arrived at using the conceptual methods of the Middle Ages while the perception of nature is resolutely positivist, making sure that *al mou'açara* (modernity) is taken for granted. This was not seen as a contradiction; in the Islamic countries, Galileo did not lead to Descartes, as was the case in Europe. Indeed, it was as if Galileo had remained Aristotelian.[17]

Radical Arab nationalism succeeded in creating a strong central state power that was officially independent internationally but that failed to transform that state power into a rule of law. This failure had ideological causes and led to an impasse that mythified and idealized the past, creating an obstacle to the emergence of a secular society. Radical Arab nationalism was mesmerized by the material and military power of the West while attaching no importance at all to intellectual thought and humanist culture, whose rare home-grown representatives were dead by the 1960s. The generation of Egyptian, Syrian, and Iraqi intellectuals educated between 1920 and 1940 was not replaced in the 1950s. Egypt ceased to be an intellectual, cultural, and artistic center in the 1960s. Populism spread to universities, which were expected to provide academic backing for the regime. The latter placed social sciences under strict control and ordered researchers to guarantee its ideological positions. University professors were enjoined to contribute to the country's modernization under the control of the administration as part of the changes that took place after independence. And this led to the appearance of militant sociology, which approved state ideology and allowed the state both to exercise a monopoly on the university and to control its staff, some of whom became fully engaged in pseudo-science. Proclaiming itself "revolutionary," the official academic frowned on the autonomy of researchers who were expected to join the single party's organisms and help fulfill the promises of authoritarian populism.

This ideology reached its zenith at the twenty-fourth annual Congress of Sociology, which convened in Algiers in 1974. This was also the year of the Conference of Non-Aligned Nations that allowed Algeria to speak on behalf of the developing countries during the 1970s. Over five hundred university professors from seventy countries, including Europe and the United States, met in March 1974 to debate sociological studies and the development of developing countries. In his opening speech, the Algerian minister for higher education and scientific research set the tone by declaring that

> sociology in our countries will never be satisfied with the simple description of objective situations, nor will it stop at the necessary decolonization of people's minds. It is its duty to persist in its ambitions and give substance to its ideas; it must, above all, impose itself as a creative science, fully suited to the task of building a solid foundation for economic, social and cultural progress. It must thoroughly reorganize its framework of methodology and supply the theoretical underpinnings that are crucial to the success of the social revolution.[18]

In other words, the minister, as the representative of political authority, was telling the assembled university professors exactly what he wanted their research themes to be. The 1974 International Congress of Sociology effectively legitimized state sociology, meaning the official thought whose role was to prevent dissent in the university. The Marxist vulgate had been mobilized to give leftist credentials to an orientation worked out by the state sociologist whose task was to construct an ideological framework that would serve as a basis for state policies. Using Marxist rhetoric to bolster the regime's revolutionary image while borrowing from the Salafist arsenal to showcase the regime's firm cultural grounding within the population, this line of thought was remarkable for the way it spread inhibiting myths that were difficult for university researchers to question without being publicly denounced.[19] The inevitable result was that university professors became much more attuned to the state's pronouncements than to society itself, of whose real evolution they knew next to nothing. It is scarcely surprising that no research whatsoever was conducted on the real situation of the country's economy, on protest movements, on social violence, on the academic level of progress of students in schools, or the trend toward Islamism. Instead, themes like imperialism, socialism, the noncapitalist path to development, the role of the peasant farmer in developing countries, and the awakening of the masses became the main research themes at the university. The social practices of daily life were utterly ignored. The scholars were not listening to society; they were instead speaking on behalf of society.

If sociology was only an ideological discourse, it is because the university and the scholars were not autonomous from the state power. Radical Arab nationalism refused all autonomy to the intermediary bodies that alone can prevent the state from cutting itself off from the people it governs. Intermediary bodies include political parties, elected assemblies, trade unions, the press, research centers, socioprofessional organizations, and so on, which provide a political expression of the contrasting interests of the individuals who make up society. Is it not ironic that populism was a stratagem that traditional political culture used to assume the cloak of modernism? Its goal was to endow the country with a modern industrial sector working in tandem with arbitrary government authority. The flagrant failures of the experience eventually made political leaders doubt the effectiveness of populist ideology. From the mid-1980s onward, they lost all faith in populism, though they remained hamstrung by its legacy. From 1950s to 1970s, they championed populism as a political vision, and the elites more or less believed in it. Ever since the 1980s and right up to the present, they do not believe in it at all, and the regimes have become ends in themselves. The radical Arab regimes lost their ideology, which was populism, and now populism has been appropriated by Islamists who use religious language to accuse the Arab leaders of betraying the Muslim people. In other words, Islamists today are bent on anachronistically reproducing the radical Arab nationalism of the 1950s. And it is radical Arab nationalism's refusal to build society on the sound basis of individual liberties that has begotten the present religious neopopulism.

Notes

1. Jürgen Habermas, *The Structural Transformation of the Public Sphere: An Inquiry into a Category of Bourgeois Society*, translated by Thomas Burger with Frederick Lawrence (Cambridge, MA: MIT Press, 1989).
2. The communists favored this approach, seemingly unaware that it was a contradiction in terms; by aligning themselves ideologically with the regime, they were de facto opposing the emancipation of the workers as a constituent element of a civil society under construction. The Arab communists were sincere militants in the national cause, but they had a major theoretical flaw. They underestimated the historical perspective of Marxism, the revolutionary character of capitalism in a feudal social order situation. This vulnerability predisposed them to be the allies of regimes that subsequently repressed them over and over again.
3. I use the notion of rent in Ricardo's meaning. We should bear in mind that political economy was built by Adam Smith and David Ricardo on the distinction between profit and rent in connection with the labor theory of value. See chapter 2, "On Rent," in Ricardo's book *On the Principles of Political Economy and Taxations*, edited by Pierro Sraffa (Cambridge: Cambridge University Press, 1966).
4. The Khalifa Affair is a classic example of this, and it reveals the peculiar logic governing the Algerian political system. Important figures within the state structure siphoned off astronomical sums of public money, which they invested in a business that went bankrupt a few years later. This—one of the most enormous financial scandals of modern times—would never have happened had there been an independent judiciary in Algeria. After the Khalifa Affair, Algeria continued to see regular cases of embezzlement of funds estimated in the hundreds of millions of dollars (the East–West Freeway, Sonatrach 1, Sonatrach 2). Had civil society been strong enough, it would have demanded full investigations of these scandals, ensuring that they never happen again. Above all, the billions of dollars that were stolen and wasted were directly financed by the state budget deficit entailing the increase of prices in the mar-

ket. In other words, the colossal sums that were lost were covered by a reduction in Algerian consumers' purchasing power. This is exactly where the political and economic culture of civil society is of such importance because within that culture the representative organisms of different interest groups (professional bodies, workers' unions, employers, political parties, and various associations) keep a close eye, day after day, on the evolution of the state budget and on the way it affects the prices paid by consumers.

5. A rational price system, establishing proportional ratios between the values of goods, is structured by the variable wage level that determines the cost of the labor force. The real wage is set by comparing its actual value with its standard value. This, in conditions of free competition and free unions, is what makes it possible to regenerate the labor force. If the price system in state-owned economy is irrational, it is because (among other things) the purchasing power of real wages has been eviscerated. This discourages young people from joining the wage-earning workforce; they opt instead to exploit the opportunities offered by speculation and the informal economic sector.

6. Thomas Hobbes, *Leviathan or the Matter, Forme, & Power of a Common-Wealth Ecclesiastical and Civill* (1651).

7. In 1974 the Algerian president made a speech in the city of Saida in which he affirmed that people who wanted to eat butter should go abroad to do so, butter being a luxury product. The next day it was found that someone had written on the walls of the city: "Anyone who wants to smoke cigars should go and live in Cuba." This sentence was referring to Houari Boumediene, who used to smoke cigars sent to him by Fidel Castro.

8. In Algeria many former combatants of the National Liberation Army who risked their lives fighting for the resistance became privileged participants in the subsequent predatory system of the new independent state. They did not change; it was the historical circumstance that changed.

9. Karl Marx and Friedrich Engels, *Manifesto of the Communist Party* (New York: International Publishers, 1969).

10. The constitutions of states observing the rule of law claim that sovereignty belongs to the people, but this is an effect of style only. In reality, sovereignty would belong to the electoral majority after an election. This fiction whereby the people are sovereign is only acceptable insofar as the minority, which does not identify with those elected, can itself become a majority a few years later. In a democracy, the notion of the people has been preserved by alternation in government that allows today's minority to become tomorrow's majority.

11. In reality, he depends on the international market; the state is his intermediary when he acquires food products and manufactured goods. And their purchase is regulated by the juggling of local currencies and local customs duties.

12. It is no coincidence that in 2001 in Algeria a citizen's protest was still endowed with structures called *arch*, thus reactivating the collective memory.

13. See Emmanuel Kant, *Idée d'une histoire universelle du point de vue cosmopolite* (Paris: Gallimard, 1967).

14. Fawzi Hussein, in *Azmat al mothakkafine* (The crisis of the intellectuals), by M. H. Heykal (Cairo, 1961), quoted in Anwar Abdelmalek, *Egypte, société militaire* (Editions du Seuil, 1962), 193.

15. See Deheveuls Luc-Willy, *Islam et pensée contemporaine en Algérie* (Paris: CNRS, 1992); and Malika Zghal, *Gardiens de l'Islam: Les oule'mas d'Al Azhar dans l'Egypte contemporaine* (Paris: Presse de Science Politiques, 1996).

16. Nasr Abou Zeid, *Critique du discours religieux*, translated from the Arabic by Mohammed Chairet (Arles: Sindbad Actes Sud, 1999), 200; and Abdallah Laroui, *L'idéologie arabe contemporaine* (Paris: Maspéro, 1967).

17. Daryush Shayagan speaks of a "yawning gulf between pre-Galilean and post-Hegelian thought." See D. Shayagan, *Le regard mutilé: Schizophrnie culturelle face à la modernité* (Albin Michel: Editions l'Aude, 1996), 85.

18. Mohammed Seddik Benyahya, "Discours d'ouverture du 24ième Congrès Mondial de sociologie," in *L'Université Bulletin de l'Enseignement Supérieur et de la Recherche Scientifique*, no. 1 (March–April 1975).

19. In 1985, in Algeria, a decree was sponsored by the party to put pressure on scholars who failed to respect the regime's political options. They were liable to prosecution in the courts. This text was never applied because the university was already so completely detached and lethargic that no critical resource remained to it.

3

Nationalism and the Nation

THERE HAVE BEEN many studies of nationalism dealing with its historical and ideological aspects. It would be impossible to mention them all; I use some only to develop my theme of Arab nationalism's failure to construct the political and economic modernity that it promised. We need to put the notions of nationalism and nation firmly in their theoretical and historical contexts. There is no preexisting path leading straight to the formation of the nation, and there is no theoretical model for it. There are, however, historic experiments in forming national groups that stand out. Unquestionably, in the nineteenth century, any human collectivity that was not politically organized as a state defined by territorial frontiers was in danger of being dominated by a foreign power. The imperialist structure of international relations brought about the birth of nationalism in the former colonies, particularly in Africa and Asia, the two continents most coveted by the European powers. Having said this, we should take note of the historic processes by which nations are built. In academic literature, there is a tendency to confuse nationalism and nation, and to assume that the one gives birth to the other. What is forgotten is that behind these notions lie historic processes that extend for centuries back.

The nation is not a theoretical model spawned by political philosophy. It is a product of peculiar historical experiences that differ widely from one another. This premise makes constant references to history, underlining the fact that mere nationalist ideology is not enough to create a nation. This has been proved beyond doubt by numerous third world experiments, especially in Arab countries. As a feeling of attachment to a community, nationalism is not new; human beings naturally share the ethnocentric emotion of belonging to a group and embracing its values. Fundamentally, nationalism is an ethnocentrism within a geographic area in which the members of the collectivity accept the authority of a central power that has the legitimacy to arbitrate the domestic conflicts and to promulgate laws. From this standpoint, nationalism is a modern ideology that emerged with the birth of states organized on the principle of monopoly of violence. When the nation-states emerged in Europe at the end of the sixteenth century, they affirmed their autonomy, which led to the Westphalian order that considers any foreigner as a potential enemy. Thereafter, the fact of belonging to the same religious faith was not sufficient to make an individual part of the same political community, as was the case with the Holy Roman Empire for Christians or the Ottoman Empire for Muslims. The Westphalian order introduced political units whose members showed solidarity with each other and loyalty and allegiance to a central power. The nation-state, appearing in the seventeenth century in Western Europe, was a historical novelty. Political conflicts within the nation were now institutionalized, and the attachment to the nation was expressed in the nationalist attitude that redirected the conflictual aspect of ethnocentrism toward the outside. In other words, there was a division between Them and Us, which was given tangible form by the presence of a clear territorial frontier keeping states apart.

Nationalist sentiment appeals to a sense of shared identity, but this sentiment is fragile and can quickly shatter when interests diverge. Ideologists of Arab nationalism like Sati al-Husri or Zaki al-Arsuzi overestimated the language factor in the formation of the nation when they pointed to the importance of a shared tongue in the German experience. These two authors failed to grasp the secularized culture of which the German language was the vehicle. They underestimated the political role of economic elites that underpinned Bismarck's project of unification. The comparison between Pan-Germanism and Pan-Arabism was wrong because Syria or Egypt had nothing in common with nineteenth-century Prussia, which was already an industrialized country by the end of the nineteenth century to the extent that it could rival the other two great European powers of the time, Britain and France. The profound social and economic transformations Germany went through in the second half of the nineteenth century allowed the country to catch up with its two rivals. Moreover, the German-speaking intellectual elite played a huge role in the formation of a secularized European culture, principally by way of the works of Immanuel Kant, Georg Hegel, Karl Marx, Friedrich Nietzsche, and so on. The German ideology of the nineteenth century was in no way confined to Johann Gottlieb Fichte and Johann Gottfried von Herder, who had influence on Arab nationalists with European training.

Nationalism in Europe appeared when nation-states reached the final stages of their formation, whereas Arab nationalism appeared as an instrument for opposing foreign domination and creating a nation. Its only resource to create it was the Arabic language; the unfolding history showed that it was not sufficient to achieve a political integration of communities for which memories of ethnocentric conflicts were still very fresh. The Arab nations reached the first stage in the nation-state building process under the conditions of the

European domination, but after they won independence they were incapable of going any further. Whether they were republics or monarchies, the Arab states were content to flaunt the outer and visible characteristics of the nation without tackling the political, cultural, and economic transformation of the collectivity. The state remained a thing apart from the people who were excluded from politics monopolized either by a military hierarchy or by a family dynasty. Sovereignty remained traditional in both cases, resting on a mystical concept of power. The education of younger generations was not planned to secularize culture or to give them the meaning of citizenship. The medieval interpretation of Islam was simply reproduced, and this prevented the birth of a society that is aware that it is a source of law. Without the political participation of the population, without the clear awareness that power is the expression of the sovereignty of the people, there can be no political collectivity in which its members enjoy civil peace. Nationalism prompts national construction, but it is not sufficient to create the nation. We have seen the conditions under which Arab nationalism took shape, influenced by the Westphalian order that imposed the form of the nation-state on a global scale. If ideologists like Sati al-Husri, Chakib Arslan, Michel Aflaq, and others mobilized the resource of shared identity to fight foreign domination, their successors—mostly military, in the postcolonial era—delayed the birth of the nation. By claiming a monopoly on nationalism, the ruling elites militarized the political field, exacerbated the warlike character of subnational ethnocentrisms, and prevented the shift from national sovereignty to popular sovereignty. If we define the nation as a sociopolitical collectivity in which the relationships between state and society are rendered peaceful, we must also acknowledge that nationalism does not automatically give birth to the nation that is still a work in progress in the Arab world. Any Arab country could break apart, like Syria today.

The Militarization of Politics

After the Second World War, the idea of an independent state became overwhelmingly popular in every country of the developing world and nationalist demands were no longer confined to a minority of militants and ideologists. Every stratum of society was touched by the nationalist fervor, which caused the collapse of the colonial empires. The penetration of the radio into cities and rural areas favored the propagation of nationalist discourse that also touched the military of semi-independent Arab states. Some of them were to rebel against the political authorities of their countries, giving expression to the people's expectations in a coherent way. The emblematic example of this, of course, is Colonel Nasser at the head of the Free Officers, who overthrew the Egyptian monarchy and sent their senior officers— who were loyal to the king—into forced retirement.[1] The rest of the army followed them in this endeavor because both officers and soldiers were attracted by the mission that was suggested to them: that of defending the national interest in the name of the people. In the Arab countries, militarization of the political field was favored by historic circumstances linked to foreign domination and the creation of Israel in 1948. Some monarchies fell; others (Saudi Arabia, Jordan, and Morocco), survived the wave of coups that hit the region in the 1950s and 1960s. The inability of the political parties to be effective in any way or to mobilize for a response to the national aspirations of the population turned the army into a candidate for the exercise of national sovereignty. The experiences of different countries were specific to each, but result was the same in every case. In Algeria a clandestine army of national liberation was created in 1954 to wage war on the French colonial authorities. In 1962, with the coming of independence, this army was institutionalized and took over the running of the state. In Egypt the army was loyal to the monarchy until the creation of Israel in 1948. The military overthrew the monarchy and sent into exile the king in 1952. In Iraq the same scenario took place in 1958, and in Syria the young officers were receptive to the rhetoric of the Baath Party.

Because they were already a hierarchical organization with bases all over the country, the military had no difficulty in driving out the former regimes. Perceiving themselves as the guarantors of nationalism, they took control of the state with the promise of strengthening the nation. Within a few years the people's image of the soldier was transformed. He ceased to be the defender of a feudal or aristocratic social order and became the son of the people, whom he was sworn to defend with his life. Political parties lost their influence in the face of a charismatic military leader in whom the masses saw their dreams reflected. The seizure of power by the colonels in Egypt, Syria, Iraq, and Algeria all followed the same track, whereby the army presented itself as the shield of the nation against foreigners and as the vanguard of the people. Hence the historical conditions of nationalist euphoria, in which the population craved a party or an institution that might express, in a radical way, its hostility to foreign domination.

In these conditions, the soldier ceased to be a mere professional whose sole competence was that of bearing arms. He had now to be "politicized," fully engaged in the battle for development. It was on the latter criterion that his chances of climbing through the ranks were decided. The army embraced the idea that technical competence was not enough. Those who had been tested over time would be able to move closer to the narrow circle of power, at the center of which was the *za'im*, the unquestioned leader chosen by history to lead the effort of catching up with the West. The superior officer's pretension to absolute political legitimacy was based on the belief that he was the one closest to the leader, whose name alone symbolized a whole political program. Ready to sacrifice his life for his country, having deliberately opted for the rigors of barracks life to the detriment of his family life and symbolizing a force that could dissuade attackers from abroad, the soldier was convinced that he was the rampart of the nation and, hence, the harbinger of the legitimacy from which all political and administrative authority was bound to proceed. This is obviously a representation, but it worked through the backing of an overwhelming majority of the population that projected all its expectations onto a providential soldier who would restore a dignity trampled on by foreign powers and put an end to social inequality.

The Arab military regimes lasted so long because they had popular support and the ideological justifications to exercise repression in the 1950s and 1960s. Opponents were tortured or put to death, especially Islamists and Communists, presented to the public as traitors to the nation because they would have links with Saudi Arabia, the ally of the imperialist United States, or with the Soviet Union, ruled by atheists. Their neutralization was ideologically justifiable from a populist standpoint since the creed of populism allowed no political dissent within the national community. One was not allowed to be an Islamist, a Communist, or a liberal; even less, a Shiite, a Sufi, a Christian, a Kurd, or a Berber. One's nationality—Egyptian, Iraqi, Algerian, or just plain Arab—was sufficient as a political identity. Colonel Ghaddafi wrote in his "Green Book," "The nation is a great tribe." The members of a tribe or a family did not disagree politically or ideologically, and there was no need to institutionalize relationships between them. In the home, parents did not need to explain the daily running of the family to their children. As Aristotle remarked, the law is useless within the family sphere, hence the futility of a separation of powers in a "national family," where there is no need to institutionalize the divisions by party, which defend the interests of diverse categories and classes. Pluralist electoral democracy was condemned on the pretext that it only benefited parasite layers of society such as great landowners and the comprador bourgeoisie. Political parties were therefore dissolved and parliamentary life was abandoned in favor of a single-party system controlled by a former army officer. There is a kind of coherence in this utopia that attempts to fashion a nation without political conflict, within a state that is controlled by military officers who reject society's political modes of expression that are, for them, ineffectual, incoherent, and liable to breed disorder. The intention of the first generation of military rulers who seized power in the 1950s and 1960s was praiseworthy, but it was naive. The Algerian president, Houari Boumediene, made a decision in the 1970s to make health care coverage completely free of charge. The idea was laudable, but ten years later, the quality of care available in Algerian hospitals had fallen dramatically because the necessary financial and human resources were not available to back up his policy. The families of the ruling elite went to Europe for their medical care whereas the people's health requirements were dealt with in hospitals that were badly organized and chronically missing basic medications. In Egypt, Nasser decreed that every student who received a university degree had the right to a job within the administration. Within a short time, the administration had become swollen, inefficient, and corrupt because the state functionaries had to live on starvation salaries. Nasser had also decided that the National Assembly, an arm of the single-party state, should be made up of 50 percent workers and farmers, as these statuses were biological or genetic. How many of these members of parliament remained workers or farmers? After they were elected, they blindly supported government policies and developed strategies to change their social status by taking full advantage of a system based on co-option and clientelism. They took advantage of this to buy property and build the futures of their own children. These workers and farmers did not betray the nation; all they did was obey a primary law of human nature: social status is not something that defines an individual in perpetuity.

The proliferation of military regimes in many developing countries led some political scientists to elaborate on such a concept as authoritarian modernization with the idea that the army was the only historic agent of revolutionary change in a situation where the national bourgeoisie was linked to speculative activities and served the interest of international capitalism. In such context, the state substituted itself for the bourgeoisie to kick-start the process of accumulating wealth. Public capital, under the army's protection, would limit the extent of private property accepted only if it did not exploit the workers. In Algeria, the National Charter passed by referendum in 1976 introduced the notion of "non-exploitative property" without clearly indicating the line that would distinguish it from "exploitative private property." With this approach the national bourgeoisie would be weakened and eventually supplanted by a state bourgeoisie, which in Egypt was usually composed of retired soldiers who received privileges as a reward for their engagement in the struggle for development. The promise to run public corporations during retirement strengthened the esprit de corps among the military, who would have effectively two careers: one as soldiers with the prospect of attaining high rank, and another one as heads of state-run organisms or companies once their military careers were over. In this way, the regimes contrived to create a new social class with multiple new benefits. Without personally owning property, the members of this social class had a standard of living that was considerably better than that of the workers and executives they supervised. So the attachment of armed forces personnel to the regime was hardly based on ideological conviction; it had a lot to do with a class-rooted interest encouraged by an authoritarian system bent on "depoliticizing" the state and reducing it to an administration whose main concern was to manage the country's material resources.

The idea was to use violence to create a future society without conflict and without violence, a society in which the distribution of wealth would not lead to competition between different social groups. Civilian elites, appointed by the military, were expected to run the state administration and to carry out a fair distribution of wealth in favor of the destitute classes. Within this framework, there was a generous and naive approach to politics that rejected social conflict as something that could actively undermine the nation's unity. The state was not a political institution; it was the administrative instrument to which the armed forces entrusted the task of social and economic development in the country. The military saw itself as a sovereign body that delegated authority to civilian elites in function of their unfailing respect to the unwritten rule of the system: the army was the only source of the authority of the state institution. The military believed that by forbidding all political activities, they fixed the contradiction between rulers and ruled. Once the state was placed at the service of the people, the leaders could have no interest that went against the interest of the people. Electoral democracy was rendered useless because the army had put an end to all divisions within society. It believed that it had put an end to the concentration of power in private hands. However, by carrying out the change of regime, sovereignty had not been transferred to the people in consequence of free elections. On the contrary, the army had held on to it and in doing so it had reproduced the same pattern of privatization of power as its predecessors. The discourse may have changed, but the reality is that Colonel Nasser took the place of King Farouk in Egypt, and Colonel Boumediene took the place of the French governor-general of colonial Algeria. They put in place a model of a state that was supposedly at the service of the people while depriving the legislative power of its autonomy and abolishing the independence of the judiciary.

The negation of political conflict that masked the still-private nature of political power rested on a consensual ideology whereby the desire for modernity went hand in hand with the values of the past. Nationalism took over the armed forces to claim for itself the mantles of modernity and tradition. In the *National Action Charter* submitted to referendum in 1962, Nasser wrote: "We must not hesitate, even for a moment, to enter the atomic age. We have a duty to rise at dawn, with those that have initiated it. . . . An unfailing faith in God and in the saints he has sent as guides and vehicles of truth to all men, at all times and in all places."[2] It is not so much God's invocation that was problem; it is rather this mystical reference to religion that perpetuates a religious thought that goes back to past centuries. Instead of confronting the religious establishment, radical nationalism sought a compromise that failed to conceal the contradictions. The first president of Algeria, Ahmed Ben Bella, who was chosen by the army after the country won its independence, declared in 1963 that socialism was not invented by Marx but by Islam, which is known for teaching values of justice in the distribution of wealth. These were not just strategies to attract the approval of the majority; the idea went deeper, echoing a historic situation wherein social groups within Algeria had widely contrasting aspirations. The revolutionary dynamic of Arab nationalism was smothered by syncretism that prevented it from secularization. For example, nobody dared to raise the issue of sharia although it could have helped to render it as a modern law. Except Tunisia, no Arab country forbade polygamy, which would have been perfectly possible according to the Qur'an, which accepts the practice without recommending it. Arab nationalism was built on compromise that may have sidestepped mainstream religious tradition like its monarchist neighbors had done but also managed to reject Mustafa Kemal's Turkish model. There was fear to undertake the task of modernizing the theology, hoping that it would change and make progress automatically with the expected economic development. Meanwhile, the place of religion in society, the secularization of the law, gender equality, and so on were all swept under the carpet.

The Arab countries began to face substantial violence in the 1980s when the compromise could no longer be sustained. The ideological synthesis could not last. It is possible that Nasser, Boumediene, and others thought that economic development would automatically include cultural change without direct confrontation with conservative ideology. But, objectively speaking, the interests of military rulers and religious conservatives coincided in their opposition to groups that called for freedom of speech and of conscience. Thus, the regime needed the support, explicit or implicit, of religious authorities that could accept the hegemony of an executive power, and the religious line was hostile to the political modernity based on religious freedom, implying also that society itself is the fount of power and the law. For the ulemas, law and authority proceeded from the will of God expressed by a ruling elite concerned by the well-being of the community. If this elite strengthened the nation's independence vis-à-vis foreign powers, and if it worked for the prosperity of the faithful, it would be blessed even though it presented itself as the actual source of power. This political/cultural dimension is consistent with the people's yearning for a just prince who would fight inequalities and defend the poor and the orphaned. The leader was seeking to play the role of the righteous ruler, claiming to fulfill a revolutionary mission, that of placing the state at the service of the people.

But politics is more than just ideas and projects that polarize opinion. It also involves material resources capable of creating a *rapport de force* that disqualifies all competing ideas. The control of the state by the military is facilitated by the existence of revenues that are external to the country's economy. There is a need of money to build dams, to open schools, to pay civil servants, and so on. If these expenses were funded by taxation, the people would end up demanding representatives of their own within the institutions that decide how the state budget ought to be apportioned. Some authors believe that this mechanism, known to American political science as "no taxation without representation," belongs to Western culture. The mechanism implies a *rapport de force* in which the protagonists work out compromises to protect their respective interests. However, the notion of interest is a universal one and not exclusive to any particular culture. The difference regarding the Arab countries has more to do with the weakness of economies that are unable to generate sufficient tax revenue to cover the state budget. For this reason, the state is economically independent of society, which depends upon it for its subsistence. Oil revenues, tourism, international aid, and remittances from emigrant workers create the kind of wealth that allows the regime to bypass any need for negotiation between the different social groups.

The army contrived to win acceptance as symbols of national unity for historical, political, and economic reasons. But, like all human associative bodies, armies consist of different generations of personnel. Hosni Mubarak was not Nasser, who had given millions of Egyptians and Arabs a dream. The difference had nothing to do with the two men's psychologies; it was more a question of the effectiveness of the symbol whose relevance was linked to history. Between these two leaders were fifty years during which the world, the region, and Egyptian society all changed. Nasser was a symbol, and as such he was the totemic incarnation of a utopia. He embodied collective feelings and desires of individuals who, beyond their differences, had aspirations and expectations that the symbol more or less satisfied. In the course of the last half century, new generations have emerged whose aspirations are intertwined with the facts of daily life: expressing oneself, gaining respect, acquiring dignity and position in society, traveling, and so on. Thereafter other symbols—such as the Qur'an, the constitution, and the rule of law—enter the equation with the promise of realizing these collective and individual aspirations. After the 1970s the Arab countries entered a postnationalistic ideological phase, a phase in which nationalism—monopolized until then by the army—

ceased to ensure the cohesion of the body politic. The generations born in the 1960s and 1970s, brought up in the culture of national unity, wanted to give their nationalism a different content. For some the meaning of their existence was inseparable from the religious norm; of course, this was in direct opposition to the behavior of others who dreamed of living in a secular society. Their confrontation was played out in the field of culture, which is the way we see the world. The predicament became public and took a political dimension as violence began to spread through university campuses. Fueled by social discontent over the living conditions of daily life (jobs, housing, and transportation), political Islam gained ground among ordinary working people and in the recently impoverished middle classes, the bedrock social base of radical nationalism during the preceding decades. Years of broken promises had led to a deep disenchantment, confirmed by an increasingly difficult relationship between the population and the corrupt state administration that governed it. The army had severed the state's link to the people who complained of the government's arbitrary behavior. In such a situation, people could not rely on the judiciary. The only way to settle a dispute with the administration was either to resort to friend or parenthood networks or corruption. This explains why the conflicts were violent since the executive power refused any kind of institutional counterweight.

The void between rulers and ruled lay at the heart of the Arab uprisings that began in Algeria in 1988, plunging the country into chaos for the next decade. The uprising took place because the people no longer recognized themselves either in their leaders or in their institutions. The regimes stemming from the coups d'état of the 1950s and 1960s did not understand that their historic task came to an end once they had strengthened the process of formation of a central power exercising sovereignty in the international scene, and the monopoly on violence at the national level. After accomplishing all this, they opposed the integration of the people into the state institutions. The 2011 Arab uprisings set off this process in the region even though the situation turned out to be more complex than expected. The collective frustration that led to rioting expressed a demand for an efficient state administration; there was a crying need for institutions where individuals could be heard by those exercising public authority, whose decisions would have important consequences on their private lives. The privatization of the state hindered the integration of members of the community into the political system and opposed the emergence of true citizenship by strangling civil society.

The paradox of a utopian society innocent of all conflict is that it leads to the most extreme violence (torture and murder). It may be useful at this point to recall Hannah Arendt's *Essay on Revolution*, in which she states that Europe only passed from its prepolitical to its political phase in the nineteenth century, underlining the fact that the prepolitical phase was based on force and violence. The state in Europe had a difficult birth, scarred by conflict and violent protests. Why should it be any different for the Arab countries in the conditions that are even more unfavorable of globalization and the interference of Western powers? The Europeans brought about a political revolution by deprivatizing political power by elections only two hundred years ago. Everything would seem to indicate that the same process is under way in Arab countries today. Consequently, the difference with the West is a historical one, and cultural specifications do not imply an unalterable essence that would make the Arab culture immovably hostile to modernity and democracy. The Arab countries are not ungovernable; they are looking for a credible government that will fulfill their aspirations and manage public life in a way that radical Arab nationalism, represented by military regimes, was incapable of doing.

The Aggressive Nature of Nationalism

The political stability of the Western nations and the peaceful competition for power through the vehicle of free elections tend to make some people—among them, scholars and journalists—believe that democracy is consistent only with Western culture. This is especially so of Arab countries because Islam does not make today the distinction between the spiritual and the temporal. What is forgotten, or underestimated, is the long historical process of national construction undergone by the European countries, which have endured revolts, revolutions, and conflicts between church and state at the cost of many millions of dead people. Barbarity is not exclusively Christian or Muslim. Among other things, it is part of mankind's nature. A reference to history is indispensable to social sciences to avoid the trap of the kind of model frozen in time, in which the Arab countries seem to be imprisoned today. Having obtained their political independence, the Arab countries found themselves confronted by the political and cultural problems of national construction, meaning the depoliticization of segments of identity competing to define the nation. A nationalist ideology can unite against foreign domination, but it loses this capacity when foreign domination is ended. In Syria, Iraq, and Egypt, Sunni and Shiite Muslims, Christians of various denominations, Copts, and others were united against European domination. The Christian community had supplied nationalist ideologists and eminent leaders since the close of the nineteenth century. Many Egyptian Copts participated in the leadership of the Wafd, the party that fought the British for Egyptian independence. But once the foreigners had recognized the sovereignty of the new state, the national identity had difficulties integrating the nation's ethnic and religious diversity, as if a non-Muslim could not be fully Egyptian, Syrian, or Algerian. Some alchemy is required to convince a Sunni Syrian that his Greek Orthodox Christian neighbor is entitled to the same rights as he is.

The confessional representations that have marked Arab societies so deeply will not vanish of their own accord from one day to the next. Moreover, the traditional societies of the past, built as they were on hierarchies of status (e.g., Muslim, Jew, Christian, black, female, young), have no inkling of the modern notion of equality. The political violence that broke out in Iraq after the fall of Saddam Hussein and the military conflict that has been ravaging Syria since 2012 show that the idea of equality between individuals of different confessional communities has not taken root. Certainly, the confessionalism inherited from the Ottoman Empire has been abolished, but the practices of the state and the cultural representations of Arab countries still perpetuate it among the people at every level of government. This mutual devaluation of one another confines group awareness to the confessional group to which the individual happens to belong. Sunnis say they are more nationalist than Shiites; Arab Christians are convinced that without them Muslims would still be under Turkish domination, and so on. Each confession claims a monopoly of nationalism, accusing the others of laxity and—when they differ ideologically—of betraying the nation.

As soon as there is conflict over political, material, or symbolic issues, the protagonists look to their respective communities for support. They distrust parties that include militants from different communities. The Lebanese example is a perfect illustration of this obstacle to universality within national frontiers. In Syria, to shield himself from a military coup d'état, General Assad surrounded himself with Alawite military men like himself, even though the Alawites represent only 10 percent of the total Syrian population. Saddam Hussein did the same with the Sunnis, preferring the inhabitants of his own village, Tikrit, to all others. This confessionalism at the pinnacle of power favors the formation of networks of clients that serve as informal and unequal middlemen between the state and the population; naturally, this makes most of the population believe that they are being bullied and marginalized. In Algeria the people of Kabylia, a Berber-speaking region, feel that they are excluded outright from the rest of the nation. The truth is, they are excluded not because they are Kabyles but because they are just like any other Algerians who have no connections with the graft networks that control the state. Community and regional solidarity are mobilized as resources to obtain from the state the rights that are theoretically accorded to every citizen, but these solidarities bring no advantage to communities; instead they bring profit to individuals who manipulate the resources of their confessional identity in their own private interest. Communities are not officially recognized (except in Lebanon) and go unrepresented in state institutions.

Not all Syrian Alawites and not all Arabic speakers in Algeria have easy access to state services, hospital beds, bank loans, and jobs or the ability to obtain a passport without trouble; for this, they must go to individuals within their community who have power to help because they belong to networks of clientelism that reach to the very summit of state power. The state integrates a part of the population through informal networks that can be used as growth areas and social bases. This structure is a source of chronic frustration and instability: it is not wanted by leaders who would wish to see a fully integrated nation within which all lesser powers are absorbed by the state and to which all citizens would swear allegiance, each on the same equal footing. Arab leaders have in mind the theoretical model of the nation, defined by sociologists as a collectivity within which all segmentation by clan, city, tribe, seigneury, or feudal domain is abolished, in such a way that the individual, freed of local political allegiances, can give his loyalty to the state. This model is a society politically integrated by the state, which pacifies the political field by means of a participation that assumes a degree of democracy. The Arab leaders failed to implement such a model. Given the formal equality that exists among its members, the model of the nation-state rests on universality and cosmopolitanism, neutral to religious or ethnic belonging as well as inequalities of status. In his relationship with the state, a man should neither be Sunni nor Shiite, Greek Orthodox Christian nor Kurd or Berber. He should first and foremost be a citizen subject to the rule of law assessed based on his behavior toward the legal system. Culturally, he can be Christian or Shiite, but not politically.

This dream of integration is only possible through a political participation guaranteed by free elections and a democratic process to which the authoritarian regime is adamantly opposed. The contradictory nature of Arab regimes reflects the incompatibility between the political/administrative structure of the nation-state and the exclusion of most of the population from its institutional machinery. As a sociopolitical framework whose integration is guaranteed by the state, the nation is a formation within which members of the community recognize themselves in a leadership they trust. Political participation is either fictional (reflecting the charisma of a leader giving the illusion that the people wields power), or effective (with the people choosing the leaders they want). The crisis of the Arab nations began when fictional political participation lost its potency. Within this context, the aggressive and warlike nature of nationalism acts as a brake on national construction since it actively prevents the pacification of the political arena. Paradoxical though it may seem, except in times of war, nationalist ideology has always—and in all places—divided rather than united people. The very structure of its ethnic and religious roots incorporates latent divisive forces that burst forth at every opportunity. As one of the resources of nationalism, religions divide because there will always be one person or one group of people who are convinced that they are closer to God than everybody else. Religion only unifies when its adherents feel threatened by the adherents of a different religion.[3] The same is true of ethnicity that is shot through with the dynamic of pure ethnic origin, a fiction to which every powerful group refers in order to establish its superiority over the rest. Ethnic conflicts are as virulent inside the group as outside it because of the segmentary logic that leads some to claim for themselves a privileged link with the origins of their ethnic group. The anthropologist Fredrik Barth has shown that ethnic frontiers are social constructions and that they take shape in function of their adversaries.[4] The ethnic group is not an organic body with immutable frontiers, he explains; it is a relationship to others that provides an identity in function of its enemies. If we do not understand this approach, we will never understand the divisions and conflicts that occur within the same ethnic group. Ethnic or ethnocentric logic is what motivates nationalist ideology to classify and rank individuals, groups, and regions according to the myths of the origins. If a political community is held together by nationalist ideology and nothing else, it will never have civil peace because one-upmanship within that framework constantly creates hierarchies whose result is the chauvinism of certain groups who claim a monopoly on nationalist purity. In the Arab countries, ethnic or religious minorities are always suspected of helping foreigners who might threaten the nation's independence. Kurds, Berbers, Maronites, Shiites, Christians, Jews—all are perceived as potential dangers to be foiled by police or army action. They are expected to forfeit their identity in public to blend into the imaginary majority or else to confine its existence to the privacy of their own homes.

Nationalist ideology is the contemporary form taken by local patriotism that has always existed and that grows out of belonging to a group and subscribing to its traditions and culture. It draws its basic elements from an identity or, rather, the awareness of an identity felt by members of the group. This springs from what Clifford

Geertz calls "primordial bonds or sentiments" that are rooted in tradition and myth of the past (kinship, language, religion, customs, neighborhood proximity, etc.).[5] Resting as it does on these bonds mobilized as resources, nationalist ideology is essentially chauvinistic; it spurns anything that it views, through the lens of its own criteria, to be foreign to local culture and ethnicity while singling out any individuals within the community that it suspects of disloyalty by reason of their origins or antecedents.[6] This creates a structural situation of confrontation and violence. It also produces a political system that must be imposed by force of arms or by a belief in some kind of meta-social principle that legitimizes a blatantly non-egalitarian structure. Ethnic origin, language, religion, and the rest are not enough to build a nation if we consider a nation to be a community that has depoliticized or neutralized its various ethnocentrisms and blended them into an ethnocentrism of national dimensions. Any community in today's world whose members are aware of their cultural or ethnic identity is likely to produce a nationalist ideology. If the community is dominated by foreigners, a nationalist ideology will invariably rise with a sense of identity. It is the first stage of the birth of a nation united against those who are viewed as alien to the *imagined* community seeking to draw political frontiers. By liberating itself from foreign domination, the community does not so much form a nation as constitute a central power to which it gives the attributes of a state, whose goal will be to build a nation. Theoretically, the concepts of nation and nationalism are mutually sustaining, but the latter does not automatically give birth to the former. The question is: does nationalism shape or does it proceed from the nation?

The specialized academic literature on this subject offers two alternatives: the first is that nationalism is the rock on which the nation is built, and the second is that the nation itself is the source of nationalism.[7] Both suggest a genetic link between the two notions.

They only differ on the direction of the relationship. For some, nationalism is as old as mankind itself; for others, the nation is a modern historical phenomenon. But none of these authors seem to grasp that nationalism alone cannot create the nation and that nationalism is not the only ideology generated by the nation to maintain a national consensus. It is not by its nature sufficient to ensure national cohesion; on the contrary, by playing on the ideas of *pure* and *not so pure*, and *true* and *false*, by classifying the members of the community by the length of time they have belonged to it or adhered to the party (i.e., whether they are early or late converts), nationalism contrives to fashion a perfect prototype of the national individual, who is well-nigh impossible to find in the real world but who, by serving as the imaginary norm, becomes the yardstick for authentic nationalist credentials. And all this prevents people from entering the political system on an equal footing and, hence, from sharing the universal benefits of citizenship. Nationalism is a source of conflict. It cannot create, of itself, any kind of peaceful consensus that would presuppose civic responsibility, solidarity, and equality; in short, it denies the people a citizenship that bestows rights and imposes duties. If potential enemies remain within the nation, in the sense given by Carl Schmitt to the friend/enemy dialectic, the political unity of the collectivity is imperiled, as has often been the case in many countries in the twentieth century. Primordial sentiments have not been enough to ensure national unity in Iraq, Syria, or anywhere else. Neither Islam nor a common language has contrived to bring Sunnis and Shiites together properly in a single country.

This approach makes it possible to define the nation in its historico-political context in relation to the mechanisms of integration that it employs to construct a pacified political space and to institute universal citizenship within national frontiers. Our hypothesis is that the nation, in the experience of Europe, where it first made its appearance, is the result of a double dynamic: that of a tradition in regard to the ethnic origin, culture, and religion ("mechanical solidarity"), and that of a demand for universality, to the detriment of subnational identities and bellicose ethnocentrisms, spearheaded by the civic culture that is the ideology of citizenship. As a pacified political space, the nation does not break with the cultural heritage of traditional society; on the contrary, it continues to revere tradition, culture, and primordial bonds, except when they may run counter to universal equality and freedom of conscience in the public sphere. "Nationalism," writes Ernest Gellner, "uses some of the pre-existent cultures, generally transforming them in the process, but it cannot possibly use them all."[8]

Much has been written about the difference between cultural nationalism of the German kind and the civic nationalism preferred by the French. This difference is an ideological representation in both Germany and France, the nation being both cultural and civic in nature. In France, the nation had to come together by integrating foreigners without sacrificing its local memory of the past; in Germany, the nation had to take a different path, putting the culture of the people first, without subordinating the political freedom of the individual to the idea of a cultural community. The starting point of the French in defining the nation was the voluntary engagement of the individual declaring himself to be a part of it. For the Germans, ethnic identity and the culture of the people were the source. Yet the French did not rule out the cultural dynamic of the homeland, and the Germans did not exclude individual autonomy and citizenship. The difference can be traced to historic conditions: France is indelibly marked by the spirit of the 1789 revolution and is a country of immigration that positively needs to integrate foreigners into its fabric; these foreigners are expected to individually renounce their cultures of origin and adhere to political principles that the French deem to be universal. This was the idea of Ernest Renan, for whom "the nation is founded on the forgetting of origins. . . . It is a plebiscite that takes place on a daily basis."[9] France nationalized foreigners living on her soil, turning them into "universal French people," whence the myth of the universality of French civilization. Germany, by contrast, used to be a country of emigration, which had no need of immigrant foreigners, having plenty of its own people. The closed German idea of a nationality centered on Germanic identity, a common language, and the law of consanguinity stems directly from this.

The nation is a human collectivity that creates a universalized political culture within geographical frontiers. All its members are formally equal, educated in the conviction that their values are universally applicable. This education directs the aggressiveness of nationalism toward the outside, painting the foreigner as an enemy who is waiting to pervert the national culture and exploit rivalries between national ethnocentric entities. The Western nations have pacified their respective spaces, but they are still at latent war with the non-Western countries. By systematically seeking to accumulate greater power than rival nations, national ethnocentrisms transform the world scene into a theater of confrontation regulated by the law of the jungle. The Americans, French, Chinese, and Russians, to mention only a few, consider that the cultures of their respective nations are more rational than other peoples' and cast themselves as the guardians of the only true human values. While they have managed to impose the supposed universal dimensions of humankind within their geographical borders (excluding immigrants, especially clandestine ones), the Western nations still balk at applying the cosmopolitan idea of Kant on a worldwide scale. National ethnocentrism is unable for the time being to imagine the dignity of mankind beyond its own national prototype. It is as if, to be a fully recognizable member of the human race, one must belong to the chosen nation. The Kantian project positing man as an end in himself has never been accomplished on a global level. Kant helped with the pacification of nations, but his teachings about pacifying the world scene found no echo beyond the much later creation of the United Nations Organization, which has no authority to force respect for its own skeleton version of international law. We need no reminding that the United Nations was only born after two world wars had left untold millions dead.

The peoples of the developing world are thus doubly victims of the denial of universality. First, for political reasons related to the conflictual situation within their nations still under construction, and second, in a world context for reasons related to anthropology. Having been destroyed locally, the colonial order was reconstituted on a global scale, leading to discrimination among human beings based on their national origins. The repression of waves of migrants and the incessant debates about immigration give some idea of the current discriminatory logic at work around the world. American political scientists talk of "failed states" instead of "failed policies," for which the leadership elites of the South are just as responsible as those of the North. The Arab states are part of this discriminatory world order, which recognizes their sovereignty and legitimates them with diplomatic relations and seats in the United Nations. Yet the leadership elites of the Arab states deny sovereignty to their peoples who do not possess the right to free elections. When the American or French presidents receive with state honors a leader who has come to power by force, they give him international recognition that is then used in his own country as a legitimizing resource. The global propagation of the nation-state model will not deliver progress in the history of developing countries unless that model is securely bound to the people's sovereignty expressed through free elections. Nationalist fervor, which originally helped populations to shake off colonial domination, contributed after independence to worship the kind of nation that flattered the individual in the abstract while mutilating him in flesh and blood. Nationalist alienation and religious alienation resemble each other: they share an adoration of totems and a deep suspicion of ordinary human beings.

CHAPTER 3

THE NATION, KANT, AND GELLNER

In his book *Nations and Nationalism*, Ernest Gellner expressed his surprise that Kant is recognized as the theorist of the nation, given that his philosophy runs counter to nationalism. For him, Kant did not invent the nation since his theory actually weakens nationalism. But Gellner's error is that he fails to establish formal links between nation, citizenship, and public space; Kant, the ideologist *par excellence* of the public space, is by that very fact the first theorist of the nation. Gellner writes: "A person's identity and dignity is for Kant rooted in his universal humanity, or, more broadly, his rationality, and not in his cultural or ethnic specificity. It is hard to think of a writer whose ideas provide less comfort for the nationalist."[a] Gellner fails to grasp that Kant is the theorist of the nation and not of nationalism. By introducing a universal dimension, Kant neutralizes the conflictual structure of nationalism and lays the groundwork for a pacified political arena. He attempts to reconcile morality and liberty by making individual desires compatible with one another through the notion of subjection to the law starting from the unsociable sociability of individuals. He supposes that the individual is responsible for his own acts and free of community allegiances. Thus he prepares the ground for a pacified social space that becomes a space for the exercise of citizenship. Abstract social links within this space are supported by a political identity in which the individual, freed of the communities that previously existed, can see a place for himself. The great figures of the Enlightenment did not create the political community, but by pacifying it they created the nation, allowing it to demonstrate that it was workable and capable of imposing itself as a universal model through a "national concordance" of which they were the inspiration. Kant had nothing to do with nationalist ideology carried through to community chauvinism, but once national frontiers are established, the community must be pacified, and to this pacification Kant made a decisive contribution. The role of the Enlightenment in the emergence of the nation does not escape Gellner. He declares that if high culture is to take root in the nation, the price to be paid is secularism. Clerics must become secular; this is the only way that the Kantian tension between ethical-religious and political-juridical approaches can be left behind. But Gellner fails to see that secularization is the process by which religious passions and an emotional attachment to one's ethnic group would have already been eliminated from society to guarantee national concordance. Nor does he understand that the process of secularization of a "high culture" is the very process of achieving universality, without which the nation would remain a bone of contention between local identities squabbling over the way national universality should be defined.

[a]Gellner, *Nations and Nationalism*, 131.

What Is a Nation if Its People Are Not Sovereign?

In the 1990s, Clifford Geertz questioned the ability of developing countries to build states under the rule of law such as existed in the West. One of his articles on the subject was titled "What Is a State if It Is Not Sovereign?"[10] Although intellectually stimulating, his skepticism is connected to the synchronic approach of anthropology that has always had methodological difficulties with history.[11]

Geertz's work is essentially focused on religious changes in Indonesia and Morocco, and he observed that these were formal as far as they concerned an adaptation of the traditional religious view of the world to the new historic realities of the nineteenth and twentieth centuries. For him, the nationalism of the Indonesian president, Sukarno, and the Moroccan king, Mohammed V, was a discursive construction that preserved the old Islamic worldview. This approach was relevant enough, but it underestimated the contradictions of a syncretism that, with time, was to provoke a crisis. This crisis made it crystal clear that the syncretism of authoritarian nationalist ideology had no long-term future or at the very least could not guarantee the building of a pacified political space. The Arab countries have been proving the truth of this ever since the 1980s.

In Egypt the regime failed to keep its promises or build a political order that ensured the hoped-for dignity and standard of living, whence the reforms first implemented by President Anwar Sadat in 1974, which terminated the single-party system and reinstated a free market and private capital. These reforms were not intended for regime change; they were simply a means of rescuing the regime seeking to gain a new legitimacy through (rigged) elections. The regime authorized the existence of opposition parties but prevented them from winning elections by stuffing ballot boxes or annulling results that went against it. It was, however, a progress because eventually stuffing boxes would not be possible. Bereft of projects like those of the 1950s and 1960s and that had offered hope, the military elites went on the defensive to save a regime that was under heavy pressure after its failure. What was actually at stake was sovereignty, the founding prerogative of a legitimate political order. Sovereignty is a belief that gives sense to a hierarchical power structure and that serves as a basis for all relationships of authority.

Along with the Westphalian order, which reached the Arab world at the beginning of the twentieth century, the monarchies (Egypt,

Saudi Arabia, Iraq, Jordan) claimed the national sovereignty; with varying degrees of success, they essentially ensured the independence of their countries. The Egyptian, Saudi, and Iraqi monarchies were recognized internationally between the two world wars since the principle on which they were based was acknowledged by their subjects. As a descendant of Muhammed Ali, the founder of the Egyptian monarchy, King Farouk availed himself of a general belief in hereditary legitimacy that made him sovereign of his country. After the Second World War, political events in the region destabilized the monarchies, especially in Egypt, where the king was accused by the army of betraying the nation. Egypt's military leadership forced a break with the symbolic political order, just like the French revolutionaries of 1789, by transferring sovereignty to the nation, but for all that the notion of sovereignty remained unsecularized. Under King Farouk, it was a fiction; under Nasser, it was a utopia; and in both cases, it had no connection whatsoever to universal suffrage. The Egyptian officers did not give the population the right to elect the president and the members of parliament. They took sovereignty out of the hands of the king, but they did not pass it on to the electorate. As far as they were concerned, national sovereignty was entirely compatible with an authoritarian regime that drew its legitimacy from a metasocial principle: God, tradition, martyrdom, army, history.

Not wishing to look like dictators wielding absolute power, Arab military leaders were careful to create revolutionary councils, or Councils of the Revolution named under the new constitutions as repositories of national sovereignty. The councils' authority rested on a popular belief in the mission that history had conferred upon the army. From this standpoint, the military did not actually bring about any revolution, given that sovereignty was not transferred to the electorate and the political order was not changed fundamentally, only verbally, because of what they did. National sovereignty was affirmed and foreigners were kicked out, but the general population remained outside the institutions of government, just as before. The discourse had changed, but the political power structure was the same as ever. For the military, national sovereignty meant the affirmation of the nation in liberating itself from colonial domination; their goal was to set up a strong central power according to the logic of the Westphalian Order, in which all states were considered equal and sovereign. Was this enough to create a stable state in which the population could see its aspirations reflected? What did the notion of national sovereignty actually mean, in a world caught up in transnational whirlwinds over which states had little or no control? What is the political value of armies in a post-Westphalian system whereby wars between states are illegal, from an international standpoint? Surveying all this, specialists in international relations, political science, and public law began to wonder if the notion of national sovereignty was not already outdated in a world that had changed so radically in the last fifty years.[12] The interdependence of economies had eroded the very idea of national sovereignty that is only effective if it is supported by a strong economy or military power. Finally, if we define national sovereignty as the capacity of a country to preserve its independence, we must accept that the Arab countries are not sovereign at all. This was conclusively demonstrated by the invasion of Iraq in 2003 and the troubles in Syria that began in 2011. Sad enough, but the only sovereign states are those that have nuclear weapons to deter any military invasion.

The concept of national sovereignty is intimately connected to the political logic of war in a conflictual international situation. By mobilizing this concept to affirm their legitimacy in their own internal political arenas, the military put in place regimes that resorted to violence to eliminate all opposition, even when that opposition was expressed by revered historic figures of nationalism. Michel Aflaq, the founding father of the Baath Party, fled Assad's Syria; his companion, Salah al-Bitar, was assassinated in London. Nasser forced into exile many Free Officers who had joined him in the overthrow of the Egyptian monarchy. In Algeria, under Boumediene, the founders of the National Liberation Front, Hocine Aït Ahmed, Ahmed Ben Bella, and Mohamed Boudiaf, were imprisoned or exiled. The same happened in Iraq. If it is the only basis for a regime, national sovereignty leads straight to state violence and repression of public freedoms, notably the freedom of expression. The military disenchanted the national sovereignty, but they made the nation sacred, generating a new class that replaced the former aristocracy. Lyrical speeches glorifying the nation served to devalue the state, which was reduced to an administrative apparatus. Above the state hovered the sacred entity of the army, its sole source of authority. In Arab republics, the army is not a state institution; it is the embodiment of the nation, the heart of a political ideology that prevents the institutionalizing of relationships of authority. Unlike the state, the nation *is* an idea, something imaginary that references a collectivity that includes past, present, and future generations. It is an abstract thing, whereas the state exercises real authority over real living people hoping to make their voices heard within its institutions. The nation is not a juridical category working under the law to regulate relationships of authority. Specialists in public law all agree that the nation has no public persona outside the state. In a democracy, any citizen can lodge a complaint against the state, which can be found to be wrong and condemned. A complaint like this against the nation is unthinkable because the nation has no existence in law, despite the lyrical speeches made in its praise. Anybody can speak in the name of the nation, but only officially appointed people can speak on behalf of the state. If we declare that the nation is sovereign, it is like saying that someone speaking in the name of the nation is sovereign. Any monarch and any colonel who carries out a coup d'état can say he speaks for the nation, awarding himself the legitimacy to appoint people to run the state. In this way, the army imposes itself as the legitimate source of the authority delegated to civil elites to direct the state's administration. As the guarantor of national sovereignty, the army is above the state, whose functionaries are mandated by it to manage the government's services. The president receives a mandate from the army to exercise an authority that is intended to carry out the precise mission of strengthening national sovereignty by creating the economic, social, and cultural conditions for it to flourish.

The theory behind this concept of sovereignty needs to be addressed in order to understand the workings and contradictions of Arab regimes that have built states on the basis of national sovereignty rather than on the sovereignty of the people expressed through the ballot box. The founders of authoritarian Arab regimes were against electoral democracy because it supposedly gave the rich a serious advantage over the rest. They attempted to build a more democratic system whereby the state could be placed at the service of the people. They claimed to be the embodiment of the nation's will to be sovereign, orchestrating coups d'états to take the exercise of sovereignty out of the hands of monarchs and aristocrats, whom they accused of corruption and collusion with the West at a time when colonial and neocolonial domination was busily repressing nationalist aspirations. The notion of sovereignty appeared in a context of foreign domination, not in one of contradictions within the political arena. Designed to strengthen national independence, it was also used to justify the authoritarian tendencies of the regime that made laws strengthening the prerogatives of the executive power. The goal was to curb any public freedoms of which the opposition might take advantage. These historic conditions explain the antiliberal nature of the political currents that emerged to achieve the process of national liberation. Colonel Nasser in Egypt and Gen. Abdul Karim Kacem in Iraq did not overthrow the monarchies in their countries on the grounds that they did not guarantee public freedoms; they merely accused them of connections with foreign powers opposed to national sovereignty. The Arab regimes did not spring from movements whose goal was to guarantee civil rights to individuals. Their principal mission was the political and economic neutralization of foreign influence. They ensured domestic civil peace by using public force (the police and the justice system) without pausing to think that they might be oppressing some members of the national community. When it comes to crackdown opponents, the police think they are dealing with traitors who betray the nation. The idea of the protection of the country does not imply the freedom of individuals. In Arabic, *ettahrir* (liberation) is the means by which *al horiya* (liberty) is achieved. This is no play on words but a question of the semantic content of a language that conveys political concepts as they relate to contemporary culture and contemporary aspiration. The aspiration is for a strong power that defends the interests of the group. Consequently, the liberal demand for a genuine separation of powers is inopportune, even harmful, because it may hamper the ability of leaders to defend the nation. Consistent with that political figure of popular imagination—the just prince who personifies and defends the pride of the group—this ideology was accepted by the majority of the people.

Arab nationalism is a blend of Westphalian sovereignty and utopia. It carries within itself a fundamental contradiction that exposes it to both Islamist and liberal criticism. It seeks to modernize the country by using the idea of the providential leader who fights evil and spreads good. This psychologization of politics offers no incentive to place institutional limits on government power. In the contemporary Muslim culture, Machiavelli's and Hobbes's works did not resonate among the social elites, and the concept of state remained to some extents linked to the sacred. The fundamental question is this: can the old Arab culture be compatible with a state in which sovereignty belongs to the people and in which the people choose their own representatives? The question is crucial as far as the very idea of sovereignty presupposes a profound intellectual break in the perception of the sacred in the public space. Such a rupture itself presupposes that the seat of the state power is perceived as empty, as the French philosopher Claude Lefort put it; or, rather, that state power belongs to the people alone per the mandate given to their representatives to exercise it, in their name, for a limited period of time. If the seat of power belongs to some transcendent entity in the name of which the king or the soldier speaks, then power belongs to the same transcendent entity and the people want leaders who will apply its will. Thus, the ballot box is perfectly useless as long as politics is not desacralized. Nasser, Kacem, and Boumediene were popular when they seized power through military force. The vox populi of the 1950s and 1960s saw the military as providential agents for the restoration of a dignity that had been trampled upon by the Western powers. The religious establishment gave its blessing to the new regime as long as it did not touch the symbols of Islam. It was in the regime's interest not to break with the old political culture, which held authority sacred; yet it was hostile to the liberal idea that society was the source of power and law, and that the people should elect its representatives to the sovereign assembly that promulgates and abrogates laws in its name. The military opposed liberalism condemned also by the ulemas who did not accept the idea of men changing sharia. The compromise with the military was encapsulated in the constitution of many Arab countries that stated unequivocally that "the *Sharia* is the chief source of the law." All this means that in the Arab culture predominating today, men are not aware that they are sovereign or that sovereignty is still locked in by a religious significance that makes it sacred.

The perspective developed in this section on the issues of nation, sovereignty, and democracy is bound to draw objections from the relativist camp, which underestimates the universal dimension of different human experiments that have influenced one another. Relativists seal cultures into an immutable essence that ignores the process of historic change, whereas their opponents tend to refer to a universal blueprint offered to mankind by Western civilization.[13] Some orientalists assume that Muslim societies are hostile to modernity because they do not share the same rationality with Europe. The flaw in this reasoning is that it separates individuals from their representations and cultures to explain something irrational regarding standards of the researcher's implicit model. The pitfall to avoid is the belief that there is one universal and rational culture that humankind should claim. Consciously or unconsciously, researchers tend to assimilate European experience with a temporal, universal model. This intellectual laziness prepares the ground for ethnocentrism leading to orientalism by way of explicit or implicit comparisons between societies open to progress (Europe) and societies closed and intolerant ones (Islam). Bernard Lewis, for example, appealed very strongly to European ethnocentrism, building his reputation on an invidious comparison between the Westerner as a free individual and the Muslim as a creature oppressed by his religion. Orientalism is misleading when it depicts Muslims as reluctant victims of their religion and culture, and when it states that Islam is incompatible to modernity on the basis of commentaries on medieval texts. It is all too easy to demonstrate that the concepts of tenth-century theologians are incompatible with modernity. It is very difficult to find Christian theologians in favor of gender equality and religious freedom in the fourteenth century. Are we allowed to conclude that Christianity is incompatible with democracy?

In this debate, the crucial question is this: how far can the modern state—that is, the rule of law—having been born in Europe, develop outside Europe? It seems that, in the wake of the profound social changes that have destroyed the old local communities, there is simply no alternative to the rule of law, either in the developing world or in Arab countries. European expansion imposed the national pattern on the entire planet. Nationalists fought for the independence of their collectivities, expecting them afterward to become sovereign nations with full international recognition. The Arab populations expressed the will to form nations organized into sovereign states that might carry within themselves a dynamic of evolution. This dynamic held the promise that sovereignty, personified by a man or a caste, would be claimed sooner or later by people whose goal is to be heard and represented in the institutions of the state. In Europe, popular sovereignty had to be imposed on kings and on ruling elites through uprisings, protest, and revolution. Absolutist monarchies and republican regimes only contented to transfer sovereignty to the electorate under intense pressure.

Readers could have the feeling that this approach is somehow Hegelian, meaning historicist, as I was told after a lecture given at Algiers University some years ago. The outlook developed in this book may be Hegelian, but it exactly reflects the subject to the extent that Arab nationalists *were* Hegelian, dreaming as they do of strong nations politically organized as states and economically fitted into the international market. Saad Zaghloul, Sati al-Husri, Michel Aflaq, Messali Hadj, Habib Bourguiba, Allal al-Fassi—all were Hegelian revolutionaries because they grasped that the only alternative to colonial domination was the creation of Arab categories of Hegelian historicism. How can we exist as a human collectivity, they correctly argued, within a structure of international relations regulated by force, if we do not form sovereign states? If the Arab nationalists were Hegelians in the past, it was because they had a sense of historical perspective in times of colonial domination. They understood instinctively that all human history since the European expansion became in some sort Hegelian. After independence, however, their heirs should have asked themselves different questions: how can this state guarantee its own independence if its market does not produce goods enough to satisfy the needs of its population? How can this state be stable if its population is deprived of the right to choose its leaders? The problem is that it is not relevant anymore to be Hegelian in a postcolonial situation. As soon as the formal independence was achieved and the state was a sovereign member of the international community, the leadership in Arab countries should have been Kantian and not Hegelian. As soon as Kant's philosophy comes to influence local political culture, the Arab world will be prepared to organize into modern societies and into a rule of law that protects individual and public freedom. In other words, if it was right to be Hegelian under colonial domination, it is necessary to be Kantian in the postcolonial period.

Notes

1. As the quintessential nationalist officer, Nasser had what Machiavelli called *fortuna*, meaning the historical circumstances that allowed him to emerge as a leader giving expression to a sense of national unity shared by nearly everyone. Did he have what Machiavelli calls *virtu*? Let the historians answer this question.

2. United Arab Republic, Information Department, *The Charter* (Cairo: National Publication House, 1962).

3. Put another way, both in Islam and in the Catholic faith there exists a constant state of one-upmanship because there are always Catholics or Muslims who declare themselves closer to God than other people. In nonsecular societies, this is immediately converted into political gain to win a symbolic or material advantage or to build up a political resource to dominate the less fervent.

4. Fredrik Barth, *Ethnic Groups and Boundaries: The Social Organization of Cultural Difference* (London: George Allen and Uwin, 1969).

5. See Clifford Geertz, "The Integrative Revolution: Primordial Sentiments and Civil Politics in the New States," in *Old Societies and New States*, ed. Clifford Geertz (New York: Free Press, 1963).

6. It is no coincidence that right-wing thinkers in Europe think of the nation solely in terms of cultural identity and tradition. From this standpoint, nationalist ideology, sometimes pushed to chauvinistic lengths, is best expressed by the extreme right in Europe, from Maurice Barrès to Jean-Marie Le Pen, by way of the Italian and German fascist movements. But it is not because it is the best expression of nationalist ideology that the right, or extreme right, is more attached to the idea

of the nation than the rival left. On the contrary, by making nationality a political issue, the extreme right tends to create a climate of civil turbulence. On the other hand, the European left sees the nation as a public space wherein nationality is a juridical rather than a political issue. The right sees itself in terms of homeland, locality, farmers, ethnic origins, and ancestral values. The left stands for universality, natural law, human rights, social contracts, a shared future, and so on.

7. Anthony D. Smith, *The Ethnic Revival* (Cambridge: Cambridge University Press, 1981); Ernest Gellner, *Nations and Nationalism* (Oxford: Blackwell, 1983); and Benedict Anderson, *Imagined Communities: Reflection on the Origin and Spread of Nationalism* (New York: Verso, 2006).

8. Gellner, *Nations and Nationalism*, 48.

9. Ernest Renan, *Qu'est-ce qu'une nation* (Paris: Imprimerie nationale, 1995).

10. Clifford Geertz, "What Is a State if It Is Not Sovereign? Reflections on Politics in Complicated Places," *Current Anthropology* 45, no. 5 (December 2004): 577–93, doi:10.1086/423972; see also Clifford Geertz, "What Is a Country If It Is Not a Nation?" *Brown Journal of World Affairs* 4, no. 2 (Summer–Fall 1997).

11. Despite its theoretical difficulty with history, anthropology makes for a better understanding of the politics of Arab countries than political science for which the issue is the state, with its constitutional basis and its legal arrangements for guaranteeing the exercise of citizenship. Political anthropology is concerned with relationships of authority, the practices of the central power, and the resources of leadership claiming legitimacy. More precisely, it pinpoints the coherences and incoherence of the process of construction of states that start with the nationalist demand for sovereignty. The danger lies in fixing this objective within an a-temporal structure in which the political anthropologist fails to see that the dynamic of change is hampered by numerous constraints.

12. See Stephen D. Krasner, *Sovereignty: Organized Hypocrisy* (Princeton, NJ: Princeton University Press, 1999); and Bertrand Badie, *Un monde sans souveraineté: Les états entre ruse et responsabilité* (Paris: Fayard, 1999).

13. See the debate between Clifford Geertz and Ernest Gellner on this issue: Ernest Gellner, *Postmodernism, Reason and Religion* (London: Routledge, 1990); and Clifford Geertz, "Reason, Religion and Professor Gellner," in *The Limits of Pluralism: Neo-Absolutism and Relativism*, ed. H. R. Hoentick (Amsterdam: Praemium Erasmanium Foundation, 1995).

PART II

The Ideological and Political Dynamics of Islamism

EVER SINCE 9/11 it has been difficult to discuss Islamism without it being associated with violent radical groups like al-Qaeda or the Islamic State in Iraq and Syria, ISIS. These radical groups are a minority when compared with a movement that is supported by a big portion of the population whose expectations and aspirations it carries. Under pressure from the Western media and Western public opinion, it is the radical wing that attracts the attention of researchers specializing in international relations. It is to the radical groups that the media turn for an explanation of the threat posed by aggressive fundamentalists to the international order, when they destabilize fragile states like Somalia, Afghanistan, Mali, and others. That terrorism is a transnational phenomenon that has amplified with globalization, drawing from it many vectors of propaganda as well as destructive weaponry. Its international involvement made it relevant to disciplines that study the conflictual nature of the current world scene. In Western universities, Islamism is a research object of international relations academic discipline. Yet sociology and anthropology are conceptually better equipped to study Islamism as an ideology that crystallizes the hopes of nonsecularized societies or societies in the process of secularization.

PART II

This book uses sociology and anthropology to study the ideological and political dynamic of Islamism from the standpoint of individuals and groups that reject the idea of separating church (or mosque) and state. As a social representation, Islamism reveals a culture that is attached to a normative model of a religion that, if it is respected, is supposed to guarantee social well-being and material progress. This aspiration is marked by historic conditions of social frustration, political revanchism, and loss of a sense of the values of traditional society. If the researcher does not take account of the expectations and values that give meaning to the lives of individuals, he is liable to view Islamism as a phenomenon outside the social existence of people who are perceived as victims of abstract forces that prevent them from being free.

It we are to avoid this line, we must at all costs avoid viewing Islamism as an institutional agency with a political rationality (or irrationality) threatening the state. This error is one often committed by political scientists trained to do research on the rule of law. Without being aware, they seem concerned by something lacking in Muslim societies while they should focus on the contradictions of the process of state building and nation building. Muslim societies are in the painful path of modernizing at their own pace with their own idiosyncrasies. They are all scarred by the convulsions of state and nation building and the monopoly of violence exercised by central powers seeking to affirm themselves. If we agree that the focus of the social sciences is historical, we must also acknowledge that they are themselves marked by history. The Islamist movement requires a pluridisciplinary approach in which anthropology, sociology, history, political science, and economics are all necessary for a proper analysis of its historic dynamic, its sociological roots, and its political effects within societies afflicted by multiple contradictions. The all-encompassing nature of Islamism is itself the expression of the nondifferentiation of social practices (total entrenchment of religion, politics, morality, and economics, for example) without autonomy of their respective fields. Islamism is a movement that opposes the trend toward differentiation in social practices but at the same time it goes along with it, seeking to influence it and negotiate the limits that separate the sacred from the profane at a time when the consequence of differentiation—that is, secularization—is genuinely under way in Muslim sociopolitical structures (though in many apparently contradictory forms). This is the approach of sociology, whose focus is on the experience of populations in a period of their history when they are seeking to balance the sacred with the profane. The Qur'an and the religious corpus, however relevant they may be from a theological standpoint, cannot help to understand the ideological and political contradictions of today's Muslim society. To some extent, the writings of Abul A'la Mawdudi, Sayyid Qutb, and other Islamist theorists do not pertain to theology. They tell us about the contradictions of Muslim societies torn between a deep concern for identity and a longing for progress. Islamism is neither the expression of a religious revival nor of a schism; it is a sociocultural and political/ideological movement that responds to the destructuring of Muslim societies following their insertion into modernity from which they are suffering intensely. The emphasis on historicity makes it possible to avoid essentialist approaches and to understand that Islamism is a reaction to modernity, to which it takes part, under conditions of political and cultural dependency. It is because it is a historical phenomenon—and not an eternal cultural essence— that the Islamist movement has become such a vector of political protest against authoritarian rule of radical Arab nationalism. It puts forward a utopia that is bound to perish after electoral victories that will reveal the depth of the gap between reality and the enchanted discourse of protest. Islamism is condemned to evolve and distance itself from the millenarian posture that promises to build an apolitical state. This is what I show in this second part, which deals with the movement's ideological and political dynamic.

4

Islamism as Cultural Representation and Ideological Will

ISLAMISM IS A WORLDVIEW with a cognitive and ethical dimension that incorporates the project of making life on Earth consistent with the divine norm that ensures well-being in this world and salvation in the next. It is a cultural representation that seeks to reconcile *being* with what *should be* by an act of ideological will. Transmitted from generation to generation, religious culture polarizes existence as *haram/halal, dounia/akhira, sadek/batel, hakika/kedb*. The semantic content of these performative notions has been structured by an ethos that draws a frontier between what is allowed and what is not allowed, between truth and falsehood, between humanity and animality.[1] The two heuristic concepts of will and representation indicate that, beyond the false consciousness, men are the agents of their history with reified concepts.[2] With all the necessary methodological precautions, the notion of representation is relevant since it is at the heart of history, which it incessantly nourishes. Peter Berger and Thomas Luckman emphasized that reality is built socially based on representations by which human beings act in the world.[3] For this approach, the concept of representation is crucial and is the basis of the social construction of reality that shows that social life goes beyond the simple biological reproduction. It emphasizes with some force that social

125

action finds its source in values stemming from consciousness. Cultural representations distinguish human societies from one another, endowing humanity with several different faces. Unlike animals, which obey the rigid and immutable laws of nature, man is open to a different form of evolution, having freed himself from the determinism that binds him to nature. Animals are not concerned by history since their existence is that of nature, which cannot change on the scale of life. This is not the case for man, who builds and invents his fate in the limits of his habitus (in Bourdieu's meaning). Representations forge an image of man that imposes itself as a norm indicating what social life should be. Man feels that it is a duty to be in harmony with this image of morality and reason. The heuristic interest of this theoretical approach is that it makes it possible, on the one hand, to pinpoint individuals as agents of the social processes with which they identify and, on the other, to integrate them into history by way of a culture that gives meaning to their existence. Whether it is inspired by Weber or Durkheim, sociology can help us understand Islamism as a set of representations that socialize the individual within the group (Durkheim) or as a network of values proceeding from subjectivity that form the basis for the morality that unifies the group (Weber).

The dynamic relationship between society, representation, and religion must be considered if we are to comprehend Islamism the way the founders of religious sociology intended to address religious beliefs. This means that we do not have to reduce its role to that of an institutional agency that would have a coherence and rationality of its own. Moreover, this perspective gives Islamism a local and global framework that is historically intelligible, in which cultural representations are politicized to explain the gap between the West and Muslim countries and to show how that gap may be narrowed and filled. Islamism is a modern ideology worked out by Abul A'la Mawdudi and Sayyid Qutb, whose teachings led to violence. With time, the Islamist movement divided into an extremist wing loyal to the teachings of the two founding fathers and a majority wing that no longer referred to them and sought to align itself with political reality with a view to transforming it by peaceful, nonviolent means. This latter wing has now entered the post-Islamist phase. It is more advanced in Tunisia today than in Algeria or Egypt.

The Cultural Roots of Islamism

Becoming aware of how far they have fallen behind Europe, the eternal rival they so despised in the past, many Muslims believed (and still believe) that they were dominated to such an extent because they had forsaken the true way of Islam. This idea was first formulated by the Al-Nahda, in the mid-nineteenth century, which called for a return to the original Islam as a shield against European expansion and the secularization that had attracted so many urban elites. Rejecting Wahhabism, which was too rigorous for the urban middle class, the Al-Nahda legitimized the material modernity and scientific discoveries of the Europeans while insisting on the central role of Islam in public life. The argument of Mohammed Abdu, the movement's principal thinker, was that the Qur'an urged the use of reason to unravel the mysteries of nature whose complexity revealed the power of God. He made it permissible to imitate the Europeans in the fields of science and technology, economics, urban administration, and institutions on the sole condition that Islam should continue to provide men with guidance. Abdu admired the Europeans; in his view the only thing wrong with them was the fact that they were not Muslims. In the minds of ordinary people, the Europeans had simply been more successful in taking advantage of the riches contained in the Qur'an than the Muslims themselves. Yet this line of reasoning, which was shared by many literate people and ulemas, remained obdurately hostile to the intellectual transformations of eighteenth-century Europe, which were rejected or ignored because of their indifference to religion. The link between the progress of science and the movement sparked by the ideas of Descartes and Kant was missed completely; instead the ulemas accepted the scientific discoveries of Antoine Lavoisier and Louis Pasteur while rejecting the modern philosophy that is at their epistemic core. Muslim culture has been marked by this contradiction ever since Abdu adopted European positivism without proposing a new theology that could accommodate the secularization of social thought. Avoiding direct confrontation with the orthodoxy represented by the sheikhs of Al-Azhar University, the Al-Nahda did not create a new theology, and thus it confined itself to proposing a puritanical interpretation of Islam, encouraging the assimilation of scientific progress to catch up with the West while resisting its domination and expansion. It was as if Abdu was saying yes to science and no to modern philosophy.

A century later the Muslim world has yet to overcome the contradictions of the Al-Nahda, whose program has been taken up again by Islamism in a simplified, radicalized form. Islamism is the message of Abdu carried by crowds expressing a collective frustration after a period of "national disenchantment" described by Héli Béji in her book *Le désenchantement national*.[4] The violence of contemporary Islamists is born of historical conditions, not of religion; it proceeds, more precisely, from the imbalance between the promise of the nationalist struggle and the reality of the postcolonial state, which was and remains a bitter disappointment. By mobilizing religion to serve as a tribune for protest, Islamism revived the argument of the Al-Nahda in different historic conditions. The former explained colonial domination in terms of the abandonment of the "real" Islam; the latter blamed the failure of the independent state on the decline of faith among leadership elites. Referring to certain verses of the Qur'an, Islamism demands a return to the "true" Islam to purify a society and state that have been contaminated by what is called social diseases imported from Europe. Radicalizing the Al-Nahda's program, it mobilizes the sacred to express contradictory expectations that borrow as much from modernity as from tradition in societies undergoing major changes. Islamism is not a millenarian movement seeking to ensure the salvation of souls in the next world; it offers instead to resolve the problem of social inequality by the strict application of religious morality. It denies that these may have existed in the past, explaining them as a consequence of the materialistic influence of the West and the lack of respect toward the values of justice, equality, and solidarity. The Islamists' scapegoat for all this is a greedy minority that has turned its back on the teachings of the divine. Islamism extends the Al-Nahda movement, adding violence. Sayyid Qutb recognized Mohammed Abdu as a master but reproached him for giving too much importance to reason and too little to the divine revelation. Abdu attracted educated bourgeois in the nineteenth century while Islamism in the twentieth century found support at every level of society, including disadvantaged young people tempted to resort to violence.[5]

Today the West is accused of propagating a materialism that has supposedly corrupted morals and influenced weak people who are victims of the perverse culture broadcast on satellite TV that can now reach the most remote villages on the planet. The Western way of life shown in films and TV series, in which religion has no place, is perceived by devout Muslims as a symbolic violence imposed by an image of men motivated by nothing more than their own material interest and pleasure, in a world where the bodies of half-naked women are used as advertising tools for selling soap and cars. The moral order championed by Islamism is deeply offended by this kind of symbolic violence invading the domestic sphere and weakening parental authority. Islamism responds to it with authoritarian methods aimed at safeguarding the supposed original goodness of Muslims whose pious ancestors (the *salafs*) still stand as an example.

This anthropological optimism is shared by a majority of the population, whose culture explains poverty, unemployment, and corruption as a consequence of the declining moral values.[6] Islamism is spontaneous sociology made up of popular representations and beliefs, seeking to find causes for behavior patterns that seem not conform to Islam. For example, if we begin with the hypothesis that God has created sufficient wealth on this planet to supply all of humanity, poverty and wretchedness can be explained by the egoism of the well off, the corruption of officials, and the greed of the materialist West that disturbs the equitable sharing of wealth according to the will of God. Under such circumstances an authoritarian state is needed to protect the basic values of a healthy society with laws that conform to morality and the true order of nature.[7]

We must bear in mind that Islamism is different from traditional Islam, which used to explain poverty by God's will. Why are the verses of the Qur'an that appeal for solidarity in the forefront today? Why are the verses affirming that God created the estates of rich and poor forgotten and those calling for fairness put forward? By declaring that poverty is of human origin, Islamism places itself squarely in an era of revolution that put pressure on the state to deal with the "social question." The state is no longer the private business of kings, princes, and aristocracy; it is now at the heart of the kind of deep public concern that leads to violent protest. As soon as people become broadly convinced that poverty has political and social origins, writes Hannah Arendt, the masses will become a political force, creating a dynamic of revolt.[8] Borrowing just as much from modernity as from tradition, Islamism is a contradictory product of contemporary history that has seen the bursting of the masses as a force in politics. By pushing the masses to take over the streets and exert pressure on politicians, Islamism reproduces the nineteenth-century European revolts, which led to political change and a proper representation of the people in state institutions. Islamism threatens social peace and smashes the ivory towers of rulers who seek to protect politics as the exclusive preserve of an elite. By mobilizing crowds, it plays a revolutionary role. However, the social energy it unleashes is handicapped by a theoretical weakness in its unrealistic political thought that refuses the autonomy of politics. Revolutionary though it may be, Islamism still lacks a coherent body of political thought that is in step with sociological upheavals in the Muslim world over the last two hundred years.

How, today, can a modern state be built if the notion of individual freedom is rejected? The rule of law is based on the concept of freedom and not on that of justice. It does not mean that the modern state is less concerned with fairness than is the traditional one. It means only that freedom empowers better people in their search for a realistic idea of justice. We can assess with objectivity freedom but not justice. Islamism is suspicious of liberty, which is suspected to lead to sinfulness and acts that go against the order of nature ordained by God. Islamism makes no distinction between sin and crime, both of which it views as misbehavior punishable by law. God is so present in this construct of social reality that he becomes a familiar personage whose rights must be respected. Thus, sin is perceived as an attack on God's rights, which is reproved by public opinion and condemned by judges; in light of this, to speak of the rights of man is an incoherence. The Islamic line of reasoning fears that liberty will lead straight to delinquency. An individual who lacks respect for the Qur'an is suspected of plotting to disturb the moral order and harm the property and honor of others. The same goes for the ruler; religion clearly indicates to him that there is a line that he may not cross in the exercise of his function. The principle behind this conception of existence is that the law must proceed from God, who is the guarantee against violations of the natural order. Respecting this principle is a guarantee to preserve the human character of society and to avoid falling into a state of barbarity (*jahiliyya*). In wilderness the animals are free, but there is no justice among them. Islam reminds everyone that men are not animals. They need a moral order to fulfill their human nature. Justice enhances this order; freedom threatens it.

The present secular culture of the West makes us as scholars take for granted the separation between religion and law, between the sin and the crime. European societies went through intellectual upheavals before secularizing the law. Secularizing the law seems to be a dreadful process to a Muslim consciousness that is afraid of the idea that society falls into anarchy. If God withdraws from Earth, there will be an open door to moral perversion. The metaphysical vacuum that Nietzsche wrote about is alarming to believers who rely on God's willingness in their everyday life. In this period of history, the believers do not trust themselves to be able to build a moral order without the guarantee of God. There is a rejection of political autonomy for fear of calling into question the moral order since the religious discourse teaches that man is incapable of settling his own destiny. Islamism is the illustration of this fear and of the cultural and social contradictions of societies transformed by European expansion.

Today's Muslim societies are searching for a way to curb individualism by appealing to duty and morality; they are also searching for a way to frame politics in the psychology of men, over which religion is expected to play a role. This apolitical representation of politics has perhaps been effective in the past in communities numbering a few thousand inhabitants, but it is bound to fail in the running of cities with populations in the hundreds of thousands who have lost touch with their ancestral solidarities. In the village, social life is embodied by the familiar faces of uncles and relatives by marriage who exercised informal control; in the city, absolute anonymity unleashes the most violent individualistic instincts. The Islamists have not yet taken account of these sociological changes; they believe that the convivial sociability of the villages of yore was solely the consequence of a respect for God's teachings and the kindness of the earlier generations. They look to psychology and religion for factors of cohesion in societies that have been completely undermined by money. And yet secularization is steadily under way in everyday life, where the inegalitarian rules of economics supersede religious morality. Everyone has firsthand experience of corrupt officials, cheating teachers, dishonest salesmen, uncles who trick their families out of their inheritance, imams living far above their means, and so on. The overexploited workers in a private company will clearly understand that their boss is a bad Muslim who does not respect the ethics of Islam even though he may have contributed money to build the local mosque. There is a gulf set between the ideal "norm" and the behavior of people who use religion for personal reasons to acquire moral credibility in their commercial transactions. Economic behavior is not detached from religion; on the contrary, it has absorbed it to give the trader or businessman a good conscience. We only have to walk down the street in Casablanca or Cairo during the month of Ramadan to observe that some behaviors (aggressiveness, waste of food, and so on) are a long way from the spirit of Ramadan as explained in the Qur'an. Void of their spiritual content, religious duties (*'ibadates*) suggest a mercantile relationship with God. Ritual obligations are displayed as a means to accumulate social capital. Credibility in the neighborhood is measured by the number of pilgrimages one has made to Mecca and by religious ostentation among people guided by an individual interest that has appropriated the religious ideal only to enjoy good reputation.

This is secularization by excess of religion. It works through the deep cultural crisis of Muslim thought that is frozen in obsolete tradition and unable to rearticulate religious culture in line with the sociohistoric changes of the last two centuries. Economics, politics, family ties—none of these pay much heed any longer to the religious ideal, which itself is unable to resist the egotism set loose by monetary exchange and the stampede for money. The fundamental contradiction within Arab societies is the fact that social practices are secularized and consciences are either not secularized at all or are not secularized enough. There is a gap between the social practices of everyday life and social consciousness. Fieldwork research in the streets in Algiers or Cairo shows the daily violence in contrast with the peaceful behavior at the mosque. Will the butcher give a scrap of meat to a half-starved woman scavenging for something to eat in a pile of trash? If the orientalist discourse on Islam repeats that the Muslim makes no distinction between the sacred and the profane, it is because this discourse pays no attention to the practices of daily life, to social relationships in the workplace, in the markets, in the courts, or in the street, where rudeness and violence are commonplace. Why has the Muslim conscience never acknowledged the secularization that is manifest in social life?[9]

A sense of existence is at issue in a situation where society is undermined by individualism and by the erosion of the values of solidarity. Caught as it is within a dynamic of rampant secularization that terrifies the faithful, religious conscience is anxious and dreams of a return to the Islam of the *salafs* (the pious ancestors) to restore a social cohesion that is threatened by the new social order. The crisis derives from this gap between the practices of daily life and a dream wherein the symbols have lost their capacity to enchant reality. The struggle between the just and the unjust, the true and the false refers to contradictory representations and visions of the world that attempt to give a kind of coherence to a society torn asunder by the divergent interests of individuals and groups. A Platonician vision lies at the base of the Islamist utopia, for which men are in error, living in a cavern where all they can see is flickering shadows. This utopia offers to free them and show them the true world, that of reason and the word of God. This paradigm, which has given meaning to the lives of Muslims for centuries past, is now in disarray. It is because of this crisis of paradigm that Islamists resort to violence and make it the only filter through which reality may be understood. The priority is to dissolve the individual into the group. The medieval religious culture, which continues to influence Islam, addresses itself to the group on which it exerts pressure to hold its members within the confines of morality.[10]

Religious discourse is fighting the concept of consciousness and thus cannot accept the private practice of faith, or a faith that is not supported by an institutional authority. In other words, medieval Islam, just like medieval Christianity, is unable to conceive of a faith unprotected by an institution or by a state. Christianity faced this crucial question at the close of the Middle Ages, when it was challenged by Protestantism: how could one be a Christian without the Catholic Church? For the contemporary Muslim, the crucial question is: how can one be a believer in a state that transforms sharia on the basis of what are fairness and freedom today? The Islamist utopia has emerged to resist the sociological tendencies that lead to the autonomy of the individual. Individuals are caught between a rock and a hard place, torn in two by a struggle between a sociological dynamic and a symbolic one. Muslim societies are under pressure to answer these crucial questions: How can we pretend that we want man to live in happiness if freedom of conscience is not acknowledged? How can we wish to build a modern world if we reject the idea of gender equality? How can we proclaim that human beings are all equal if we exclude religious minorities from the Muslim ideal? How can we reconcile the essential goodness of God with the intolerance of believers and the authoritarianism of political regimes? These questions are swept under the carpet, proscribed by a religious discourse that denies human anthropology and takes refuge in the myth of mankind's overall goodness. Finally, the great problem of Muslim societies harks back to the crisis of a theology that is incapable either of renovating the symbolism of the sacred or of inventing a new way of believing that would be compatible with sociological development. In the absence of philosophy, which ceased to exist with the demise of Ibn Rushd, Muslim theology completely dried up; it has long been no more than repetition by rote of the thinkers of many centuries back.

One of the failures of Arab nationalism relates to its inability to set up schools of modern theology open to philosophy, history, and social sciences at large. The Arab regimes have prohibited all public debate on religion in order to gain the people's support. Intellectual aridity has prevented creative thought from any consideration of social sciences or any alternative theology that might restore meaning to religious symbols that have been detached from the sociological conditions of everyday life and even from their own first objectives. The few attempts made in the twentieth century to reverse this trend were roundly condemned as heresies; this was the case of Ali Abderrazak, who suggested separating political legitimacy from religion, and (more recently) of Mahmoud Mohammed Taha, who proposed that a distinction be made between the Medina and Mecca verses of the Qur'an, with a view to working out a new theology centered on *mou'amalates* (everyday social practices). The former was condemned by the sheikhs of Al-Azhar University, who banned his book, and the latter was hanged in Khartoum in 1985 by the Ga'far Numayri regime under the pressure of the religious establishment.

Today, if any religious scholar tries to propose a new interpretation of the sacred text, he will face the anger of the crowds. Religious debates take place in the public in such a way that literate elites have no other choice but to outbid one another in dogmatism. This explains the return of Hanbalism, a rigorous doctrine that was neutralized by Abu al-Hasan al-Ash'ari when he established a tradition of compromise between celestial demands and terrestrial necessities. Al-Ash'ari was a former *mu'tazila* who had a wide philosophical culture and was familiar with Aristotelian and Platonician thought. A new al-Ash'ari is needed today who would be aware of the intellectual progress of philosophy and would found a new theology superseding the dogmatism of Hanbalism that belongs to the tribal past. But this, unfortunately, is not the way Muslim thought is headed.

The excessive religious fervor that has gripped the cities and rural areas of the Arab world is not a sign of theological renewal; on the contrary, it indicates an intellectual impoverishment when compared to the erudition of the *fuqahas* (religious lawmakers) of classical times. The leaders and ideologists of the Islamist movement all have superficial knowledge of the theology of al-Ash'ari and Abū Hāmid al-Ghazali. Stripped of spirituality, their discourse is essentially ideological with a reference to the sacred, which gives it credibility among the masses. Neither Sayyid Qutb nor Abul A'la Mawdudi had the erudite training of classical Islam. Nor did they have any education in religious sciences. Qutb was a literature professor and Mawdudi was a journalist. Their knowledge of Islam, based on memory, barely exceeded that of a young student, and that is exactly what explains their appeal to the popular masses. They took over the eschatology contained in the Qur'an to produce a political ideology that narrowed the spiritual range of the holy text. They revisited the biblical tale of original sin, which is also taught by the Qur'an, to emphasize the fact that man is haunted by temptations that can bring about his ruin, a ruin that is translated today in terms of social inequality, poverty, and corruption. The objective of this ideology is to prevent a fall similar to the original one, the cause of which may be found in the decline of faith among the westernized leaders and elites of Muslim countries. This discourse rests on the assumption that the Muslim individual is good, but his goodness is threatened by the egotism of certain individuals of weak character or influenced by values that are incompatible with the message of the Qur'an.

CHAPTER 4

The Making of Islamist Ideology: Sayyid Qutb and Abul A'la Mawdudi

Islamism was originally developed as an ideology by two thinkers who reinterpreted Islam's popular representations as a variety of utopia, Abul A'la Mawdudi (1909–79) and Sayyid Qutb (1926–66). They formulated an ideology to express the political will to make the world in conformity to cultural representation of Islam, proposing an alternative to capitalism (rejected because of its political freedoms and social inequalities) and socialism (also rejected for its indifference and hostility to religion). They formalized Islamic popular representations and in doing so framed them with references to verses of the Qur'an and to facts borrowed from natural science. Mawdudi and Qutb had a strong influence on the poorer urban classes that had benefited from the mass schooling of the postindependence years. Their works were readily available in bookshops and were sold for next to nothing. Written in language that was easily understood, they were highly didactic and were illustrated with examples drawn from everyday, ordinary life. There was no classical erudition or Muslim mysticism in Mawdudi and Qutb; this made them easily accessible to teenagers and adults who could barely read. The burden of their books was that Western civilization was trying to impose on the Muslim countries its own ways of thinking, with institutions built on the negation of the spirituality of the individual.

According to Mawdudi and Qutb, Islam offers a shining alternative to Western materialism, which turns men into robots and women into sexual merchandise. They assert that Western society, by making the practice of religion into a private activity, had mutilated man and reduced him to the level of a consumer guided by physiological instincts alone. Islam rejects this debasement and places God at the heart of society, preventing man from forgetting his humanity. Without God, the individual is no better than an animal; with God, he is a human being free in his actions and free to submit to divine law. In the 1970s, this discourse was the principal rival to the pan-Arab nationalist and socialist ideology, which it accused of aping the secular ways of the West. Prior to 1967, it was in a clear minority in the Arab countries, whose masses were patiently awaiting the modernization promised by the military elites in Egypt, Syria, Iraq, and Algeria. However, the military defeat in June 1967 gave the ideas of Mawdudi and Qutb a new appeal among ordinary people, notably young people. With the 1967 defeat, radical Arab nationalism had reached its limit, along with its failure to keep its promises of modernization. The Islamists claimed loudly that the victory of Israel—a small country with only three million inhabitants—over an Arab nation numbering 100 million and backed by vast oil resources was a sign and a warning from God for Muslim societies that had strayed from the way of truth and righteousness. Others, more narrowly, saw the defeat as a mark of God's fury over the assassination of Sayyid Qutb by Nasser's regime a year earlier in 1966.

Qutb wielded huge influence over the Islamist movement; he coined an ideology of combat whereby he politicized relationships with those he called "the hypocrites": namely, Christians and Jews. The crux of his theory was that the hypocrites had twisted the word of God as revealed to the prophets Moses and Jesus. The Prophet Mohammed had restored the original verity of monotheism, and the hypocrites opposed him just as they had earlier falsified the messages of Moses and Jesus. Qutb wrote: "Is it not logical that those who have twisted the Word of the Bible should now be perverting the Book revealed to Mohammed? In truth they have not changed for they continue to seek ways of evading the real issues, of shirking the truth and of spreading counter-truths."[11] Qutb's commentary has nothing to do with the theological debate between the branches of Abraham's monotheism; instead it set up a straight political rivalry, clearly designating the enemy—Jews and Christians—who are enjoined to acknowledge that their beliefs are unfounded and far distant from the word of God revealed to Abraham. This rivalry, says Qutb, must lead to a war of religion, ending with the total victory of sincere Muslims over the hypocrites, the Jews and Christians who embody evil. Once someone is declared as an enemy of God, there is no possible room for compromise, and the only solution is to reduce him to obedience by forcing him to submit to inferior status (*dhimmi*) and paying a tax (*jizya*) to the faithful of Islam.

The theological divergence with Jews and Christians is seen by Qutb as a betrayal of the word of God by those he calls the hypocrites, who are supposedly animated by jealousy and perfidy. The Qur'an may not be kind to Jews and Christians, whom it accuses of turning away from their prophets, but it made clear that God himself will take care of their punishment beyond the grave. At no point does the Qur'an ask Muslims to avenge the injustice done to God by those Jews and Christians who refuse to convert to Islam. Indeed, it is unequivocal about this: "They are a community of the past. To them, what they have acquired and to you what you shall earn. You will not be asked to answer for their acts." (Qur'an 2:134). In another verse, the Qur'an recommends that there should be no quarrel over Allah and no claims of a monopoly in Him: "Would you quarrel over Allah when he is our Master and your Master? Unto us the recompense for our actions, and unto you, the consequences of your own; for we are faithful unto Him." (2:139).[12] God, not man, is the only judge of religious differences between those who believe in the monotheism of Abraham. Concerning the disagreement between Jews and Christians, the Qur'an states: "Allah, on the day of resurrection, will judge this dispute between them"[13] (2:113). He will also judge, in the other world, the theological disagreements among Muslims, Jews, and Christians.

The Qur'an claims that Islam is the extension of Judaism and Christianity, and this claim is itself a factor of peace. By contrast, however, Qutb pushes for demonization and war, accusing the Jews and Christians of betraying Moses and Jesus, both considered as Muslim prophets whose message was deformed by Jewish rabbis and Christian priests who lied to those who followed them. For Qutb, the mass of uneducated Jews and Christians were led into error by rabbis and priests who hid the fact that their true religion is Islam, not Judaism or Christianity. Even though the Qur'an disapproves of Jews and Christians and appeals to them to convert to the new religion, it lays the foundations of peaceful coexistence among all the People of the Book. "There shall be no constraint in matters of religion," says the Qur'an (2:256), meaning that force should not be used to convert people to Islam. And the Qur'an insists on this issue of religious freedom in 109:6: "To you your religion and to me my religion."

Islam's adhesion to Abrahamic monotheism clearly indicates that the new religion does not demonize Jews or Christians, who shall be respected as People of the Book and invited to correct their beliefs. At the beginning, Islam had to convince the Jews and Christians that the new religion does not deny their faith; it merely brings a few corrections. Qutb would have none of this tolerance; on the contrary, he advocates a thoroughly belligerent interpretation of the Qur'an, demanding that Jews and Christians reconvert to their supposedly first religion, Islam, on pain of being reduced to the status of *dhimmi*. He wrote: "It would have been better had the Jews and Christians of Medina been the first to declare their adhesion to the new Islamic mission, since the Koran generally confirms and corroborates the Tora; their Holy writ announced the coming of Islam and they themselves awaited it to ensure the victory of Allah's religion over the idolatry of the Arab tribes."[14] This reasoning is based on Qutb's idea that humanity must have but one religion, Islam—the one supposedly revealed by Moses and Jesus, altered by the Jews and Christians, then restored by Mohammed, the last of the Prophets.

Qutb's understanding of the Qur'an deforms its meaning, as the following example shows: The Qur'an: "The Jews and the Nazarenes will never be satisfied with you until you follow their doctrine." Qutb's commentary: "The Jews and the Christians will continue to fight you and will give you no peace unless you abjure your mission, turn away from the truth and abandon your convictions to follow them in the errors earlier exposed."[15] And Qutb likens an injustice done to God to an injustice done to the faithful: "Injustice takes a multiple form: association in the cult in an injustice, aggression of others and transgression of the Law are all injustices."[16] The sacred Qur'an loses its substance here, crushed by the conflicts of the different social groups of the Arabian Peninsula in the time of the Prophet Mohammed. All the battles, defeats, friendships, and betrayals of early Islam are described without the smallest reference to their symbolic dimension, which reveals the opposition of good and evil inscribed in the anthropological makeup of mankind. For Qutb, man is not simultaneously good and bad; as far as he is concerned, good men are sincere Muslims gathered around the Prophet and faithful to the word of God, while bad men are Muslim hypocrites, Jews, and Christians. The former are victims of the latter because they wish to preach the word of divine justice and human equality; consequently, they are under constant attack from the enemies of God and his messenger, the Prophet Mohammed. The tolerant and humanist aspect of the Qur'an is entirely ignored by Qutb, who calls the Muslim to his duty of jihad against all unbelievers—beginning with what he calls "sociological Muslims," hypocrites who do not respect the five pillars of Islam.

For Qutb the fate of all humanity was decided in the Arabian Peninsula, which, according to him, contained different peoples during the seventh century. He failed to understand that the Jews and Christians that the Qur'an is talking about were actually Arabs—the majority of whom were later converted to Islam. There were no "Jewish people," no "Christian people," and no "Muslim people"; there were only Jewish, Christian, pagan, and Muslim who were Arabs. It is a retrospective error to endow these peoples after the fact with national identities that they did not have in the time of Mohammed. Speaking of the enemies of Islam, Qutb writes: "Today, just as before, their stratagems lead the nation far from its Koran and its religion, which constitute its war chariot and its armor in battle. They will be untroubled for as long as this nation remains cut off from the source of its power and vision."[17] The word "*umma*," incorrectly translated into English as "nation," defines a community whose members are united in the same faith; the moment one changes one's religion, one changes one's community. The anachronistic translation of the word "*umma*" by the word "*nation*" makes it lose its flexibility, as if the men who fought Islam in its earliest years were unchanged today. Qutb's text gives the impression that the Jewish and Christian "peoples" have swarmed together in Europe and America and have taken up the struggle that their ancestors lost to the Prophet Mohammed in the Arabian Peninsula. He analyzes the colonial domination of the nineteenth and twentieth centuries and the creation of Israel in Palestine in 1948 from an exclusively religious standpoint. He calls for a planetary struggle to save humanity, which is on the edge of the abyss due to a loss of moral values brought about by the machinations of the spiritually decadent West.[18]

Analyzing twentieth-century international relations in the light of the conflicts that took place in the Arabian Peninsula at the very birth of Islam, Qutb viewed Western imperialism as a new crusade, more powerful technologically, economically, and militarily than those of the Middle Ages. Islam has been aggressed, he says. It has been dominated because Muslim societies had fallen into *jahiliyya*, the time of ignorance that preceded the coming of the Prophet Mohammed. Qutb writes: "It is because they have fallen into the same errors as the people of Israel that Muslims are thus condemned to division, powerlessness, small-mindedness, indigence, trouble, and perdition. They must return to the faith and pledge obedience, for they can only recover the grace of God on condition that they once again show themselves to be loyal to the pact established with their ancestors, holding to it and remembering it."[19] The concept of *jahiliyya* is important in the discourse of Qutb, who considers that the forces of evil have forced humanity into retreat and into a pre-Islamic state of *jahiliyya*. "It is clearly visible that the entire world is steeped in *jahiliyya* and that too of an order whose evils are not diminished or attenuated even by marvelous material comforts, luxuries and high level inventions."[20] Consequently, the struggle is global as well as local, against leaders who imitate the pharaohs who see themselves as Gods. How is it, wonders Qutb, that a tyrant like Nasser is so popular in Egypt and the Arab world? The explanation for him is that contemporary Muslim societies have distanced themselves from Islam. They are run by leaders who have usurped the divine sovereignty of God and have insisted that their peoples adore the photographs of themselves plastered all over public buildings, streets, and homes. "The basis of this *jahiliyya* is a rebellion against the Sovereignty of God on Earth, which is a special attribute of the Godhead. This *jahiliyya* has passed the reins of sovereignty into the hands of man, assigning the overlordship of men to other men."[21] For Qutb, obedience to the Arab regimes and life under their authority are illicit from the point of view of the *fikh* (Islamic law), thus the need for jihad, for violent action until time as the *taghout* (tyrant) is brought down.

From this springs the theory of the vanguard (*takfir oual hijra*). "It is necessary that an official vanguard should come into existence, determined to perform this tremendous task, moving steadily forward through the vast ocean of *jahiliyya* which has encircled the world."[22] The notion of the vanguard that awakens the masses and leads the way for them is borrowed from Vladimir Lenin, who believed that the revolution could only be brought about by a vanguard of militants utterly committed to the task. The similarity with Lenin is not confined to this notion alone: it also extends to the concept of *jahiliyya*, whose communist equivalent would be alienation. In political practice, Qutb is close to the communist model in which the alienated, exploited worker is incapable of freeing himself without a "dis-alienated" vanguard to show the way forward. Although he was not aware, Qutb was influenced by communist ideology whose concepts he changed by the substitution of religious semantics for Marxist ones.[23] Qutb is the activist for whom revolutionary violence is the only way to bring awareness to the millions of believers who have strayed from the right way. He is the mastermind of Islamist violence legitimized canonically. It is true that the authoritarian Egyptian regime forced the radicalization of the Muslim Brotherhood by its savage repression of the 1950s and 1960s, using imprisonment, torture, and executions. The violence propagated by Qutb's discourse derives as much from his interpretation of Islamic dogma as from the process through which he passed and of which he was to some extent the product. Many Muslims have been troubled by the affirmation that Muslim societies fell back into *jahiliyya* (ignorance of God) since they had accepted the authority of the state. The Muslim Brotherhood, to which Qutb belonged, had to backtrack to establish its opposition to him. The Brotherhood Muslim organization published a book in 1977, supposedly written by its former supreme guide, Hassan al-Hudaybi, in jail and before his death asserting that the mission of the organization was to preach the real values of Islam and not to judge other Muslims.[24]

Qutb was much influenced by the thought of Mawdudi, who can be seen as the first author of the discourse of political Islam. Certainly, the ideologization of Islam begins with Jamal al-Din al-Afghani and Mohammed Abdu in the nineteenth century, but these two thinkers of the Al-Nahda sought to make Islam compatible with political modernity (nationalism, nation-state, democracy) whereas Abul A'la Mawdudi rejects modernity, accusing its proponents of confining religion to the private sphere and of seeking to detach it from political and juridical life. Moreover, he attacks the idea of Western secularization just as violently as he reproves traditional quietist Islam, which he berates for its cooperation with political powers that are hostile or indifferent to Islam. In the 1930s he championed a system in which politics merges with religion in a state run by a pious figure who would apply the laws of God. "The chief characteristic of Islam," he writes, "is that it makes no distinction between spiritual and secular life."[25] He takes no account of the histories of the Muslim dynasties in which there was necessarily a separation between political leaders and religious men—the former being military leaders and princes and the latter being the ulemas, called *"ahl el hal oual 'aqd"* (those who have the power to bind and unbind). Mawdudi rejected this model, which had imposed itself over centuries, confusing Islam with the history of Muslim societies. Islam would disappear altogether, he believed, if the religious powers did not control the state—the only organ capable of imposing the laws willed by God. His fear was that India, his home country, would become independent, and Indian Muslims, who were a minority there, would find themselves governed by representatives elected by the majority—that is, Hindu leaders. It was the special nature of Indian Muslims that made Mawdudi hostile to democracy that would force Muslims to obey non-Muslims. "Acknowledging that someone is a ruler to whom you must submit means that you have accepted his *Din* [religion]. He becomes your sovereign and you become his subject. *Din* means the same thing as state and government."[26] On this basis he affirms that democracy is *kufr*, impiety. The legitimacy of the chief should not depend on the number of people who have voted for him but on the depth of his knowledge of divine law. Mawdudi never called for revolution by the masses, preferring top-down reforms to bottom-up movements, which he feared would create disorder and benefit only nationalists and communists. The economic and political program of his Jamiat-e Islami party did not favor measures of social justice such as agrarian reform, preferring the rule of divine justice taught to the masses by the religious elite. Consequently, he rejected elections because they presupposed that elected leaders would promulgate laws, usurping the prerogative of God. He attacked the British and French parliamentary models on the grounds that they gave the national assembly the function of law making, thus proclaiming itself sovereign. This, he believed, amounted to trespassing on the territory of God, who is the sole sovereign and ordainer of the laws of nature and society. He translated the word "sovereignty" as "*hakimiyya*" and popularized the slogan "Al hakimiyya li Allah" adopted by all Islamists. It is quite true that the concept of sovereignty is of religious origin in the sense that Abrahamic monotheism views God as the master of the universe, but the concept evolved significantly with the emergence of the nations-states in which the ruler recognizes no human authority superior to its own. This does not imply a substitution of himself for God. However, Mawdudi refused the semantic evolution of this concept and did not grasp that it was an entirely new notion around which the nation-state could be built. The Arab word "*hakimiyya*" reflects the majesty of God, who is master of the universe and does not conform to a notion of political sovereignty unknown to the *fikh* and Muslim philosophy.[27]

Mawdudi's knowledge of the sacred texts is rudimentary; this is made clear by his commentary on the Qur'an, which he interprets in such a way as to develop a socioreligious interpretation of Islam presented as an alternative to capitalism and socialism. Rejecting both out of hand, he offers an authoritarian ideology based on a literal reading of the Qur'an. His argument is marked by a rationale suggesting that the universe is a clock set by divine law, guaranteeing the harmonious functioning of nature, to which human beings belong. If man intervenes to modify this mechanism and its social rules, he will introduce disturbances that will bring about anarchy. According to Mawdudi, human happiness will follow once society respects the "natural" laws from God. These laws have been called into question by the modernist aspirations of liberty and equality in secularized Western societies—which has impacted on young people in Muslim countries. The thought of Mawdudi is thus an attempt to restore a traditional order with its natural and divine basis; for him this is willed by God and best preserved if sharia is applied. He writes: "Man's status in the universe having been determined thus, it follows logically that he has no right to lay down the law governing his conduct and decide the right and wrong of it. This is a function which properly belongs to God."[28]

If there is a single author who has pushed the ideologization of Islam to its limit, stripping it in the process of its spiritual and mystical dimension as well as its theological richness, then that author is Mawdudi. He knew the British political institutions better than the Islamic culture of the ulemas of India. He was in total disagreement, politically and theologically, with them. One of the best critics of his work, Sayyed Vali Reza Nasr, observes that "his discourse produced an ideological orientation that was indigenous on the surface but was actually based on the very culture he sought to reject."[29] He built his discourse on Islam around his knowledge of Western political life, which he criticized via a literal reading of the Qur'an. Deeply affected as he was by the historic conditions of India under the British rule, he was appalled by the idea that the nationalists of the Congress Party and the Muslim League aspired to an independent Indian nation politically organized along the same lines as Great Britain itself. The ideology of British institutions, notably parliament, was in his view totally foreign to the beliefs and feelings of the Indian population, especially Indian Muslims. He rejected the model of the nation-state founded on the allegiance of its members to a central power, which he suspected of marginalizing religion. Paradoxically, he was against the partition of Pakistan and India, probably out of nostalgia for the Mogul Dynasty, which reigned in Delhi until 1857. Nevertheless, once the independence of Pakistan was proclaimed, he accepted the fait accompli and participated with his Jamiat-e Islami group in several elections, winning some seats in the parliament. To this end, he argued for a single-party government controlled by a pious man (*salih*), who would be an informed interpreter of the divine law and an instrument of God's will on Earth.

Attracted as he was by the authoritarian political model, Mawdudi was a typical example of the modern Muslim integrist, for whom religion should dominate every aspect of life in society in both public and private spheres. After the partition of India and Pakistan, he went so far as to declare that the marriage bonds of Muslims who had remained in India and the transmission of their inherited property were illicit according to sharia because authority in India was exercised by non-Muslims.[30] This caused consternation among Indian Muslims and provoked a violent reaction from the *ulemas*, who answered that sharia is not as rigid as Mawdudi understood it. Its methodology contains concepts that allow it to adjust to human life wherever it is taking place. The concept of *darura* (necessity), for instance, gives Muslims the possibility to be citizens of a state run by non-Muslims. Mawdudi ignores the intricacies of sharia according to the *ulemas*, who considered him a politician and not a religious man. Several times they challenged his writings and declarations. One of these *ulemas*, Mohammed Manzur Nu'ami, reproached him with having misunderstood Islam, pointing out that the latter was "not a government establishment, but a movement for the promotion of faith and piety."[31] Another *'alem* (plural *ulema*), Wahiduddin Khan, emphasized that "religious worship should serve as a means for personal reform and not as a vehicle for establishing worldly power."[32]

Mawdudi was a politician who developed an authoritarian ideology that he justified by recourse to religious doctrine. For him, the ideal regime under which Muslims should live was a theocracy directed by a pious figure who would apply sharia. Mawdudi and Qutb were very influential on the postindependence generations, attracted by a religious discourse hostile to Western countries accused of marginalizing religious faith. A "political Islam" was subsequently constructed around their work, based on a rudimentary knowledge of Islamic theology and an elementary knowledge of Western thought; this made possible its spread among vast numbers of young Muslims living the contradictions of underdevelopment and above all the oppression of authoritarian single-party regimes, so many historical factors that were bound to lead to violent confrontation. Islamist militants pushed the teaching of the masters to its logical extreme, finding in their work religious arguments to refute concepts such as sovereignty, democracy, freedom of expression, human rights, emancipation of women, and so on, on the pretext that these values carried the seed of something dangerous. In the past, stability in Muslim societies was ensured by the monopoly of the word of God held by the ulemas or the saints. This monopoly was called into question by mass education that in the last half century had allowed many young people to gain direct access to the Qur'an and the religious corpus. The authority of the ulemas was diminished, and they were accused by the Islamists of collaboration with the regimes they opposed. As in Lenin's formula defining communism as the Soviets plus electricity, Islamism is the Islamic corpus plus public education in mathematics and physics. In the 1970s, the thousands educated at universities in medicine, biology, chemistry, and so on used the discourses of Mawdudi and Qutb to propagate an apolitical conception of politics.

Islam is not the only religion to have spawned integrist spinoffs of the kind that have remained minorities in the West Christianity (Monseigneur Lefèbvre in Europe and the Christian Evangelists in the United States). The question is: why has the integrist trend in

Islam won over so many people at every level of the population? There are two possible answers. The first is that cultural representations in Muslim countries, as in medieval Europe, are structured by the religious corpus inherited from past centuries; it gives moral standards about the human behavior and human actions. Mawdudi and Qutb politicized this corpus by pushing it to its logical extreme. The second reason, which is linked to the first, is that the teachings of the religious culture have remained indifferent and impermeable to the intellectual advances of the last two hundred years, ignoring the progress of philosophy and the social sciences, and this has prevented the birth of the kind of modern Muslim theology that alone could stand effectively against religion's integrist attitudes. The ulemas of Pakistan and India as well as those of Egypt condemned the works of Mawdudi and Qutb for their Kharijite orientation, but they never developed a modern theology that would have prevented the ideologization of the sacred text. If we add to this mix the social conditions of Muslim countries facing unemployment, a rising cost of living, housing shortages, and so on, we will understand why this integrist discourse has spread so widely through populations disappointed by the postcolonial state after many decades of independence.

Toward the end of the 1970s, Islamist euphoria increased following the 1979 victory of Ruhollah Khomeini in Iran, which gave hope to the followers of Qutb and Mawdudi with a more aggressive edge, aimed at the violent takeover of the state. Paramilitary groups were formed in secret ready to launch jihad against impious regimes. In 1980, Egyptian president Anwar Sadat was assassinated; in 1982 in Syria, armed groups started an uprising in Hama; in Algeria the same year, military barracks were attacked. On university campuses Islamist students defied the authorities by refusing to accept mixed classes, using violence against anyone who opposed them. The 1980s saw the development of a violent, aggressive form of Islamism, despite heavy repression by security services. In the mosques, Islamists

CHAPTER 4

returning from the war in Afghanistan against the Soviets declared that because of their faith in God, Muslims could vanquish the world's most powerful armies, including those of Israel and the United States of America. In Syria, Egypt, and Algeria, Islamist pressure grew very strong, leading to widespread violence and repression. The struggle against Islamist violence became the state's chief priority. Military checkpoints in the cities and frequent arrests of activists suspected of terrorism gave the impression of countries at war with themselves. The rise of the Islamist movement reached its peak in the early 1990s, with wholesale assassinations of policemen and secular intellectuals and bloody attacks on foreign tourists. In Algeria hundreds died every week for a decade, with more than 150,000 losing their lives.

Paradoxically, all this violence induced most Islamists to adopt a more peaceful approach, distancing themselves from extremist groups operating in the shadows. In Egypt, personalities close to the Islamist movement offered a vision of Islam that was totally different to that of Sayyid Qutb. At the 13th Political Science Congress at the University of Cairo (December 4–6, 1999), Islamist personalities were invited to present their views. One of them, Selim El-Awa, criticized Qutb, affirming that he had betrayed the heritage of Hassan al-Banna, the founder of the Muslim Brotherhood organization.[33] The new Islamist vision, by contrast with that of Qutb, was provided by Ahmed Kamal Aboul Magd.[34] A new Islamist tendency had been born that embraced both democracy and sharia, proclaiming that Islam meant peace, tolerance, and respect for human life. But the verbal condemnation of violence is not enough as long as religion defines the person's political identity. If a movement proposes to establish a political order willed by Islam, this signifies that anyone against that order is against Islam and against God. In nonsecular societies, this is tantamount to a symbolic—or even physical—death sentence. Again, the declared objective of building a state based on sharia presupposes restrictions on the liberties of non-Muslims (of the Egyptian Copts, for example, who form 12 percent of the population) and of those Muslims who view religious faith as a private matter. The political ideology of any religious movement installs a belligerent state of mind by tracing a double line of demarcation between believers and nonbelievers and between true and false believers. It bred symbolic violence by justifying and preparing physical violence against people seen as different from Muslims or supposedly against Islam. If ideology creates a hierarchy in society based on religious criteria, it is no surprise that it unleashes violence, and there is no point in issuing communiqués condemning it.

Toward Post-Islamism?

The new Islamist discourse is the sign of a growing awareness of a contradiction between the goal of building a peaceful society and the violence used to implement this task. A new post-Islamist ideology is emerging with equally strong attachments to democracy and respect for human life. Young members of the Muslim Brotherhood in Egypt took up this task, breaking with their organization to advocate the compatibility of Islam with democratic values. Aware of the dilemma of the ideology of their elders (condemnation of violence when their discourse logically led to violence), they created in 1996 a party named the al-Wasat Party, an ideological halfway house between secular thought and the heritage of the organization's founder, Hassan al-Banna.[35] Their originality lays in their open determination to break with the goal of an Islamic state, substituting for it a civic state with Islamic references. Considering themselves politicians attached to Islam as a civilization and not a religion, they rejected the idea of a political order that is hostile to democracy and the values of citizenship. The young leaders of the al-Wasat did not present themselves as men of religion preaching about what was licit and what was not but as militants defending the values they wished to share with all Egyptians, whatever their differences. They did not confine Islam to its religious aspect; for them, Islam was an ethic, a culture, a civilization, a way of living one's humanity, whether one was a fully practicing believer, an occasionally practicing Muslim, or a non-Muslim (Jew, Copt, or whatever). The only people they rejected were atheists who declared themselves hostile to religion. The Muslim civilization, they averred, had always been inclusive of Christians and Jews, some of whom had contributed its cultural and political ascendancy. The militants of the al-Wasat Party abandoned the Islamist label to present themselves as a party founded on citizenship, not religion. They included Copts in their ranks and affirmed that the constitution of Egypt should not prevent non-Muslims and women from taking part in presidential elections. They provoked deep hostility not only from the mother organization that had condemned them in 1996 but also from the Mubarak regime, which refused to allow them to participate legally in the nation's political life.[36] The Muslim Brothers accused al-Wasat of discounting the originality of Islam and endorsing the secular intellectuals who sought to separate religion from politics. This accusation was fully coherent with the position of the organization, which considered Islam to be a totality with no separation from the state. Neither did the Muslim Brothers wish to compete with political parties, seeing themselves as above them and preferring *irchad*, the orientation of the entire nation toward the values of Islam. They refused to indulge in politics because they did not recognize the autonomy of politics. However, when the Mubarak regime fell in February 2011 under pressure from the popular demonstrations of Tahrir Square in Cairo, the Muslim Brotherhood was forced to imitate al-Wasat, hastily creating a party called Justice and Freedom. They implicitly recognized an approach to politics that they had previously mistrusted. For them, as men of religion, politics was a divisive element whereas their vocation was unity.

The Islamists are bound, sooner or later, to recognize politics that deals with the heterogeneity of society. This evolution is already perceptible not only in Egypt but also in other Arab countries where Islamists take part in elections. Leaders explain to party members that the implementation of sharia is the final goal but, in the meantime, a compromise with the secular section of society is necessary. Rachid Ghannouchi, the Islamist Tunisian leader, explained that society had to first be educated and prepared before it would accept—voluntarily and in its own interest—the imposition of sharia law.[37] This strategy of postponing the final objective avoids a head-on collision with the secular movements. It also allows Islamists to gain some experience of government that they lack dramatically. Ghannouchi had already begun this process in the 1990s during his exile in London, in the course of which he wrote several books, the most quoted of which is *Public Liberties in the Islamic State*.[38] This new approach seeks to demonstrate that the Qur'an defends the human rights, freedom of speech, and equality between men and women.[39] Under his leadership, the Ennahda Party, with a majority in the Tunisian National Assembly, accepted compromises in the makeup of the new constitution approved by the secular movement. At a national convention held in May 2016, Ghannouchi declared that the Al-Nahda is not any more an Islamist party. It is a democratic party based on Muslim values.[40]

The Islamist discourse has changed also in Algeria, where the FIS (Front Islamique du Salut) was involved in the violence that afflicted that country in the 1990s. Ali Benhadj, the number two figure in the party who declared in 1989 that "democracy is impiety," completely changed his position, concluding that democracy was the only political regime that could accompany Islam.[41] In a long letter addressed to Algerian president Abdelaziz Bouteflika following his election in 1999, Benhadj gave his opinion on the causes of the bloody crisis, and on the prospects for peace and on democracy.[42] With copious references to Western writers (Adelard, Voltaire, Jean-Jacques Rousseau, Thomas Jefferson, Alexis de Tocqueville) he eulogized democracy, which, he claimed, was always of vital concern to the best-advised caliphs. Thus, he turned the argument against his detractors, self-proclaimed democrats whom he accused of intolerance toward the Islamists. He tried to show that tolerance is a virtue of collective life; it prevents, he said, recourse to violence if differing views can find a legal field for fair arbitration. Ali Benhadj's entire case rests on legitimate elections, which he believes to be in no way contrary to the tenants of Islam. Quite the reverse, Islam recommends it, he writes, because "human experience has shown that the seizure and monopolization of power by force are the chief causes of civil wars and internal armed conflicts. We ignore the will of the people at our peril." Emphasizing the humility that leaders should display and the compatibility of Islam with the democratic system, Ali Benhadj quotes the example of the companions of the Prophet. Caliph Abu Bakr declares: "Help me if I do good, and correct me if I stray from the path of good." Caliph Omar: "If one of you shall see any deviation in me, may he correct me." Caliph Othman: "Should you find in the Book of God good cause to bind my feet, then do so." And from this Benhadj concludes in the same letter: "Actually, Islam does not make rulers sacred, but respects them as long as they observe the agreement they have made, and devoutly apply the dispositions of Islamic law." Twelve years of imprisonment and prison isolation following a verdict handed down by a military tribunal led Ali Benhadj to a fervent appreciation of the rule of law, which—had it been in place—would have provided him with a lawyer to protect himself against the arbitrary executive power of which he was the victim.

After the annulment of the elections won by their party and the crisis that resulted, the FIS militants had to endure a repression that involved thousands of people. The extrajudiciary kidnappings, torture, and executions to which they were subjected led them to adopt the views on human rights of the nongovernmental organizations, which proved to be powerful allies. Having experienced government repression and show trials, they learned the underlying sense of human rights, which in turn revealed the virtues of an independent judicial system. On its Website, the FIS declared itself

> a political party that, without ever pretending to have a monopoly on Islam, militates for the construction of an Islamic state which it sees as an instrument in the hands of the people who would permit the organization of a society based on Islamic values. The Islamic state that the FIS wishes to build in Algeria is a state of law and justice, an independent, free and sovereign state, in which the individual citizen and the people in general enjoy full freedom.[43]

This is a clear change of tack, with compromises that offer a way out of the impasse dictated by Qutb and Mawdudi. The fact that an Islamist party was acknowledging that it did not have a monopoly on Islam is itself a huge step toward the pacification of society.

The political program of the Islamist Moroccan PJD (Parti de la justice et du développement) went even further, affirming that the "state within Islam is a temporal state, its decisions are humane and its duty is to adopt a maximum of objectivity in the management of the affairs of society." Saadeddine Othmani, the former secretary-general of the party, published a book in which he made a distinction between religion and politics. "Moroccans," he wrote, are deeply attached to their religion and a lay society in which religion is marginalized is unimaginable in Morocco, let alone an anti-religious lay society. On the other hand, a lay society managing public affairs objectively is not, in my view, anti-Islamic. Within Islam there is a certain distinction between religious and temporal matters. The proof is the *hadith* wherein the Prophet states, in substance, "Let me regulate your religious affairs, and regulate matters of everyday life yourselves." In other words, temporal affairs, which have to do with public management, must be handled with the tools of modern, objective management."[44]

In contrast to the Al Adl Wa Al Ihssane party of Sheikh Abdessalam Yassine, which was not recognized by the authorities, the PJD was respectful of the monarchy, acknowledging the king's quality of commander of the faithful. The Moroccan state, an Islamic state that has been in existence for more than twelve centuries, affirms the PJD, which, after winning the elections, runs the government under the sovereign authority of the king. Saadeddine Othmani, the party's ideologist, explains that the Moroccans are unconcerned by the debate over the caliphate and that the monarchy has never been extinguished. Morocco, he states, is one of the few Muslim states where the Islamic *imarat* has never ceased to exist.[45]

There is an attempt from Islamist parties to account for the socio-political complexities of Muslim societies. Many Islamist leaders are convinced that violence is not the solution to build the Islamic state. Without doubt, there is a conciliatory tone that aims to give another image of Islamist parties. Ghannouchi keeps repeating that the Tunisians are Muslims with different levels of practice of their ritual duties and their convictions. Once an Islamist acknowledges that two Muslims can have different views on religion, the way is clear to pluralist politics. Taking part in election campaigns, criticizing one's opponents without threatening them with death or hellfire, being part of national assembly side by side with deputies who are hostile to the public influence of religion—this is the reality of post-Islamism. From this standpoint, the Arab world has already entered a post-Islamist period; indeed, the Islamist parties in Morocco, Tunisia, and Jordan are participating in elections where there is no mention whatever of Mawdudi or Qutb. This is not a discursive strategy to outmaneuver the secularized elements of society and international opinion. Rather, it is a genuine evolution that is affecting the entire Islamist movement, which has learned the lessons of Algeria's experience of ten years' lethal struggle.

Islamism trapped itself between religion and politics in its attempt to build a state that would serve as a coercive support to the faith, supposed to be self-sufficient to eliminate inequalities and conflicts within society. How can a society without conflicts possibly exist? The Islamist utopia is a dream of a nonconflictual society whose members give up their personal interests. How can such a society be possible? Confronted with this question, the Islamist movement divides into two tendencies: one, in the majority, seeks to use institutions and elections to rule the state; and the other, an extremist minority, opts for clandestine cells and violent action. Even though the international media focus more on violent extremist groups like al-Qaeda or ISIS, Islamism is steadily changing to find a way to deal with politics without violence, searching a path toward post-Islamism.

The first scholar who used the notion of "post-Islamism" is Asef Bayat, who conducted fieldwork in Iran during the 1990s. However, post-Islamism does not mean the end of Islamism; rather, it is the continuation of a battle for a religious utopia waged by political means, which translates as an implicit recognition of politics as a constituent dimension of society.[46] It is no coincidence that the expression "post-Islamist" was coined by observation of the Iranian experience. Despite its authoritarian bent, Iran's regime was forced to compromise with a society in which certain major segments took serious issue with it. Opposition appeared even among the mullahs and ayatollahs, who felt that any requirement to make political concessions damaged the purity of the religious ideal, and this naturally gave rise to the idea that the separation of religion and politics might be the best way to respect the tenets of Islam.[47] Since the 1990s the debate in Iran between Islamists and secular intellectuals on the role of religion in politics has been intense, attaining an academic level rarely achieved at any time in Arab countries. Nevertheless, even among the most devoutly religious people, there has been a demand for the separation of politics and religion to protect the sincerity of the faith. Strangely enough, secularization is a demand in Iran from some clerics who see that religion is best respected when it is separated from the state. Abdolkarim Soroush is a former revolutionary guard who explains that forcing someone to go and pray in the mosque or obliging a woman to wear the hijab against her will is incompatible with the Qur'an's requirement of sincerity in the expression of the faith.[48] As Olivier Roy has pointed out, Islamism has failed in Iran; it may not have lost control of the state, but neither has it succeeded in creating an apolitical state founded on the Islamist utopia.[49] Iran is not a religious regime; it is an authoritarian one that uses religion as a way of legitimizing itself. The country is categorically in a post-Islamist situation because the mullahs have failed to build the ideal society they promised, and their ideology no longer inspires the enthusiasm of the younger generation of Iranians. The regime is underpinned by the export of hydrocarbons, which allows it to have populist economic policies. It also maintains itself by mobilizing anti-Western, third world resentments, transnational Shi'ite solidarity, and a Persian nationalism revitalized by the war imposed by Saddam Hussein's Iraq in the 1980s. Iran is now set in a post-Islamist perspective obstructed by Western aggressiveness that does not help it move forward.

The example of post-Islamism par excellence is the Turkish AKP (the Justice and Development Party), which, after breaking with the Islamist discourse of former years, now declares itself to be a Muslim party fighting to promote the Qur'an's values of justice within the framework of a peaceful and democratic competition for power. In Turkey, the military establishment—which is strongly attached to the heritage of Mustafa Kemal—has bound Islamism to be pragmatic and to be more lenient with civic rights. The religious movement Hizmet helped toward this evolution. Centered on the spirituality of Turkish Sufism, the Hizmet movement is radically different from Islamism of Arab countries. It offers a "civil Islam" compatible with the secularization of the political space. Fethullah Gülen, Hizmet's leader, writes: "If a state gives . . . the opportunity to its citizens to practise their religion and supports them in their thinking, learning and practice, this system is not considered to be against the teaching of the Koran. In the presence of such a state there is no need to seek an alternative state."[50] Hizmet threw all its weight behind the post-Islamist evolution of the AKP, breaking with the populist Islamism of Necmettin Erbakan, which was closer to that of the Arab countries.[51]

Born in Anatolia, this movement has taken root all over Turkey and among the Turkish diaspora abroad. It has its own newspapers and reviews and finance institutions for religious instruction where its own interpretation of Islam is taught.[52] Supported by the powerful Turkish Federation of Businessmen and Industrialists, it has had a decisive influence on the post-Islamist evolution of the AKP, which has won three general elections in a row since 2000. The attachment to puritan, ascetic values by Turkish business leaders has created an affinity—in the sense that Weber uses the word—between Turkish Islam and capitalism, which has barred the way to religious populism. This is the main difference between Turkey and the under-industrialized Arab countries where populism makes use of religion to reject all social differentiations. If we compare the economies of Turkey and of other Arab countries (e.g., Egypt, Algeria, Libya), we note that Turkey has a stronger economy. In Egypt, in Algeria, in Saudi Arabia, and others, the economy is still underdeveloped and the rent (oil revenues, international aid, and remittances of migrant workers) is the main source of national income.

Also in contrast to the Arab countries, Turkish nationalism was crystallized by the hostility to Islam of the Ottoman Empire, which was viewed by the Young Turks as being the root cause of Turkey's failure to keep up with Europe. It was the nationalists who abolished the caliphate in 1924, throwing the Muslim world into profound disarray. One of the reactions to this abolition was the creation in 1928 of the Muslim Brotherhood in Egypt, whose central demand was for the re-establishment of the caliphate. Turkish Islamism could not express this demand without directly opposing the very idea of the Turkish nation, so Islamism had to accommodate history by affirming its attachment to the nationalist heritage of Mustafa Kemal, who abolished the caliphate.

The AKP has succeeded politically because it has sought to reconcile religious and nationalist tendencies in Turkey. Any attempt to compare the Turkish AKP with an Islamist party in any of the Arab countries should consider the country's degree of economic development, the role of private capital in the production of wealth, and the ideological conditions inherited from its past. The Turkish case shows that it is not relevant to link the Islamist phenomenon automatically with the sacred text and religious corpus. Instead, it should be viewed in the light of the contemporary history of Muslim societies that have all taken different paths in the construction of independent nation-states.

Islamism will have to face several major obstacles in the future: (1) the naivety of its ideology ("Islam is the solution; the Qur'an is our constitution"); (2) the regimes in place that, notwithstanding their exhaustion, will fight for their survival as in Syria; (3) Islamist extremists who discredit the movement; and (4) the Western powers that dread any instability that threatens their geostrategic and economic interests. The first of these obstacles is the overriding theme of this section on Islamism and the process of its political socialization. Post-Islamism represents the abandonment of ideological naivety and the formulation of a coherent political discourse like that of the Egyptian al-Wasat movement, which makes a straightforward distinction between religion and politics. It is not the only movement to do so; other Islamist parties have chosen the same path, notably in Tunisia and Morocco, where they have won elections and become pragmatic about reaching compromises with other political forces at work in their countries. This moderation erodes some of their popular support, creating the conditions for religious one-upmanship. In Tunisia, the *salafists* accuse Ennahda of straying from its promised program "to satisfy lay forces that are hostile to Islam." The phenomenon was repeated in Egypt when the Muslim Brotherhood was in power. The al-Nour Party preached hardcore *salafism* in order to delegitimize the actions of the Muslim Brotherhood's Justice and Freedom Party. If these movements of self-proclaimed *salafists* exist on the political scene and win seats in the National Assembly as they did in Egypt and Tunisia, it is because they have support from many sections of society. Therefore, there is an "electoral demand" for them to exist that delays the post-Islamist dynamic of the movement.

This brings us back to the persistent cultural elements that oppose the evolution of the Islamist discourse. The shift toward post-Islamism did not originate from a decision by the party's leaders. To be in any way significant, it had to reflect a shift of the Islamist electorate toward political pluralism. No political party can exist unless it is rooted in society and expresses a visible ideological trend. The example of the al-Wasat Party, which only won 3.7 percent of the vote in the 2012 Egyptian legislative elections, clearly indicates that it was too far ahead an Islamist electorate that did not identify with its discourse. The Islamist electorate did not like the idea of Copts and women participating in presidential elections, nor did it want the separation of religion and state to be as absolute as al-Wasat proposed. The Justice and Freedom Party of the Muslim Brotherhood won the election but lost votes and was forced to form a coalition in the National Assembly with the other Islamist party, al-Nour, which had attracted a considerable share of its electorate. The rhetoric of the al-Nour Party drove home the message that the Muslim Brotherhood has strayed from the original Message of Hassan al-Banna and have been warped by lay influences. The failure of al-Wasat and the electoral setback of the Muslim Brotherhood in 2012 meant that their post-Islamist shift had not been accepted by a part of their electorate that preferred the harsh religious discourse of the 1960s and 1970s, now appropriated by the parties preaching *salafism*.

The lesson to be learned from all this is that the political order draws all its legitimacy from the culture of the population. If, in the mind of the average voter, there is no distinction between the ethical and the juridical, if his conscience does not separate the ethicoreligious from the politico-juridical, then the autonomous political sphere, which is the basic requirement for a democracy and a rule of law, will never be established. Arab societies are profoundly afraid that modern politics will diminish Islam, which for centuries past has given meaning to the lives of individuals. These societies are in search of a new culture to establish a proper balance between their earthly necessities and God's commands. A new theology is needed to satisfy consciences while promoting the human rights and freedom of speech based on the separation made by *fiqh* (Muslim law) between *'ibadates* (religious practices and the relationship between God and the believer) and *mou'amalates* (social relationships). This task belongs to theologians and social scientists whose duty it is to

create a modern culture structured by the principle of the universality of man.[53] The challenge is to avoid the idealization of the past and
culture.

The academic hostility that greeted the work of Mohammed Arkoun and Nasr Abou Zeid indicates that the religious establishment is
unwilling to address new problems and produce new theoretical
approaches that will modernize the cultural heritage of the past. The
intellectual battle of the years to come will be hard fought, given the
importance of what is at stake: namely, the meaning given by believers in the Muslim world to their own existence. The biggest problem
is that Islamic theology is frozen in the culture of the Arabian Peninsula of the seventh century. The theologians do not understand
that even though the content of God's message does not change, the
culture in which it is expressed does. It was already debated at the
beginning of Islam between the *mu'tazilas* and the orthodox Han-
balites. The former believed that the Qur'an was created by God for
man, blessed with reason to understand and interpret it according to
his time, whereas for the latter the word of God is eternal in its formulation. The triumph of Hanbalism over the *mu'tazilas* made
sacred and unchallengeable the culture and history of the revelation.
And this in turn severed Muslims from the dimension of secular
thought that enriches man and makes him the creator of cultures,
symbols, meanings, and interpretations of religion that suit his times.

Notes

1. Clifford Geertz attempted an outline of linguistic anthropology in the
book he edited, *Meaning and Order in Moroccan Society: Three Essays in Cultural
Analysis* (Cambridge: Cambridge University Press, 1979).

2. These two concepts echo the title of a book by the German philosopher
Arthur Schopenhauer (1788–1840), without adhering to the metaphysical dimen-
sion contained in it, which offers a partially critical view of Kant's philosophy.
Schopenhauer, *The World as Representation and Will* (Cambridge: Cambridge
University Press, 2010). Sociologists have used the concepts to analyze the social

action. I cite the examples of Raymond Aron, who wrote an article titled "La classe sociale comme représentation et comme volonté," *Cahiers internationaux de sociologie*, no. 38 (1965); and Pierre Bourdieu, in one of his texts on the sociology of the family, "La parenté comme représentation et comme volonté," in *Esquisse d'une Théorie de la pratique: Pre'ce'de' de trois e'tudes d'ethnologie kabyle* (The Hague: Mouton, 1971).

3. Peter Berger and Thomas Luckman, *The Social Construction of Reality: A Treatise in the Sociology of Knowledge* (New York: Anchor Books, 1990). In its general project and outcome and in spite of certain divergences, sociology was constructivist at its origin, from the moment it attempted to "denaturalize" society by demonstrating the evolution of social existence within the limits of representations that appeared natural to the individual.

4. Héli Béji, *Le désenchantement national* (Paris: Maspéro, 1982).

5. Condemning violence even against European colonizers, Abdu disapproved of Col. Arabi Pasha's action against the British. In Algeria, his disciple Abdelhamid Ben Badis was also opposed to insurrection as a means of winning independence from the French authorities.

6. Anthropological optimism is an assumption stating that men are basically good but they undergo bad influence from outside. It opposes anthropological pessimism, which states that men are simultaneously bad and good by nature. In the first case, society needs an authoritarian rule and in the second one it needs a rule of law that empowers everyone to defend himself.

7. Paradoxically, the idealization of man is the basis of an authoritarian ideology that considers repression the only way to stamp out deviations that result in social inequality. Authority is designed to generate the image of the ideal believer, not to ensure the freedom of ordinary individuals. Islamism is against individual liberties not on account of Islam itself but because of the same anthropological optimism with which the regimes of Nazi Germany and Soviet Communism began, as Hannah Arendt has so clearly shown. The reverse of this is anthropological pessimism, founded on the theory of man's original egotism, which is compatible with democracy inasmuch as it builds counterweights that give the individual the means to defend his rights and interests.

8. Hannah Arendt, *On Revolution* (London: Faber, 1962).

9. In answer to this question, I hypothesize the decline of Muslim theology that, ever since Abu al-Hasan al-Ash'ari, has simply repeated itself over and over without adding any new thought. Muslim theology has been frozen in time since the twelfth century, when it banned the study of philosophy.

10. Religion is not enough to ensure moral order in a context where the preoccupations of the individual override those of the group. Muslim societies have not yet grasped that the autonomy of the individual is an aspiration and that a new morality needs to be devised based not on reason and justice but on conscience and liberty. The persistence of this culture has led to the belief that

Islam does not separate religion from politics. This belief gives these two categories a rigidity that empties them of human content. They become disembodied forces functioning with the logic of robots, leaving no room for maneuver for individuals who passively submit to them. Man can live with reified forces like this but students of social science should distance themselves from such reified representations of social existence.

11. Sayyid Qutb, *Ma'alim fi Tarik*, Al Hidaya al Islamiyya, s.d., p. 141.

12. Quoted in Qutb, *In the Shade of the Koran* (Markfield: Islamic Foundation, 2001), 204.

13. Ibid.

14. Ibid., 111. There is an enduring myth among ulemas that Islam was forecast by Moses and Jesus. This myth refers to a fake gospel, called the Gospel of Barnabas, in which Jesus said that after him a prophet named Mohammed would come to correct the sacred text. When history is denied as social science, the myths take over culture.

15. Ibid., 183.

16. Ibid., 192.

17. Ibid., 140.

18. Sayyid Qutb, *Milestones* (Karachi: International Publishers, 1981), 44.

19. Qutb, *In the Shade of the Koran*, 150.

20. Qutb, *Milestones*, 49.

21. Ibid.

22. Ibid., 51.

23. Olivier Carré points out this parallel with Lenin in his *Mystique et Politique: Lecture révolutionaire du Coran par Sayyed Qutb, Frère Musulman Radical* (Paris: Les Editions du Cerf et Les Presses de la Fondation national de Science Politique, 1984). This is one of the best books on the thought of Sayyid Qutb.

24. Hassan al-Hudaybi, *Du'at la Qudat* (Preachers, not judges), Cairo, 1977. According to Sayed Khatab, this work was a fake concocted by the ulemas of Al-Azhar under pressure from the Egyptian security services. Even if this is true, it does not change the fact that Qutb is a controversial figure. Yet it is hard for the brotherhood to condemn him publicly because he is popularly seen as a martyr unjustly assassinated by the Nasser regime. Qutb is acknowledged by the brotherhood as one of its martyrs. See Sayed Khatab, *The Power of Sovereignty: The Political and Ideological Philosophy of Sayyed Qutb* (London: Routledge, 2006).

25. Abul A'la Mawdudi, *The Islamic Way of Life* (Leicester: Islamic Foundation, 1986), 9.

26. Abul A'la Mawdudi, *Let Us Be Muslims* (Leicester: Islamic Foundation, 1985), 295–96.

27. See Khaled Abou el Fadhel, *And God Knows the Soldiers: The Authoritative and Authoritarian in Islamic Discourses* (Lanham, MD: University Press of America, 2001).

28. Abul A'la Mawdudi, *The Ethical Viewpoint of Islam* (Lahore: Islamic Publications, 1953), 33.

29. Sayyed Vali Reza Nasr, *Mawdudi and the Making of Islamic Revivalism* (New York: Oxford University Press, 1966), 33.

30. If we follow this line, it means that Muslims living in Western countries have an illicit earthy existence unless they fight until the Western population converts to Islam or they leave. Their marriages and their property inherited from their parents are not in conformity with sharia.

31. Mohammed Manzur Nu'ami, *Tabligh Jamaat*, quoted in Nasr, *Mawdudi and the Making of Islamic Revivalism*, 59.

32. Quoted in ibid., 65.

33. See William Baker, *Islam without Fear: Egypt and the New Islamists* (Cambridge, MA: Harvard University Press, 2003).

34. Ahmed Kamal Aboul Magd, *A Contemporary Islamic Vision* (Cairo: Dar el Shuruq, 1991). The publication of this book led to a historical debate with the journalist Sayyed Yacine in the *Al-Ahram* newspaper.

35. See Clement Steuer, *Le Wassat sous Moubarak: L'emergence contrariée d'une groupe d'entrepreneurs politiques en Egypte* (Paris: Fondation Varenne/LDGJ, 2012).

36. The request for approval for their party, regularly submitted since 1996, was consistently rejected, and the fall of Mubarak had to intervene before al-Wasat could have any official existence. What worried the Egyptian regime was the appearance of an Islamist movement with a coherent and credible discourse that could attract the secularized classes of society. The Arab regimes preferred Qutb's version, which gave them legitimacy as fighters of violence and defenders of tolerance to a post-Islamist plan articulating a political discourse that respects individual freedoms. Qutb offered a secure logic that made it possible for them to bring in financial aid from Europe to avoid the seizure of power by extremists who might directly threaten Western countries.

37. Noureddine Jebnoun, "Tunisia at the Crossroads: An Interview with Sheikh Rachid al-Ghannouchi," foreword by John L. Esposito, ACMMCU Occasional Papers, Georgetown University, April 2014.

38. Rachid Ghannouchi, *Al Hurriyat el 'amma fieddawala el Islamiya* (Beirut: Markaz Ed-Dirassat el Wahda al 'Arabiya, 1993).

39. On Ghannouchi's vision of democracy from the point of view of Islam, see Azzam Tamini, *Rachid Ghannouchi: A Democrat within Islam* (Oxford: Oxford University Press, 2001).

40. *Le Monde*, May 26, 2016.

41. *Al Munqid*, no. 23, 1990.

42. This letter can be read on the FIS's official Website, www.fis-infor.net.

43. Text of the FIS Convention, Brussels, 1998.

44. Saadeddine Othmani, *La religion et la politique: Distinction et non séparation* (in Arabic) (Casablanca: al Markaz al-Thaqafi, 2009).

45. The *imarat* is the king's authority in his quality of *amir el mou'minine* (Commander of the Faithful). Othmani is referring to the history of Morocco, reminding the reader that Morocco was the only Arab state that was not under the rule of the Ottoman Empire. The Moroccan king used to claim to be the rival of the Sultan of Istanbul, declaring himself as the Commander of the Faithful, meaning the leader of all Muslims.

46. See Asef Bayat, *Making Islam Democratic: Social Movements and the Post-Islamist Turn* (Stanford, CA: Stanford University Press, 2007); and Asef Bayat, ed., *Post-Islamism. The Changing Faces of Political Islam* (Oxford: Oxford University Press, 2013).

47. See Mahbooubeh Bayat, "L'Etat et la religion dans les débats intellectuels en Iran de 1990 à nos jours" (PhD thesis, Institut d'études politiques de Lyon, Lyon, 2011).

48. Abdolkarim Soroush, *Reason, Freedom and Democracy in Islam* (Oxford: Oxford University Press, 2000).

49. Olivier Roy, *The Failure of Political Islam* (Cambridge, MA: Harvard University Press, 1994).

50. See "An Interview with Fethullah Gülen," *Muslim World*, special issue on Islam in contemporary Turkey: *The Contribution of Fethallah Gülen*, vol. 95, no. 3 (2005).

51. On the principal Islamist movements in Turkey, see Ahmet Kuru, "Globalization and Diversification of Islamist Movements: Three Turkish Cases," *Political Science Quarterly* 120, no. 2 (2005).

52. On the Hizmet movement, see Greg Barton, Paul Weller, and Ihsan Yilmaz, eds. *The Muslim World and Politics in Transition: Creative Contributions of the Gülen Movement* (New York: Bloomsbury Academic, 2013).

53. The Syrian thinker Muhammad Shahrur is completely involved in this crucial intellectual work. See *The Qur'an, Morality and Critical Reason: The Essential Muhammad Shahrur*, translated and edited by Andreas Christmann (Leiden: Brill, 2009).

5

Islamism and Democracy

THE DECLARED AIM of Islamists is to establish a state that represents the people, founded on the ethics of the Qur'an—and on sharia, which indicates the right way. They are not against democracy per se, provided it does not give elected representatives the right to trespass on the domain of God, specifically the laws relating to questions of marriage, divorce, and inheritance. This law is locked into the sacred, thus forbidding man from adjusting it in tune with the evolution of society. Islamism rejects the secularization of the law, or at least that part of civil law that concerns the family and inheritance. On one hand, Islamists want a modern state to serve people and, on the other hand, they disavow that the state wields full and complete sovereignty for fear that it will modify sharia. This incoherence is linked to the fundamental contradiction that runs through Arab societies that dream of a modern state while refusing the ideology of the modern state. Muslim societies are in the middle of the conflict between religion and state, with its many implications. Religion and the state fight to control the same individual, who is at the same time believer and citizen. To whom should this person swear allegiance: to God or to the state? Which law should be implemented to bring about social peace: the religious one or the secular one? Modern forms of politics stem from the inability of religion to manage life for men and women belonging to social groups whose interests are opposed. In Europe, it took two or three centuries for Christianity to acknowledge this incapacity and accept the secularization of the state. It is devoutly hoped that the process will not be so lengthy for Muslim societies, torn as they are between their attachment to religion and their need for viable government. In the pages that follow, I address the contradictions inherent to Islamism and the gradual secularization of sharia under the pressure of social dynamics.

Democracy and Political Participation

In the long term, the relationships between state and society are built through a process that puts in place institutions for political participation and integration—giving the population the impression, true or false, of being listened to and represented in the sphere of political decision making. To this effect, Islamism presents itself as a demand for political participation, voicing expectations that belong as much to modernity as to tradition and highlighting the need to appoint God-fearing leaders as guarantors of public morality. The moralization of the state signifies that a battle is being fought against corruption and against the declining morals of an elite accused of importing foreign values into society. This discourse wins considerable approval for the Islamists who propose to entrust state leadership positions to people who have given public evidence of their piety, notably by regular daily attendance at the mosque. Thus, they call on faith and the fear of God to place the state at the service of the population, which is what most people want. An important section of the population seeks to build the rule of law by using religious faith alone, which it believes to be an effective tool to place the state at the service of the people. In this perspective, Islam becomes a political resource in the hands of people with the prospect to be represented in the state institutions and the elected bodies.[1] Islamism conveys the hopes and expectations of the many who aspire to greater justice from an administration that is often indifferent to the fate of the poor. Its aim is not to prepare believers for eternal life but to transform the state into something more nearly resembling the mythical model of the *salafs*, the pious ancestors. Utopia is a key concept for the understanding of political movements with religious discourses because it reveals the gulf between the reality of ordinary life and people's aspirations. The harsher the reality is, the more magical and far-fetched the dream of escaping it.[2]

For the Islamists, social antagonisms are created by those whose faith in God has diminished, thus frustrating religious values and the rules of justice and solidarity. It is enough to neutralize these impious individuals, who are supported and encouraged by the West, to rebuild the ideal city of the *salafs*. The Islamists spread the message that all believers are brothers who must banish their disagreements to strengthen their unity. In this fraternal society, there is no need to create institutions and political counterbalances to settle conflicts of interest. If it is true that God created the rich and the poor, it is just as true that the former must share God's gifts with the latter. If this sharing does not occur spontaneously, the state must assume responsibility for it, ensuring social justice according to the laws of sharia. This is a populist reading of the Qur'an, but other readings are also possible, which the historic situation and the cultural representations will either impose or reject. Islamism is a form of populism that seeks to unite the people into a homogenous body purged of inequalities and divisions. It has similarities with radical Arab nationalism and Marxist populism, founded as they were on revolutionary utopias that fascinated the masses in times of extreme economic and social upheavals. When it resorts to violence, the populist utopia seeks to have done with a social order it views as innately unjust by taking revenge on the authors of that injustice—

namely, the leadership elites and their Western accomplices. This is reminiscent of the revolutionary movements of contemporary history, which impose themselves as the authentic voice of a majority of the population that is excluded from the political arena.

The popularity of the Islamists is largely attributable to their utopian aspirations whereby reality is eclipsed by an imaginary world that banishes the harshness of daily life. Individuals cannot project themselves into anything like a realist future and cannot escape a present that crushes them inexorably. Islamism gives people the opportunity to criticize the state, to denounce wrongdoing, and to commend the right (the command of good and the rooting out of evil), and it allows the public expression of political opinions hostile to a corrupt, single-party government and its censorship of the press. The intense pressure from Islamists pushed regimes like those of Algeria and Egypt to put an end to single-party systems. They have been delegitimized by sermons given at the mosques by young people educated in state schools rather than in religious ones. In effect, the mass education of the postindependence generations spawned a new brand of middle class that was dissatisfied with the quietist tradition of the imams and the ulemas, who urged obedience to the legal authorities, quoting the Qur'anic verse: "Oh believers, give obedience unto God, and unto his Prophet and unto those among you who exercise authority" (Surat 4, v. 59). Having had direct access to Islamic scriptures and the writings of Mawdudi and Qutb, many young university graduates of medicine, physics, chemistry, and so on moved into the mosques to direct prayers and preach a blend of religious ethics, elements of scientific knowledge, and denunciations of the government. They politicized the religious imagination by modernizing it, using the mythical past to paint the outline of a better future. The mosque became the focus of huge excitement, uniting believers against the state, which was denounced as being divorced from the true values of Islam. The fiery sermons of the "new imams" were not about abstract theological issues; instead they enjoined the state to listen to the views of the faithful. This discourse was conveyed by people who worked as doctors, teachers, lawyers, and engineers and who, at evening prayer in their local mosques, referenced the *salafs*, to whom mythology attributed virtues that were shamefully lacking in the present crop of Muslim leaders. To enthusiastic audiences they made themselves the champions of political participation, calling for the installation of an ideal state governed by virtuous men prepared to listen to the voice of the people. Their sermons exalted the figure of the just prince, particularly Omar Ibn al-Khattab, "Omar el Haq," whose behavior they held up as an example to all God-fearing public servants. In the 1980s the sermons of opposition imams were recorded on cassettes that were widely distributed and listened to both in public and in private; the model for this was the famous Egyptian preacher Sheikh Abd al-Hamid Kishk, who was widely popular from Iraq to Morocco, where he had many imitators. Here are two stories related and commented upon by a young imam who attracted large crowds to the mosques of Oran in 1989.

"Caliph Omar Ibn al-Khattab was walking home from the mosque when he heard the weeping of a child and the lamentations of a woman in a nearby house. He knocked on the door; the woman opened and explained that her son was hungry and she had no food to give him. Shocked, Omar the Just—as he was known in Arab tradition—asked the mother to follow him to *byit el mal*, where the wealth of the state was stored up, to feed herself and her child." The mosque audience wondered at this edifying example of justice and uprightness and began to dream of leaders like this for Algeria. The imam finished his sermon by making a comparison with the Chadli Bendjedid government, "whose ministers," he declared, were "impervious to the suffering of their brothers. These are the ministers and generals who take money from the state treasury to send their wives and daughters to have their hair dressed in Paris."

The second story, told by another imam in another mosque, refers to the condemnation of the activities of the intelligence service by the vox populi.

One day, Omar Ibn al-Khattab heard shouting nearby and was curious to find out what it was. He climbed a wall and surprised four adults drinking alcohol. Before he began to chide them, one of the four, who had recognized him, spoke out: "O Omar, we are indeed at fault, but so are you. Indeed you have committed an even more serious transgression. You have climbed the wall to take us by surprise, instead of knocking on the door and waiting for someone to come and open it." Omar did not agree and proposed that they should argue the case before the Prophet. Having heard both sides of the case, the Prophet found both parties guilty: the drinkers had disobeyed the edict against alcohol and Omar had spied upon them (*jawssassa*), which is forbidden by Islam.

The imam drew his conclusions: "Spying is forbidden by Islam, gentlemen of the intelligence service," he said, directly addressing the plain-clothes officers present in the congregation who had been sent to report on him. Given the repressive role of the "political police" of the intelligence services, this anecdote is clearly aimed at denouncing the regime's surveillance activities against the people.

Whether these stories took place during the life of the Prophet or whether they are the fruit of the collective imagination is unimportant. What matters is the impact they had on believers who judged the state by which they were governed according to moral criteria illustrated by stories of this kind. Their function is to highlight the gulf between the state as it actually is and what it ought to be. At Friday prayers the most eloquent and charismatic imams contrive to use the linguistic wealth of the Arabic language to bring alive the experiences of the Prophet as if they were present in flesh and blood during his time. Many people come out of the mosque with tears in their eyes, with the feeling of having taken part in a kind of collective therapy. Over and over again, the spiritual depth of the Qur'an and the exuberance of the Arabic language induce something akin to ecstasy in the mosques.

The ideal state promised by Islamism is the antithesis of the corrupt, authoritarian regime. The brutal reality generates dreams of a state ruled by devout and God-fearing leaders guaranteeing fairness for the poorest and weakest. This offers a strong potential for change and the challenging of authoritarian regimes cut off from the people they rule. Does all Islamist protest bear the seed of a democratic project? This is not an easy question: it involves linking the demand for political participation to the problem of democracy while taking account of the contradictory aspirations of the people and the unstable situation of Arab countries.

The challenging theoretical problem about democracy is that many people think it is a natural result of a humanist culture that anyone with a little common sense is bound to accept. We overlook the political history of Europe, its wars of religion, its popular uprisings and revolutions, which ultimately placed institutional limits on the holders of public authority. This was far more than a battle of ideas. The same goes today for the Arab countries where the struggle involves not only contrasting abstract ideas but also collective destinies linked to living conditions that must be analyzed through sociological research and anthropological observation. The choice in this matter is not just a theoretical one, between two abstract models. By placing Islam and democracy on parallel paths, we place two reified categories in opposition to one another that are emptied of their human substance and their historical content, forgetting at the same time the conditions in which real people are forced to live.

CHAPTER 5

Democratization is not the application of a theoretical model; it is, rather, a historical process whereby political protest uses the resources available to defend material and symbolic interests in society divided into rulers and ruled and rich and poor. In nineteenth-century Europe, the bourgeoisie used economic capital as a political resource to put pressure on the state. Workers resorted to strike action, paralyzing factories in order to make their voices heard and to have independent unions. In the Arab countries, where the bourgeoisie and the proletariat are sociologically weak, parts of the population readily use religion to put pressure on political leaders. Islam is a resource for sparking the dynamic of political participation. Will this dynamic yield democracy? The future will tell. The low result of the secular parties in free elections is explained by the media as resulting from Islam's religious hostility to democracy and its values. This theme is a recurrent one of orientalist literature that approaches Muslim societies in isolation from history and applies an ethnocentric European bias that confuses theology with anthropology. It is perfectly true that the medieval interpretation of Islam is incompatible with democracy; the same could be said of Catholicism in the time of Pope Gregory the Great. What orientalism passes over in silence is the fact that the Muslims of five centuries back and those of today are not the same; nor is Islamism the return of medieval Muslim tradition, even though it borrows its language. It is true that the Islamists put forward a literal interpretation of the Qur'an that contradicts their declared project of Islamizing modern society. The contradiction they bear will lead to adjustment with reality and the perspective of Muslim democracy following the model of Europe Christian democracy. The Islamist elites will eventually understand—indeed, many already do—that the thought of Mawdudi and Qutb leads to blind alleys.

It is irrelevant whether the Qur'an allows democracy or does not, knowing that democracy can be accepted or condemned from a reli-

178

gious point of view. Men act in function of their cultural representations and of a cognitive framework conveying values that give meaning to their social relationships and their actions. Obviously, the Qur'an supplies a normative system, but because mentalities and aspirations evolve with time, the norms are unconsciously reinterpreted.[3] Likewise, political aspirations hinge on practices (in Bourdieu's sense of the word) that are given legitimacy by a system of symbols (in Geertz's sense of the word). The force of the sacred text lies in interpretations devised to demonstrate the soundness of the ideological views and the legitimate nature of the expectations of the social groups. As with any religion, Islam exists only through men and women who live and practice its tenets, giving it a meaning that proceeds directly from their history and culture. These men and women are not robots programmed to apply religious norms with absolute rigidity. If this were the case, there would be no such thing as human history. And as with any sacred text, the Qur'an has different meanings put forward according to the historic situation. The violent use of Islam could be explained by the frustrations pertaining to social mobility provoked by the formation of classes, the accumulation of fortunes, and the transmission of skills and knowledge through the schooling system. Arab societies are caught in a dynamic of profound upheaval and are under pressure of markets and globalization. An ongoing class struggle has dragged the sacred into the battles of the profane. Islamism is a language of conflictual situation in which the issue is the inclusion or exclusion of certain social groups from economic, political, and cultural life. The repression of Islamists will never bring social peace and stability as long as the governments fail to integrate the majority of the population into the state institutions and modern economy. Islamism is a thermometer that takes the temperature of the social body; it is not the fever that grips it.

Journalists and university professors, some of them living in Arab countries, sometimes wonder why electors vote for Islamist parties when common sense recommends that they vote for democratic ones. These journalists and professors, who belong to a middle class sheltered from the urgent problems of everyday life, themselves aspire to freedom of thought and speech, electoral alternation, and equal rights for their children, male and female. This is emphatically not the case for poorer members of society, who are more sensitive to calls of social justice and solidarity and indifferent to the demands of the middle classes, which appear to them completely abstract. Each attributes a different meaning to democracy; the former applies political criteria and the latter, social ones. All individuals and social groups are acutely aware of their immediate interests, which they seek to realize in the full respect of the values that give meaning to their existence. Poor people will vote for a party that promises to satisfy their social needs or to be consistent with their dreams, rather than for another party that is more concerned with electoral alternation, gender equality, freedom of the press, and so on. The mother of a family is more receptive to a discourse that promises work for her unemployed husband than to one that offers equality of gender. Can we say that a vote for an Islamist party is a vote against democracy? Is it irrational to vote in this way, as many journalists say? Is it irrational from the point of view of the jobless man whose perception is that democracy gives more importance to freedom than to justice? Without having to read Habermas, the poorest people know in their bones that democracy is linked to the rules of the market, founded as it is on competition of a purchasing power that they do not possess. They prefer an authoritarian regime that will make sure they have jobs, housing, and health care to a regime that will tell them that these expectations will be met by the market based on purchasing power. People who vote for Islamists do not make an irrational choice; in sociology, there is no "cultural idiot." In first elections, secular parties would be collateral victims of the hostility to the free market that poor people fear.

It is probable that, in the long term, democracy will improve the economic situation. But in the long term, we will all be dead, as economist John Maynard Keynes liked to say. There is a popular adage, widespread in North Africa, which says the present is certain, but the future is not (*"hiyni el youm oua ktoulni ghadoua,"* meaning, take care of today and tomorrow will take care of itself). If to be rational is to protect one's own interests, the Islamist parties' overwhelming electoral success with the underprivileged classes is anything but irrational. The Islamists probably will not keep their electoral promises because unemployment will not just evaporate with the wave of a wand. Yet voters will not discover this until they experience it first-hand, until they have been disappointed by Islamist politicians who have overestimated their ability to respond to social demands. If they remain in opposition, they will never have to cope with the daily management of the state and will remain in the realm of magical immediate solutions to the difficulties of existence. Countries that have never known what it is like to have free elections and freedom of expression may expect their first elections to be won by the party that promises the most. And if those promises are backed by religious discourse, presumably those first elections will be won by Islamist parties.

In democratic competition, Islamism constitutes an electoral offer formulated with a vision of the world that finds an echo in a population that expresses an electoral demand. As with the logic of the market, an offer without a corresponding demand gets lost in the economy. Popular demand is what makes parties win in free elections, and it is popular demand that decides whether a state will be authoritarian or democratic. For historical reasons, the demand in Arab countries is burdened by populism, but that is likely to change as it evolves over time. Today the demand is confused, expressing both a wish for political participation to place the state at the service of the population and for a rejection of the "democratic threshold" beyond which the political system will become democratic.[4] If it is true that democracy presupposes electoral alternation, it is no less true that it depends on pluralism and freedom of conscience guaranteed by the law. Pluralism has existed before in Muslim history, but we are more concerned with the political pluralism that appeared in Western democracies. Pluralism is intrinsically bound to secularization. Peter L. Berger has clearly described the link between these two categories: "The phenomenon called 'pluralism' is a socio-structural correlate of the secularization of consciousness. This relationship invites sociological analysis."[5] This assumption is a crucial one in the approach of democracy built on the notion of the rule of law as forged by modern philosophy.

Arab societies are in a predemocratic stage for sociological reasons (a very weak middle class), economic reasons (the market excludes most of the population), and cultural reasons (social consciousness lags far behind secularization within society).[6] Looking more closely, we see that it is not Islam that runs counter to democracy in Arab countries but the social imbalances and inequalities that nurture populist utopia and violence. Poverty has always existed in Arab countries, as elsewhere, but urban concentration and the rapid enrichment of a few by way of speculation and corruption have given today's poor a deep sense of injustice. Without returning to the theory of the prerequisites of democracy formulated by Seymour Lipset more than half a century ago, it is obvious that democracy has a greater chance of gaining a foothold when the middle class is sociologically and culturally strong enough to lower tensions within society.[7] Unfortunately, this is not the direction in which academic research on the Arab countries is currently tending; the focus now is on the theme of Islam's visceral hostility to democracy as proven by the failure of nonreligious and democratic parties in recent elections.

Take the example of Saudi Arabia. What are the chances of that state (which proclaims that the Qur'an is its constitution) will ever have democratic institutions? The first obstacle in this monarchy is the presence of colossal financial resources that give the reigning dynasty the means to impose itself on a society divided into family clans that naturally compete in the hunt for privileged relationships with the state. Even the most underprivileged Saudi citizens benefit from the state's financial support that permits their integration into a circuit of distribution and consumption of imported goods, all thanks to the kingdom's oil revenues.[8] The second obstacle is the dominant discourse of the ulemas who are highly paid to broadcast the Hanbalite dogma from which the Al-Saud dynasty draws its religious legitimacy.[9] Notwithstanding their role, the ulemas do not ensure the survival of the Saudi monarchy; rather, the monarchy depends less on ulemas than on oil and on the support of Western countries that are concerned about the stability of the international oil market.

Democracy is not a theoretical model; it is a political relationship fashioned by a historical process and by the *rapports de force* between the state and the different social groups. Speculating on the ideological difficulty of setting it up in Muslim countries is to set aside the histories of Arab societies and their contradictions. Islamism does not reject democracy—if by democracy is meant the expression of the popular will and the control of leaders by electors. Instead, it claims to offer a better government than that of democracy, a government in which the rulers will serve God by serving the people they govern. How can this be possible without citizenship and civil rights, without the freedom of the subject under the law, without popular sovereignty, and without a secularized judiciary?

The Islamists support the principle of free elections (including votes for women) and they do not reject the idea of electoral alternation. But if they win majorities in national assemblies, will they not be tempted to make laws that limit freedom of expression in order to impose their own interpretation of religion? The contradiction between Islamism and democracy will find a solution when Islamism is forced to evolve by reality, which will demonstrate that freedom is not the consequence of a crushing victory over religion. Islamists fear democracy because they think it arrogates too much power to man. This anthropological dread will only dissipate with experience that demonstrates that meaningful political participation depends entirely on freedom of expression. Experience will make Islamists abandon the idea that the establishment of a state at the service of the people depends on a supposedly right interpretation of the Qur'an. The nature of the relationships between the state and the population is influenced by the structuring of society, by the level of development of the economy, and by the history of the country. In the case of countries with oil-driven economies, the ruling elite has a decisive advantage in imposing itself on the population.

The *Al hakimiyya li Allah* Slogan

Paradoxical though it may seem, the popular use of the slogan *al hakimiyya li Allah*, meaning "all power belongs to God," written on banners brandished by crowds during the demonstrations of the 1980s, was a sign of a nascent process of modernization, of looking for a way forward. The marching crowds were not calling for a theocracy but for a state with leaders who would be aware that power did not belong to them but to a higher authority, God, a word by which their aspirations for justice and equality are expressed.[10] Behind this verbal sophistry lurks the longing for a state that represents the people, where authority exists to serve the common good and not the interest of the ruling classes. The incessant demand for divine sovereignty expresses a democratic aspiration, yet the people must invoke God to make themselves heard. God is a symbol behind which stands a population claiming a right to what it wants—and what it wants is certainly not a theocratic state but a just social and political order like that willed by God, in which the faithful are respected in their dignity. Divine sovereignty is perceived as the means by which leaders can be kept honest and corruption can be stamped out, which would make it possible—according to the faithful—to create jobs and improve living conditions.

The utopia that radical Arab nationalism had conveyed in the 1950s and 1960s was reborn in the religious language that was mobilized to bring the postcolonial state closer to the people. The demand was about honest leaders who would not abuse their functions to enrich themselves. The reference to God was an attempt at limiting the scope of political power in a situation where the constitution is not sufficient to do so. It was within this context that the demand of divine sovereignty had to be addressed; it was put forward for improving the general living conditions of the people. It was not a theological debate between ulemas; it was a cry of rage from the street, expressing real anguish about real life with crucial questions. The crowds marching beneath this banner were not defending some theological doctrine; they were defending their own real and present interests and their desire to take part in the running of the state, with the belief that if pious men were allowed to wield power in the name of God, they would run the state for the common good and in the best interests of the collectivity.

The modern notion of sovereignty is emerging but differently than in Europe since Islam does not have a formal clergy. Muslim societies are not experiencing the same quarrel that marked the history of Europe when the Roman Catholic Church refused to recognize the full and complete sovereignty of monarchs. The Catholic clergy fought the secularization of the political space in order to defend its monopoly on salvation. By contrast, in the Muslim countries of today, most believers support the right of divine sovereignty to wrest power from a civil or military oligarchy. The goal is not to build a theocracy but to bring the relationship between rulers and ruled into balance because most of the population does not see itself represented by leaders they feel are illegitimate because they have failed to keep their promises for jobs, housing, and the improvement of daily living conditions.

The claim of divine sovereignty has a profound motive about a state privatized by an elite that has imposed itself by force of arms or by rigging elections. Affirming that God is the source of power fits the aspiration of people inasmuch as God belongs to everyone. God condemns injustice, inequality, and corruption, all of which are charges leveled by the people at today's political leaders. Since "God" is synonymous with "justice" and "equality," the Islamists assume that sovereignty must be taken out of the hands of the corrupt and given to those who, in the name of God, will reestablish a just order. When an Egyptian or an Algerian is denied his right, or what he believes to be his right, and cannot go to a civil court to plead his case, he invokes God. Thus, God conveys a demand for dignity and the rights of people in the face of a corrupt and arbitrary administration. In the absence of an effective constitution and an independent judiciary, God becomes the rallying point for moral struggle. Thus, to affirm that sovereignty belongs to God is to announce that sovereignty belongs to all (*vox populi, vox dei*) and not to a mere handful of individuals. The affirmation does not spring from the Islam of the Book but from a political situation endured by ordinary people who reject the idea of a privatized state.

Obviously, there is a utopian aspect to this discourse but we should not forget that it is being used against authoritarian regimes that have refused the transition from national sovereignty (which affirms the independence of the state in international relations) to popular sovereignty (which allows people to choose their own representatives freely). Because this transition has not occurred, divine sovereignty has gained currency as an effective way to denounce the exclusion of the people from affairs of state. In the lexicon of Arab political regimes, the concept of national sovereignty—heavily eroded though it is by globalization—is just as abstract as divine sovereignty. Both refer to metaphysics that exclude the citizen from the political life of his country. An Arab military leader who mounts a coup d'état and claims to wield power in the name of the nation is basically no different from an Islamist leader who claims to wield power in the name of God. Consequently, the notion of divine sovereignty is hardly a step backward when compared with that of national sovereignty. Above all, Islamists (apart from a small minority) do not question the national character of sovereignty; nor do they demand the abolition of frontiers to rebuild a Muslim empire ruled by a caliph.[11] Nevertheless, they attract attention to the need for a reference—or at least a norm—that will convey the idea of legitimacy. The authoritarian Arab regimes, having exhausted their historic legitimacy, are faced with the total absence of any basic norm, for which they compensate with state violence in Egypt, Syria, Algeria, and elsewhere. The demand for divine sovereignty may be fueled by the lack of legitimacy of the political order it opposes, but it does not itself offer any institutional alternative to fill the vacuum. Are Islamists aware that even though God is sovereign, he will not run the state, and that someone or some institution will do it? One of the crucial questions the Islamists are facing pertains to the autonomy of man on Earth. Who should rule on Earth: God or man?

The slogan of divine sovereignty is relevant and politically efficient as long as the Islamists are in the opposition to authoritarian rule. If they win elections, they will discover that God, who is master of the universe, has left room for men to exercise sufficient sovereignty to manage their own earthly affairs. Although it is a powerful popular slogan of protest, *al hakimiyya li Allah* opens no new perspectives for the management of a state that seriously intends to represent its population. It cannot be institutionalized even though it is inscribed in the constitution. The expression *al hakimiyya li Allah* has been invented by Abul A'la Mawdudi based on flawed reasoning. Mawdudi ignores the semantic evolution of the Arabic word "*hukm*" and of the French word "*souveraineté.*" This expression does not belong to Muslim religious corpus and has no theological foundation. In theology, the claim is made that power belongs to God, but exactly what power is meant? According to Islam, as in other monotheist religions, supreme power belongs to God alone. He is Malik, owner of Earth and Heaven. Yet he remains the Creator of the universe, commanding man to respect his will on pain of punishment in the afterlife.

There are other possible readings of the Qur'an that, while paying due respect to the word of God, permit believers to exercise a political sovereignty that would in no way compete with the majestic power of Allah. This infinite power is above all the human contingencies through which history unfolds. If God had not left autonomy to man, his existence in society would resemble that which prevails in the animal kingdom, where life is ruled by natural law. The power of God is not incompatible with man's autonomy, which supposes that he exercises a power on Earth that does not compete with the divine. Mawdudi, for his part, confuses *hakimiyya* with the categories of divine, political, and legislative power. In the holy texts, God is the master of the universe, and from this standpoint the legislative function of man does not rival the transcendence of God.[12] Mawdudi gives the concept of sovereignty a meaning that attributes to God the political power of governing the state. At a stroke, the master of the universe is reduced to the status of chief of state, a sovereign involved in the conflicts of men. Thus, Mawdudi led his readers into an impasse that has narrowed the theological scope of the Qur'an ever since.

Mohammed Abdu tried to accommodate Islam with political modernity but failed to carry the ulemas with him. They repeated what they had been taught, that the destiny of man is determined in advance by God. Whatever that destiny may be, the believer must prepare his future in the next world by acknowledging the authority of the ulemas and by fulfilling his duties to God (prayer, fasting, almsgiving, etc.). In this interpretation of the holy texts, God is the architect of history, which repeats itself generation on generation with a pattern to be followed—that of the Prophet and his companions, to whom hagiology attributes the greatest virtues in order to paint a portrait of the perfect man blessed by God. All believers seek this blessing, investing in *'ibadates* (religious obligations) to pay their spiritual debt and gain entrance to Paradise.[13] However, *'ibadates* fulfilled are not sufficient to guarantee everlasting life. The anxiety of Muslims about this is soothed by the invocation of *"Tawakkalna 'ala Allah,"* which signifies that the believer places himself in the hands of God and of the wise who know the secrets of Holy Writ. This interpretation has for centuries constituted the only permissible reading of the Qur'an, which structured the culture of Muslims to perceive that the power of God was omnipresent in their daily lives, just like the rising and setting of the sun, the falling rain, the cultivation of the land, and the cycle of birth and death. Even the strength of the central power of the state, with its police force and army, was viewed as a manifestation of divine power since God gives power to whoever he wishes. A profound crisis within Muslim societies finally came to the surface when this interpretation, which left no room for doubt, began to crack in the nineteenth century with the decline of the Ottoman Empire and the European period of domination. In the last two centuries, there have been three ideological discourses aiming to address the modernization of Muslim societies: the Nahda, nationalism, and today's Islamism.

In Mawdudi's understanding of *hakimiyya*, there is a fundamental, crucial incoherence because of his confusion of two paradigms: the Qur'anic concept of *hakimiyya* and the political notion of sovereignty. Mawdudi wrongly translates the latter as *"hakimiyya,"* which has to do with judgment in Arabic. *Al Hakem* is the judge who arbitrates in a dispute between two people. *Al hakimiyya li Allah* means that God will judge in the fullness of time, on the day of the last judgment *(yawm el hisab)*, the acts of men during their time on Earth. Several verses attest to the meaning of word *"hukm"* with absolute clarity: "God judges! No man may oppose his judgment. He is swift to decide" (12:41). "God will judge between you on the day of resurrection" (4:14). "Conform to that which has been revealed to you. Have patience, until God shall judge. God is the best of judges" (10:109). "God judges in all justice; others judge nothing. God is he who hears and sees all perfectly" (40:20).[14] The word *"hukm,"* deriving from the verb *"hakama"* (root: *"hkm"*), is translated by all the dictionaries as "judgment" or "arbitration."[15] The word for law court in modern Arabic is *"el Mahkama,"* and the football referee is called *"el hakem."* Even though in some cases it has kept its original meaning, the word *"hukm"* has developed semantically by spawning the word *"hukuma,"* meaning government or political power.[16] This evolution may be understood in relation to the former principal function of the government, to render justice in conformity with the symbolic order protected by the ulemas. Before the nation-state and its omnipresent administration, human communities were relatively autonomous, particularly outside the cities. The rural periphery was not managed by government as it is today. The word "government" is new and has been translated as *"hukuma,"* the body that dispenses justice and whose prerogatives have been extended with the administrative meshing of territories. The ongoing secularization in Muslim societies has also affected Arabic vocabulary, as we have seen with the word *"malik."* Mawdudi was preoccupied with the word *"hakimiyya"* and even rejected its semantic evolution. He forged the expression *"Al hakimiyya li Allah"* in the sense of the modern word "government" and not "judgment," as in the Qur'an. To avoid anachronisms of this kind, the Qur'an should be read with the meaning of the words when they were written and not with the meaning of the words as understood today. To understand the holy texts, we must read them in their own words, not in ours. If we fail to account for diachronic changes in the language over time, this can only lead to anachronisms like that of "*Al hakimiyya li Allah.*"

Mawdudi made a mistake when he translated the modern concept of sovereignty as "*hakimiyya,*" accusing the parliaments of democracies of seeking to substitute themselves for God, which is emphatically not the case because liberal ideology is in no way hostile to the majesty of God. The American president ends his oath of office by saying "so help me God," which is the exact equivalent of a much-used expression in the Muslim world, "*Tawakkalna 'ala Allah.*" The error of Mawdudi originated in his confusion of the natural order, which obeys immutable laws, with the social order, which is subject to historic change. The sacred texts speak of a sovereign God who is lord of the universe, whereas liberal ideology speaks of the sovereignty of the state because the state makes laws to organize the political and social life of the country. From this standpoint, the notion of the sovereignty of the state is new—and it needs a new word in the Arabic language.

Mawdudi was not aware of this side of the question, just as he failed to grasp that men have always and everywhere exercised sovereignty even though they did not have clear consciousness of it. Sovereignty has always been wielded in the name of a metasocial principle (nature, God, monarchy, nation, the market, and so on). Men have always exercised sovereignty for themselves, even if they have done it in the name of the God they worship. They have always made laws and set out rules for themselves. In modernity, they have actually become aware of the human sovereignty; even so, this access of awareness is part of a long process. It is not a sudden break. It will take different forms. The *fuqahas* exercised sovereignty in early ages of Islam when they created the *fikh* (Muslim law) based on the Qur'an and the hadiths by practicing *ijtihad*. They made laws not in their own names or yet in the name of the faithful but in the name of God. Their authority was neither political nor religious but academic, meaning that they were recognized as experts in religious science. This is the meaning of the Arabic word " *'alem*," the plural of ulemas, "those who know." When the *fuqahas* made laws, they were not in full agreement among themselves, thus creating the old tradition of juridical pluralism within Islam, attesting to a culture of creative debate that does not exist today. Nobody at that time questioned the *fuqahas'* "academic" legitimacy in the production of laws and in the interpretation of the verses of the Qur'an and the hadiths of the Prophet. Nobody yelled the slogan *"al hakimiyya li Allah"* in the streets. Political powers—princes, emirs, and army chiefs— acknowledged that the *fuqahas* had the prerogative of interpreting divine law, thus the description given to them of *"ahl el hal oual 'aqd"* (those who have power to bind and unbind). In the classical scheme of Islam, the political powers do not trespass on the domain of the *fuqahas* and ulemas; neither do these latter interfere in affairs of state, which are the prerogative of the prince, except to pronounce on what is lawful and what is not. No Muslim state has ever been governed by ulemas in the name of God. The classical Muslim state is one of a monarchy with religious legitimacy, not a theocracy within which the prince would run the kingdom in the name of God.[17] This idea is foreign to the classical tradition, which assimilates it to the Christian papacy reproved by the Qur'an. Running counter to the same classical tradition, Mawdudi spread the idea that the best political regime is a state ruled in the name of God by a pious man as if in Islam someone could say "I exercise in the name of God a power that belongs properly to Him."

This is the understanding that Mawdudi gives to the expression *al hakimiyya li Allah*, meaning that sovereignty belongs to God, who passes it on to a man in order that he may exercise it. But God, in the theological sense of master of the universe, cannot delegate his sovereignty. According to the Qur'an, the Prophet Mohammed did not possess divine sovereignty; he was merely the messenger of God. Those who succeeded Mohammed at his death were not even messengers, they were political leaders. Mawdudi is very far from Islam since his interpretation would lead to the appointment of a pope. Sheikh Ali Abderrazak published a book in Cairo in 1925 in which he explained that the Prophet had two qualities: that of prophet, chosen by God to deliver the correct message, and that of political leader and founder of the first Muslim state. At his death his successors inherited his political function and not his quality of prophet. Therefore, Ali Abderrazak concludes that all the Muslim dynasties from the Umayyads to the Wahhabis cannot claim any religious legitimacy. Abderrazak's lesson is that God's power cannot be transmitted to men.[18] Muslim countries cannot avoid the secular meaning of sovereignty. Already in 1802, Muhammed Ali, Pasha of Egypt, had asserted the virtual sovereignty of his country by seceding from the Ottoman Empire, with which he had subsequently negotiated as an equal. The structure of international relations and the *rapports de force* prevailing on the world scene in his time made it essential that states should be able to assert full sovereignty on pain of annexation by another state.

The Islamist parties involved in electoral competition have tried to redefine this burdensome expression of *al hakimiyya li Allah* inherited from Mawdudi. Having agreed to participate in elections, they needed to conceptualize the power vested in representatives democratically elected in national assemblies. In a document dating from 2002, exiled Algerian Islamists explained the position of the party as follows: "The FIS pledges to work for the establishment of a civil and pluralistic political system based on the following fundamental principle: supreme and absolute sovereignty belongs to God, and power belongs to the people."[19] This represented a leap forward for Islamists, who thereby acknowledged that power belongs to the people.

The progress was relative however, because the same text made it clear that "the democratic dogma which attributes supreme sovereignty to the people . . . conflicts with the Islamic belief that reserves supreme and absolute sovereignty exclusively to God."[20] The text also contrasts this "democratic dogma" with the democratic practice of attributing the source of power to the people, which delegates the exercise of it to freely chosen representatives. However, even though this distinction constitutes progress in the Islamist discourse, Mawdudi's error in the translation of "*hakimiyya*" is reproduced yet again. Following his example, the writers of this text cite the verse of the Qur'an that says "power belongs to God alone. He has commanded you to adore none but him. Such is the true religion; but most have no knowledge of it" (12:40). The meaning of this verse again depends on the word "power." Is this a correct translation of the word "*hukm*" in the verse? Moreover, whatever the translation, the verse says "power belongs to God." What is power exactly? Is it the power to run a state? The Islamist discourse is confronted here with an epistemological obstacle that prevents one from acknowledging the autonomy of human politics. It is a paradox that men claiming to be religious do not read the Qur'an as a text in which the power of God is transcendent and eternal whereas the power of men is contingent and historical. Despite their good intentions, those who wrote the text quoted above still failed to make a clear break with Mawdudi, even though they tried to escape the impasse into which his thought invariably leads.

The rule of law and democracy demand a theological renewal that Mohammed Abdu tried unsuccessfully to achieve in the nineteenth century. Having pinpointed the contradiction inherent in the *qadirite* (fatalist conception) reading of the Qur'an (sovereignty belongs to God alone), Abdu wrote that if we put forward this understanding of the Qur'an, it means that God wanted the decadence of Muslim civilization and the ensuing European domination of it. This reading of the Qur'an is wrong, says Abdu, because it frees the believer of his responsibilities and prevents him from improving. He offered an alternative interpretation that was audacious for the time, in which he explained that history is a sequence of events that have human causes.[21] Referring to Ibn Khaldun and to European authors like Oswald Spengler, Abdu declared that the failure to keep up with Europe originated in the fatalism of Muslim tradition. God, he said, gave every freedom to man who is sovereign on Earth. Muslims had not taken advantage of this sovereignty. Abdu used the word "*sayyada*" for sovereignty, not "*hakimiyya*." "Islam is a religion of sovereignty (*sayyada*) of authority (*sultan*) and of unity between this world and the hereafter."[22] In politics, the word "*sayyada*" translates best as sovereignty, if one understands by that word the power of the electorate to choose its representatives. The Islamists of the FIS, in the document quoted above, used *sayyada* in this sense, in affirming that *hakimiyya* belongs to God and *sayyada* belongs to the people. Thus, the constitution of a democratic Muslim state could contain as its first article: "Supreme power belongs to God and sovereignty belongs to the people. Sovereignty is delegated to elected representatives with a mandate to promulgate laws in the name of the people, within the framework of the *ijtihad* of sharia, natural law, reason, and universal values." In other words, *al hakimiyya li Allah wa al siyyada li sha'ab* (power over the universe belongs to God and sovereignty belongs to the people). Such an article in the constitution would be compatible with democracy, which would eventually emerge behind the words of Muslim culture to describe the new reality: the autonomy of politics. Under pressure of events, this line of thought has evolved in the discourse of Islamists influenced by liberal theology who, at the same time as they reject the theocratic state of the monarchies and the state ruled by military officers, dream of a civil state that would proclaim that *al hakimiyya* belongs to God and that *sayyada* belongs to the people. This concept would be the profane equivalent of *hakimiyya* and the translation of the Western concept of sovereignty. If the concept of *sayyada* enters Islamist political culture, the dead end into which Mawdudi led, it will be bypassed.

The political language changed dramatically in the Arab countries, including that of the monarchies. When a reality comes to existence, the word to describe it follows. The question, however, is why the Islamists objected to democracy and not to "*mamlaka*" (monarchy). The meaning of "*mamlaka*" is linked to the notion of property. Property is *melk*, and in the Qur'an, God is *Malik*, or owner of the universe. The translation of the word "king" as *malik* is blasphemous if we follow the reasoning of the Islamists. Exercising the authority in the name of God, the head of the Ottoman Empire had the title caliph or sultan and not *malik*.[23] As a result, the contemporary Arab monarchies, called *mamlaka*, are imitating the medieval European monarchies with the idea that the king (*malik*) is sovereign in his kingdom. The king of Saudi Arabia or of Morocco is closer to the model of Henry VIII of England or Louis XIV of France than that of Caliph Omar Ibn al-Khattab or the Ottoman Sultan. Mawdudi should have objected to the qualification of *malik* that the Arab kings gave to themselves. In the Qur'an, there is one *malik*: God. In the past, the kings were either sultan, emir, or caliph, not *malik*. In Arabic, "*soltane*" means authority. The Muslim sultan of the classical age does not consider the kingdom as his property or as the extension of his own private domains. Rather, he is the owner of the military force that has enabled him to take power to defend the just order willed by God.

Before and during the French protectorate, the Moroccan monarch's qualification was "*sultan*" (meaning "authority"). After independence, it was suppressed in favor of *malik*, to reflect the hereditary evolution of the monarchy (*mamlaka*). Yet, according to Islamic dogma, only God is *malik*. One of the first articles of the Moroccan constitution, abrogated in the 1990s, stipulated that the king held his authority from the nation and was accountable to God alone. The dynasty of Saudi Arabia, which never felt the need for a constitution, based its legitimacy on Wahhabism, supposedly the sole true interpretation of Islam. Despite the changes they have brought about, the monarchies continue to wrap themselves in the mantle of tradition that shields them from the accusation of usurping the sovereignty of God.

The word *"malik"* has since been secularized, and nobody today thinks that Arab kings are trespassing on the domain of God by using the title. Often, *Malik* is preceded by the word *"jalalat"* (*jalalat el Malik*, "his majesty the king"), though in the Qur'an only God is "majestic." Criticism of the word *"malik"* is inopportune today in the sense that its semantic content changed. Neither the king, called *malik*, nor the sovereignty of the state trespass on the prerogatives of God. However, it is worth noticing that Mawdudi criticized the democratic form of government by declaring that sovereignty belongs only to God while he avoided reminding the Arab kings that only God is *malik*. Among these monarchies, of course, was Saudi Arabia, ruled by a *malik* with whom Mawdudi had good relations—so good, indeed, that the Saudi monarchy generously financed his movement.

THE HISTORICAL DIMENSION OF THE CONCEPT OF SOVEREIGNTY

Sovereignty was originally a religious concept, meaning that the power belongs to God, master and owner of the universe and all nature, of which all human societies are a part. Medieval culture used to teach that the laws that regulate relationships among men correspond to the laws of nature and both are dictated by God. Being indissociable from nature, man would lose his humanity if he did not obey the rules willed by the Creator. Sovereignty has an aura of magic, originating as it does in the monotheistic religions that state that

God alone is sovereign. The political philosophy of "human sovereignty" was coined by Jean Bodin, a sixteenth-century French philosopher who inspired the young French monarchy to sever itself from the tutelage of the pope and the Holy German-Roman Empire. The French king wished to be "emperor in his own realm" (*empereur dans son royaume*), refusing to recognize any power as greater than his own, save that of God. Endowing himself with the divine right (*le droit divin*), the king was declared majestic in his capacity to make men submit to royal decrees. From the sixteenth century onward, the young French monarchy sought to assert itself against the *potestas* (secular power) of the Holy German-Roman Empire and the *auctoritas* (religious authority) of the papacy. This process lasted several centuries and resulted in the conquest of sovereignty by the monarch, who proclaimed himself sovereign while claiming divine legitimacy for his authority. By the seventeenth century, the French monarchy was fully sovereign in the sense given to this concept by Jean Bodin one hundred years before, when he defined it as the faculty of promulgating and abrogating laws. The notion was not supposed to be against God; instead, it was designed to resist the emperor and the pope by asserting that there is no *human* authority superior to that of the king within his realm. This idea was so radical that in England the king was able to proclaim himself head of the Church. As the Church's oldest daughter, France did not go quite that far; nevertheless, the French monarchy demanded the political allegiance of all French bishops. The metaphysic of religious sovereignty began to fall apart in Western Europe with the rise of patrimonial monarchies and the Westphalian order.

The 1789 French Revolution transferred sovereignty to the nation while preserving its mystical character and theatrical symbolism. The French Revolution radically denied that this faculty could belong to a single individual, king or otherwise, and declared in the 1791 constitution that the nation was sovereign. The concept of national sovereignty was born within this historical context, emphasizing two aspects. First of all, the state is independent from any foreign power. Second, all members of the nation swear allegiance to the leader of the central state power. This concept became generalized with the Westphalian system. However, its secularization will be complete only with the victory of the universal suffrage, with the idea that the electorate is sovereign by virtue of its quality to be the source of power and to choose representatives to make laws in its name. Thus, the sovereignty belongs to people who pass it on to representatives acting on their behalf.

Having been born into this period of European history, the concept of sovereignty was unknown to the *fuqahas* and did not belong to Muslim culture. The Muslim monarchies were slightly different from those of Europe. In their case, the king was politically sovereign, but the ulemas retained the prerogative of interpreting sharia. In a way, they possessed a legislative power that escaped the king. He was a political leader because of the nobility of his family tree, which was often invented in the aftermath of a military victory. The kings of Morocco and Jordan claimed to be descendants of the Prophet, which entitled them to a religious legitimacy that could enforce the people's obedience. In Saudi Arabia, Wahhabism appropriated sovereignty by declaring that its interpretation of Islam was the only true one.

Third world nationalists discovered the concept in the course of their anticolonial independence struggles, which were aimed at creating national states respected by the international community. Adhering to the Westphalian system, the nationalists of developing countries put forward the concept of "national sovereignty" to exist politically at the international level. But it was the leaders who were sovereign, claiming to speak on behalf of the nation while refusing to hold free elections. The sovereignty was national, not popular. The constitutions state that the sovereignty belongs to the people but the constitution is a text solely intended to provide the regime with a juridical bedrock, not to guarantee the balance between the executive, the legislative, and the judicial powers that are the underpinning of a democratic system.

The Question of Sharia

Whenever Islam is discussed, either by academics or among ordinary Muslims, the issue of sharia is bound to arise even though the Qur'an uses the word on only two occasions. The concept of sharia represents an ideal of justice linked to the metaphysical dimension of Abrahamic monotheism, which teaches that existence on Earth is no more than a brief episode in the life of an individual, that life will unfold fully in the next world, either in heaven or in hell, according to the degree of conviction in the individual's religious faith. The Qur'an threatens men and women with eternal damnation in the next world if they do not respect the elementary principles of religious ethics during their time on Earth. Sharia is a collection of principles—few of them contained in the Qur'an—that call on the individual to obey certain moral precepts on pain of God's wrath. Although it distinguishes between them, sharia encompasses 'ibadates (ritual duties) and the mou'amalates (behavior in daily life). Prayer is said to drive away ill intentions. Sin and crime are mixed and condemned in the same way; divine reprobation is invoked to guarantee the moral order of society. The Muslim believes that if he disobeys sharia, he will provoke God's anger and be pronounced guilty on the day of the last judgment. He lives in a state of fear that has had lasting effects on popular culture; sharia is the road that leads to paradise as long as the rules contained in the Qur'an are applied and respected, which is the condition of a happy life in this world.

For many centuries, sharia—a magic word with a very broad semantic content—has influenced popular knowledge about society that is torn between two opposite poles: the first, morality and religion (leading to goodness and truth); and the second, instinct and untruth (leading to evil and falsity). Individuals are submitted to a degree of tension that they try to overcome by discursive practices and by the magic of symbolic words describing an ideal social order from which injustice and selfishness must be completely absent. For the average Muslim, sharia is a model of justice, and it is impeded by the malevolence of some people and the influence of the West. The ordinary believer does not distinguish between sharia and *fiqh*; he is unaware that Muslim law is a human construction based on the Qur'an, the hadiths, and a highly refined conceptual methodology. The idea frequently surfaces that sharia is a blueprint for perfection that applies to sincere believers who have the qualities willed by God. Sharia is perceived as a fair law for a perfect society. For the average believer, if it was applied today to the letter, the courts would have to condemn half the population to death. The conclusion is that young people need to be educated in the ways of the true Islam in order to prepare future generations to respect sharia. This vision is widespread among the population, which sees sharia as the ideal norm for which the imperfect law of the state is substituted today. This vision is the basis of a political program that promises to abolish social inequalities and to give the poor "their due" by curbing the greed of the rich and the arrogance of political leaders. Its demand expresses a hope and fuels an ideological discourse denouncing the current governments. The demand for sharia is beyond the obedience to a law; it pertains to a utopia since people do not know what exactly sharia is, a word enveloped in semantical cloud in Geertz's phrase. Its purpose is *el haq* (justice) and *el haqiqa* (truth), which means a quest for an ideal.

Sharia is not viewed as a mere corpus of juridical rules; it is also the source of knowledge and ethics at the heart of the dialectic of true and false, good and evil, signifying man's incessant struggle to attain the former and flee the latter. With its special linguistic quality, the language of the Qur'an reinforces the perception of two opposite poles in perpetual conflict, the one normative that must be known, attained, and imitated and the other real that is to be overcome, tamed, or avoided. The Arabic language lends itself to this exercise; it functions as a tool for discovering the hidden reality of things through a tension that gives the believer a choice between the true and eternal world and the temporary world before his eyes, following the popularity of the Islamist discourse that deals with the eschatological dichotomy between good and evil. The desire to eliminate this dichotomy gave birth to the Islamist utopia. The objective is to set up a state determined to deter bad behavior and bring back to the right way indicated by the Qur'an. Sharia means right, straight, and law (in the juridical sense but also the geometrical one, hence the word "*shara*'," meaning a broad straight road or boulevard). It means also legitimate and legal decision, and in a state ruled by a just prince, legitimacy equals legality.

There is also a millenarian dimension to sharia that announces the promised Messiah (*al Mahdi el Mountadar*), who will reestablish justice on Earth by the application of divine law. For most Muslim believers, sharia represents the sociopolitical order of a true Muslim society obeying the principles of justice set out in the Qur'an. This representation became self-evident with the crises of Muslim societies dominated by the West. Many Muslims firmly believe that their economic, political, and cultural backwardness has a single cause: the marginalization of sharia, a virtual world of justice that gives a shape to utopia and a voice to the people's expectations. At this time in the history of the Muslim world, the sacred is mobilized to face the consequences of social change entailed by European domination. Muslim society finds itself still dependent on the former imperial powers even in the postcolonial period. Sharia is a rallying cry that can express frustrations and the yearning for modernity in religious terms: equal dignity for all, a just state, and a genuine response to the challenge of the West. However, the religious discourse blurs these aspirations by chaining civil law to religious morality and politics to psychology.

The demand for sharia law is also a rejection of the secularization of the juridical norm, as if the Muslim conscience, refusing the laws of men entirely, was unwilling to obey any laws other than those decreed by God. The idealization of sharia—whose contents are unknown to most believers—is not without contradictions. People view it as a collection of divine rules that cannot be modified and do not imagine that it is linked to culture. They refuse to consider that divine law could change to better serve its spirit. They do not accept the idea that sharia, written by *fuqahas* based on their reading of the Qur'an, is a human law bearing a medieval culture. On certain points it clashes with the aspirations of young women today, who do not wish to live under threat of repudiation by their husbands throughout their married lives. Sharia authorizes men to marry up to four women on condition that the ceremony takes place under the auspices of an imam who recites the *fatiha* (the first verse of the Qur'an) in the presence of two witnesses. Today, women are not content with this religious form of that wedlock, but it is nonetheless perfectly legal per the criteria of sharia. For women, however, it has no legitimacy since they demand an official transcription of their marriage from the town hall so that they cannot be divorced by their husbands without financial compensation. The Arab states have complied by introducing modifications discouraging husbands from repudiating their wives for no good reason. Indeed, in many cases repudiation has been abolished altogether and replaced by a divorce procedure that takes due account of the interests of the wife and that lasts many months, to allow time for the husband to change his mind. These reforms have not established juridical equality between men and women; however, they have gone as far as society would permit, given that Muslim culture is still heavily patriarchal in character.

Some find reforms like this insufficient; others see them as an attack on religion. Yet they have been rendered possible because families have found themselves caught between anxiety about the fate of their marriageable daughters and their attachment to the patriarchal ideology that is so weighted in favor of their sons. When it comes to matrimony, families have different strategies for boys and girls. In the first case, they are in a position of strength; in the second, they are in a position of weakness. If a newly married girl separates from her husband, her family invokes sharia in the conviction that God is just and loves justice. Whatever the case, each side believes that sharia, properly understood, will defend their interests. The protagonists in family conflicts do not call sharia into question; instead they criticize the opposite party's disrespect of it. A mother who torments her daughter-in-law will deplore the fact that her own daughter is being oppressed by her mother-in-law. Conflictual social dynamics broaden the rights of individuals that are guaranteed not by sharia but by family solidarities that impose their own interpretations of Muslim law. By defending their own daughters, families have improved the status of young girls in general, whose opinions are now considered by their fathers when young men propose marriage. The progressive formation of a private space strengthens the public expression of affection by parents for the children. Today, no man would dare to ask a father for the hand of his daughter as a *second* wife. This would be perceived as a grave insult, even though sharia permits polygamy. The family model that now prevails throughout the Muslim world is that of the nuclear family, to the detriment of the extended family (*'ayla*), which traditionally gathers under the same roof several married brothers with their children and grandchildren. Under the influence of other factors, this sociological development has facilitated a change in the legal age of marriage (sixteen to eighteen for girls; eighteen to twenty for young men, depending on the country) to account for the capacity of a young mother to raise her children.[24] People dream of sharia, but everyone says what it should be according his or her own interests. In daily social relations between people, sharia has a somewhat variable geometry.[25] It remains a symbolic reference, and everyone claims that he is acting in accordance with sharia: some prefer to stress its literal application whereas others fall back on what they think is the better understanding of its goals.

To comprehend exactly how large the gulf is between what is said and what is done in Arab countries, we must undertake field research and listen to the people involved in law cases who give their own versions of sharia and of what they expect of it. We must go to any law court and hear how grievances are framed. There we will find a woman who has been abandoned by her husband, imploring the judge to apply sharia in the interests of her young children. We will find an old mother, accompanied by her son, petitioning for the divorce of her daughter-in-law, accusing her of not respecting her in the way prescribed by sharia. We will see battered women begging the judge to tell their husbands that sharia forbids conjugal violence. It is as if, according to sharia, everyone is more or less in the right; and this is actually the case because sharia is based on a *concept* of justice, and everyone is free to form her own idea of what that justice might entail. The mother-in-law finds it unjust that her son's wife does not respect her, and the husband who beats his spouse can easily find a verse of the Qur'an to justify his behavior. Everyone puts on his side of sharia, accusing others of not respecting it.

The issue of the law must be addressed with the view of "culture" as "social system." The question is how to convince people to accept that there is no such a thing as a divine law outside of consciousness given by God or by nature to men, and accept that society is the only source of law. For political reasons, the Arab regimes cannot say that sharia, as a legal system, has fallen in disuse. For example, the right to own slaves has been banished from social life and memory. The Qur'an does not recommend slavery but does not forbid it neither. The sacred text encourages people to free slaves, but it is not a religious obligation. If there is no slavery in contemporary Muslim societies, it is because the idea of equality among men is more present in human minds today than it was in Arabia in the seventh century.[26] It is the same for Qur'anic rules called *huddud*, which punish robbery and adultery. Men and women accused of crimes of this kind are viewed as having committed offenses against the moral order willed by God. With the exception of a small minority, Muslim opinion seems firmly behind the idea that a thief should be sent to jail rather than having one of his limbs amputated. On the other hand, the crime of adultery is deemed morally reprehensible, but it belongs to the realm of private life.[27] A man who runs after women is frowned upon, but a man whose wife is unfaithful to him is even more frowned upon if he does not divorce her. In many Arab countries—from Morocco to Iraq, but not Saudi Arabia—the sentence of death by stoning for adultery would be unacceptable to most of the population. Whether it be in Morocco, Egypt, or Syria, corporal punishment as decreed by the Qur'an has no part in state-generated regulations. The modifications made to Muslim law—which some have considered insufficient and others feel to be outright offenses against religion—have not met with real resistance on the part of most of the population. These modifications spring from the real sociological change that took place in recent decades.

The same reasoning can be applied to the status of women who are considered by a significant body of Muslim opinion as being inferior to men. There are verses in the Qur'an that assign an inferior juridical status to women, but there are also verses that recommend that women should be respected, protected, and treated justly. It is worth asking why some verses have fallen into oblivion whereas others remain in use. The relevance of Qur'anic verses is directly related to mentalities as they evolve over time. It is no coincidence that, of all the many branches of the *fiqh*, only those dealing with family rights and successions have survived. The patriarchal culture keeps alive the code of personal status that governments dare not alter. Only Tunisia, following Turkey, forbade polygamy. If the discourse of the Islamists and the sermons preached in the mosques give such great importance to the question of women, it is because Muslim society has been structured for centuries on an ideology whereby men are the sons of men and reproduce themselves by using women. The reproduction of society depends on the postulate that women are inferior to men; they are no more than a means of reproducing the group within the traditional patrilineal framework. Sharia family laws persist today because they confirm the patriarchal representation on which society rests. As long as Muslim culture is imbued by this representation, any modification of legal dispositions concerning women's rights will be perceived as illegitimate. Law and legitimacy of the symbolic order are closely linked and mutually supportive. The sociological mutations taking place today will call into question the symbolic order as women become progressively more included in the production of material goods and services as workers, teachers, doctors, and so on, because all these working women will expect to be treated justly and properly in the workplace and at home.[28]

Cultural change is under way in Arab societies that lost the traditional social coherence and that are in a quest for the new one. The autonomy of the person is emerging through the extension of the wage-earning sector. The social logic of the group is fading away while the personal interests are more put forward in families. The individual income is no longer a family property; sooner or later, this will drive a contractualist logic that respects the subjective rights of individuals to an ever greater degree.[29] As the old solidarities of family relationships are declining, the members of the group are more and more aware of their rights, and many rules of sharia will be publicly questioned in the future. However, it will take time because many believers will resist the secularization of the law; they are caught between the fear of eternal damnation and the need to take care of their own interests. The confusion between sin and crime continues to mark the juridical culture of a society that has hitherto depended on the sacred to impose the required moral values. This confusion is not absolute, and the Qur'an opens perspectives of evolution as it distinguishes between ritual duties owed to God (*'ibadates*) and social relationships (*mou'amalates*).[30]

Even though it prescribes sanctions, the Qur'an always leaves the door open to repentance. In the juridical verses, the Qur'an recommends various punishments but also pardons if the guilty one repents. For example, it authorizes the *lex talionis* (an eye for an eye) but recommends material compensation to the family of the victim in lieu of executing the perpetrator of the crime. The pain of death for adultery is valid on condition that four witnesses come forward and swear they have seen "the pen in the ink pot," as the *fuqahas* charmingly describe it. Where is the woman who will be physically unfaithful to her husband in the presence of four potential court witnesses? In general, the Qur'an seeks to render justice to the victim of a crime while preserving human life. The same concern for evenhandedness or fairness is clear regarding polygamy—which is deemed technically lawful but is not recommended. A man may have up to four wives on condition that he treats them all fairly, but the verse adds that "God knows you will not be fair."[31]

With time, Muslim societies will find a balance between Heaven and Earth. In the meantime, before religion loses its public character, there will be crises and violence, of which Islamism is one of the foremost manifestations. Change is historically possible because the Qur'an is not unequivocal; it is susceptible to many understandings according to period of time. Many verses of the Qur'an can be interpreted in the light of other verses that contradict them; for example, there is a verse that obliges Muslims to kill "miscreants, Jews, and Christians," and another verse stipulates that taking the life of another person is no different from killing all humanity. There is a hadith that condemns apostates to capital punishment ("he who changes his religion, kill him") and yet there are verses of the Qur'an that say the exact opposite:

"There shall be no constraint in religion" (2:256)
"Your mission is not to constrain them in the faith" (50:45)
"Had God willed it, the whole universe would have embraced the
    true faith. Would you then force men to convert?" (10:99)
"Remember! You are only here to repeat the word of God. You have
    no authority to exercise over them" (21:22)

Are there true and false interpretations of the sacred texts? Religion is not above the conflicts and the antagonisms that shake society. In this perspective, Islamism, with its claims on behalf of sharia, is linked to the predicament of Muslim societies. Even though the Qur'an offers some flexibility in social relations, Muslim theologians took the path of intolerant orthodoxy. As a result, official Islam has been reduced to a perpetual repetition of what the ancestors recorded. The same phenomenon has affected the *fiqh*, which has lost the intense creativity of its origins. No theologians and no jurisconsults have ventured to innovate for fear of being accused of heresy. And yet the companions of the Prophet were fearless in interpreting the verses of the Qur'an in a spirit of absolute equity. Omar ibn al-Khattab stopped the amputation of the hands of thieves during a year of drought because of shortage of food for the poorest; he also temporarily forbade Muslims to marry Christian and Jewish women (though the practice was authorized by the Qur'an) after being petitioned by Muslim women who could not find husbands.[32] Since the caliph Omar's time, very few religious leaders or theologians have followed his example; the tendency has been toward inexorably greater rigor and against new interpretations. As far as there is no institution within Islam that exercises a monopoly on the interpretation of the early texts, all theological debate and all religious controversy takes place publicly in the mosques. Naturally, this forces the theoretical level of religious knowledge down to the lowest common denominator. The ulemas routinely use the mass of believers as a political force to isolate people seeking to break out of the routine of tradition. In a period of identity crisis, religious debate and the discussion about sharia have little to do with the academic controversies at which theologians and specialists excel; instead, they follow a logical pattern whereby public opinion—mobilized in exactly the same way by ulemas in the past and by Islamists today—is used to disqualify and threaten any individual who might be interested in a different way of looking at the Qur'an. The question of sharia is not a theological one; it has more to do with politics and the balance of power in the field of knowledge.

The modernization of Muslim law and the eventual integration into it of fresh juridical norms depend on the capacity to bring forward new interpretations of the holy text that would consider the change that society has undergone during the last century. The juridical techniques and methodology already exist. An adequate intellectual level among the ulemas is required to move forward knowing the influence they have among the masses. The Qur'an has hitherto been read literally, for once, by the Hanbalite tradition based on verses revealed in Medina, where the Prophet and his companions were under siege waging wars. Unlike the Medina verses, the Mecca verses are peaceful, seeking to win the hearts and minds of people for the new faith. To impose the warlike verses, the Hanbalite ulemas found a technique known as abrogation (*naskh*). If two verses are contradictory, they took the view that the latest one abrogates the earlier. In this way the warlike verses gained the upper hand over the peaceful and tolerant ones. Some theologians suggest that since the technique of abrogation exists in Islam, it should be used to put forward the peaceful verses revealed in Mecca. For having declared that the verses revealed at Mecca are universal and addressed to the whole of humanity, and that those revealed in Medina are not any more relevant, Mahmoud Mohammed Taha, the Sudanese theologian, was hanged by a regime calling itself radical Arab nationalist.[33]

To conclude this section, I quote one of the best Western specialists in Muslim law to help readers understand the theoretical and historical issues at stake.

All Muslim penal law carries the very visible imprint of the genius of Mohammed. His rigor in regard to religious offenses stems from the need to protect the young religion of Islam. His severity in regard to common law crimes reflects the idea of intimidation and making an example that prevailed in his time. The *talion* was a survival from pre-Islamic barbarism, regulated and softened by legal compensation. So Muslim penal law is a repressive system whose character lies somewhere between private vengeance and public or divine vengeance, between the ideas of expiation and intimidation that correspond to the theological–political concept of repression.

CHAPTER 5

The harshness of Muslim religious and common law punishments reflect the twin ideas of intimidation and social vengeance, whereby the defense of society is achieved by fear. It is worth noting that in this system, there is little concern for the rehabilitation of the criminal and that the crime is viewed in its material rather than its intentional aspect. But our own penal law had exactly the same defects right up to the 18th century. Again, the use of torture is unknown to Muslim law and the arbitrariness of punishment is sensibly reduced by the existence of the *hududs*. If we go back to the 7th century when it was founded, the repressive Muslim system turns out to be a remarkable piece of work that does honor to Mohammed's genius for adaptation. We can only regret the general stagnation that followed the great effort of construction accomplished by the lawmakers of the first three centuries and the regression due to the restoration of the *talion* by Ibn Saud in Arabia in the twentieth century.[34]

Notes

1. The concept of "political resource" is crucial to the analysis of the *rapports de force* that determine levels of political participation. Political resources are as many as varied: loyalty, charisma, beliefs, money, violence, and so on.

2. In his fieldwork implemented in Algeria in the late 1950s, Pierre Bourdieu noticed that the poorer people were, the more ambitious and fantastical their dreams became. For example, a railway employee with decent housing and a regular income dreamed that his son could obtain his certificate for employment in the administration. Conversely, the jobless man living in a slum dreamed that his son might become a surgeon, even though he was too poor to feed the boy properly. See Pierre Bourdieu, *Travail et travailleurs en algerie* (Paris: Mouton, 1963).

3. One of the postulates settled by phenomenology and hermeneutics is that texts, sacred or profane, are interpreted according to the aspirations, wishes, and culture of the reader who interprets them, consciously or not.

4. The "democratic threshold" is supposed to have been reached when participation corresponds to the definition of democracy arrived at by Joseph A. Schumpeter: that is, "an institutional arrangement for making political decisions,

whereby individuals acquire the power to decide by means of a competitive struggle for the people's vote"; Schumpeter, *Capitalism, Socialism and Democracy* (New York: Harper, 1943), 269. It includes, however, freedom of speech and a separate judiciary that will ensure real competition in electoral campaigns. This definition is condoned by many political scientists. See Philippe C. Schmitter and Terry Lynn Karl, "What Democracy Is . . . and Is Not," in *The Global Resurgence of Democracy*, 2nd ed., ed. Larry Diamond and Marc F. Plattner, 49–62 (Baltimore: John Hopkins University Press, 1996), 50.

5. Peter L. Berger, *The Sacred Canopy: Elements of a Sociological Theory of Religion* (Garden City, NY: Doubleday, 1967), 126.

6. The idea of "stage" has nothing to do with historicism. Europe imposed on the rest of the world the model of the modern state and there is no alternative to it. The historical experiences to achieve the modern state and democracy, however, will be different in each country.

7. See Seymour M. Lipset, *Political Man: The Social Basis of Politics* (Baltimore: Johns Hopkins University Press, 1981).

8. See Chaudhry Kiren Aziz, *The Price of Wealth: Economics and Institutions in the Middle East* (Ithaca, NY: Cornell University Press, 1997).

9. See Mouline Nabil, *The Clerics of Islam: Religious Authority and Political Power in Saudi Arabia* (New Haven, CT: Yale University Press, 2014).

10. One of the innovative theses of Durkheim's religious sociology was that society worships itself by worshiping God. See Emile Durkheim, *The Elementary Forms of Religious Life*, trans. Karen E. Fields (New York: Free Press, 1995).

11. In the conflict between Morocco and Algeria over Western Sahara, Moroccan and Algerian Islamists do not have the same position and each camp supports the official position of its government. Even though the dream of the *umma* has never faded from the Muslim imagination, Islamists belong to national spaces just like everyone else. As for the caliphate, it is called for by a small but violent minority, which makes newspaper headlines.

12. By swearing on the Bible, the elected representatives of the American people swear allegiance to God; they do not compete with him in the making of secular laws, which may be abrogated by other elected representatives in the future.

13. In Arabic, the words "religion" and "debt" are very close, and ordinary people think that they are synonymous. In fact, they are not. Playing on this confusion, the ulemas used to teach that men must pay their debt to God, implying that religion means debt. Thus, the faithful view their religious obligations as so many "debts" to pay before they can arrive in Paradise.

14. All these verses using the word "*hukm*" say that nobody aside from Allah may judge of men's beliefs, meaning that no authority on earth may decide the fate of any person in the next world. This prerogative belongs to God and God alone. It constitutes one of Islam's great theological divergences with Catholicism, which has a clergy that judges the faith of Catholics in order to prepare

their souls for salvation. In Islam, salvation is a personal not an institutional affair. Islam is opposed to the institution of a clergy interceding between God and the faithful, thus definitively removing from men the faculty of judging other men's relationships with God. Only God is *hakem*, and only God will judge in the next world. There is no room here for an interpretation of the Qur'an that would divide the sacred (God's domain) from the profane (man's domain). Nevertheless, the Qur'an offers a potential for the construction of a place wherein man is free and autonomous, submitting only to the judgment of God in the next world. When the Front Islamique du Salut (Islamic Salvation Front, FIS) was created in Algeria in March 1989, many people pointed out that there was no party or institution within Islam that ensured the "salvation" of believers. The institution that ensures the salvation of souls is a Christian idea, they objected.

15. See Abdou el Mannan Omar, *Dictionary of the Holy Koran (Arabic–English)* (Amsterdam: Noor Foundation, 2004); and Mustandir Mir, *Dictionary of Quranic Terms and Concepts* (New York: Garland, 1987).

16. In a book published in 1925, Ali Abderrazak uses the word *"hukm"* in its modern sense of government power.

17. See Patricia Crone, *God's Rule: Government and Islam* (New York: Columbia University Press, 2004).

18. The religious authorities of the time condemned this work, and his book has been forbidden.

19. Quoted from texts on the convention held in Belgium in 2002, from the Website http://moutamar.ennour.org/index.php.

20. Ibid.

21. Mohamed Abdou, *Rissalat Et Tawhid: Exposé de la religion musulmane,* French trans. B. Michel and Cheikh Mustapha Abdel Razik (Paris: Geuthner, 1925).

22. M. Abdou, *Tafsir al Manar,* 2nd ed. (Beirut: Dar al Ma'rifa), 1:11. It is interesting to note that in the Arabic language *"sayyed"* means the master, the overlord in a lay sense; in the Maghreb, in some families, the father is called *"sidi"* by his children. Saints are also called *"sidi."* The meaning of the term has been completely secularized and now evokes a higher human authority. There is a popular spoken formula that denies this quality of overlordship to man, but in a polite and modest way: when a person is called *"sidi,"* the proper response is a humble one: "Only God is lord and we are his servants."

23. The question of the caliphate was discussed by the ulemas of the classical age, who warned that the caliph was not God's representative on earth. There is no Islamic equivalent for the Catholic representative on earth, the pope. The Qur'an teaches that all men are God's representatives. Consequently, the caliph is he who "replaces" the Prophet (*khalafa* means "to replace" in Arabic). In 1925 Sheikh Ali Abderrazak wrote a book in which he explained that the caliphs inherited the political functions of the Prophet but not his religious attributes. The book was banned and Ali Abderrazak was condemned by Al-Azhar, where he

had studied. His work was regarded by the monarchies as deeply subversive since it denied them all religious legitimacy.

24. As far as sharia is concerned, as soon as a girl has breasts and can feed a child, she is ready for marriage. The age conditions laid down by the law have been accepted by city-dwelling Muslims today, whose main preoccupation is that their children, whether boys or girls, should continue their studies up to the age of eighteen and even beyond.

25. See Lawrence Rosen, *The Anthropology of Justice: Law as Culture in Islamic Society* (Cambridge: Cambridge University Press, 1989).

26. Abul A'la Mawdudi defends slavery in his book *Al Islam fi muwajahate ettahadiate* (Islam and its challenges) (Kuwait: Dar al Kalam, 1978). Other Islamists support the idea that prisoners of war should be enslaved but they do not convince the majority of Muslims who are perfectly indifferent to the matter.

27. In Saudi Arabia and Iran, the punishment for adultery is the death sentence—for women only, of course.

28. I have addressed these transformations in my book *Les mutations de la société Algérienne: Espace familial et crise du lien social en Algérie* (Paris: La Découverte, 1999).

29. In a private interview, a notary in Oran told me that the right of succession currently prevailing in Algeria is vigorously opposed by people who think it is unjust that a family heritage should include uncles, aunts, cousins, and nephews. He offered the example of a family that had sold a piece of property belonging to a father who had died. By law the family had to share the proceeds of the sale with uncles, aunts, and cousins, whom they hardly knew. The reason: when the father bought the property fifty years earlier, he registered it in his own name and in the name of his wife. The wife died before her mother, who, in accordance with Muslim law, inherits from her deceased daughter's half share. When the deceased wife's mother died, her children and grandchildren inherited this share. Finally, when the property was liquidated, the proceeds were shared between the brothers and sisters but also with the uncles, aunts, and cousins. The direct heirs found this process totally unjust because the piece of property had belonged to their father, who had bought it entirely with his own savings.

30. Except for the fast of Ramadan, there is no condemnation by legal courts in case of disrespect of religious duties such as praying. People who do not go to the mosque or do not pray are not punished by the judge. There is, however, an informal social pressure exercised on people who "forget" to go to the mosque, especially on Fridays.

31. Based on this verse of the Qur'an, President Habib Bourguiba of Tunisia made polygamy illegal when his country achieved independence.

32. See Mohammed Charfi, *Islam et liberté; Le malentendu historique* (Paris: Albin Michel, 1998), 162.

CHAPTER 5

33. Threatened with death by his opponents, the prophet fled from Mecca and took refuge in Medina, where he and his followers organized the resistance to establish the new religion, of which he was the messenger. The revelation took place first in Mecca and later in Medina, under different historical circumstances. See Mahmoud M. Taha, *The Second Message of Islam*, trans. Abdullah Ahmed An-Naïm (Syracuse, NY: Syracuse University Press, 1987).

34. Louis Milliot, *Introduction à l'étude du droit musulman* (Paris: Sirey, 1953), 763–64.

6

The Ideological and Political Perspectives of Islamism

IN THE TWO PRECEDING CHAPTERS we discussed the cultural origins and ideological contradictions of Islamism. In this final chapter we put all this in perspective within the context of the ideological breakup of Arab societies that have lost their cultural coherence after encountering the West. The heterogeneity of society is irreversible and will only increase with globalization and the transnational currents that undermine it. Sandwiched between globalization that imposes its own rhythm and its own values, and a past still alive in memories, Arab societies are now struggling to reconcile a utopian identity with a dream of modernity. They express anger at a secularization process that they perceive as a conspiracy fomented by the West and supported by local groups. The ulemas of the Al-Nahda movement, particularly Mohammed Abdu, believed they could resolve this problem by blaming Sufism for perverting the rational content of the Qur'an. Helped by the sociological transformations that had been under way since the nineteenth century, Al-Nahda delegitimized Sufism, which for centuries had associated sainthood with the idea of God. The vacuum left by Sufism was filled by political and religious hopes expressed by Islamism. This shift in the direction of Islamism may appear regressive in comparison with the consistent discourse of Al-Nahda and with the modernization project of radical Arab nationalism. Nevertheless, Islamism will act in the long run as catalyst to the secularization process. History has its own way of reconciling ideology with reality, often at the price of sufferings that may later appear to have been completely unnecessary.

The Cultural Heterogeneity of Contemporary Arab Society

In January 1992 the Algerian army canceled the election won by the Islamists and arrested thousands of militants of the Islamic Salvation Front. This sparked a bloody conflict that lasted ten years and cost more than 150,000 lives. In July 2013 the Egyptian army deposed Mohamed Morsi, the Islamist president who had been democratically elected one year earlier, and imprisoned hundreds of members of his party. These two coups d'état summarize the political equation of Arab republics and the impasse in which they are with no hope of change in any direction. The military coup d'état of July 2013 in Egypt, which put an end to the country's experience of Islamist government, and the Algerian coup of January 1992 annulling the elections won by the FIS both pose the question of whether national politics can function without the Islamists. To proscribe the most electorally important political grouping in a country is tantamount to choosing force as a way of regulating the political contradictions of society. The rejection by the army of electoral victories of Islamist parties discounts their electoral weight. Drawing its strength from religion, Islamism will never be reduced by the police methods used by Arab regimes that today are paying the price for their failure to modernize the country and to reform Muslim theology.

Condemned by their own failure after a half century of bad management of the state, these regimes stubbornly refuse to broaden political participation. Moreover, they block any kind of political transition, asserting that Islamists are enemies of democracy. They accuse them of endangering civil peace by threatening everyone who did not accept their political view of religion. They claim that the country, except for a small minority, is not ready for universal suffrage. This political position of the military is shared by fringes of the population, which are generally anxious about Islamist denunciations of their way of life. This fear was doubtless amplified by the ideological struggle then under way, but it was real in its effects because it bred deep suspicions among Egyptians. Countries like Egypt, Algeria, and Syria (the latter in much more violent ways) have been undermined by the contradiction between a majority section of the population that votes for the Islamist parties and a minority that favors the separation of religion and politics. In this confrontation, the Islamists have with them not only the greater number but also the greater potential for popular mobilization. Their opponents are administration officials, business managers, liberal professions, and people who favor the private practice of religious faith. Even though they are not in favor of the authoritarian regime, they see the army as a protective shield against the Islamist threat. Taking advantage of the ideological and cultural rift that divides society, the army opts for the status quo, posing as the only source of legitimate power capable of preserving the so-called unity of the nation Democratic transition stumbles across this divide.

Just after the electoral victory of the FIS in December 1991 in Algeria, Saïd Sadi, leader of the RCD party (Rassemblement pour la Culture et la Démocratie) who was disappointed by the results, answered a question by the journalist Malika Boussof from the channel 3 of the national radio: "I've gotten the wrong society." He had not expected that a majority of his compatriots would vote for an Islamist party that he considered to be running against the tide of history. Sadi's own party had proposed a program for the separation of religion and politics in the tradition of Rifa'a al-Tahtawi, Mustafa Kemal, Tahar Haddad, Ferhat Abbas, and others. The opposite camp swiftly confirmed that he had indeed "gotten the wrong society" and that he was not a real Algerian. In periods of crisis like this, mutual rejection reaches a paroxysm—as it did in Egypt, where, after the coup d'état of Gen. Abdel Fattah el-Sisi, his supporters declared that the Islamists were "not true Egyptians." If the accusations of *false Algerian* and *false Egyptian* continue to this day, it means that the sentiment of nationality is not yet strong enough to bring the members of the community together. It means also that democracy is not perceived by people as a tool for alternating governments but as the total victory of one camp and the total defeat of the other. The latter is compelled to withdraw and utterly change its views and behavior. We may conclude that national construction is incomplete.

The results of the elections of 1991 in Algeria and 2012 in Egypt, which accurately reflected the political opinions prevailing in both countries, showed that the Islamist parties won about 55 percent of the vote, and the secular parties about 20 percent. If the elected representatives of the 55 percent had established the literal rule of sharia, the secularized social groups and Copts in Egypt would feel seriously threatened. Paradoxically, universal suffrage and a free vote frighten the classes that naturally defend such liberal values as freedom of expression and equality among citizens. It is the opponents of these values—that is, the Islamists—who call for free elections, taking democrats at their word and forcing them to confront their contradictions. The electoral figures indicate that Arab societies simply lost both social cohesion and cultural coherence. This is clearly expressed by Rachid Ghannouchi, the Tunisian Islamist leader:

> The secular background of the Tunisian elite was formed under special circumstances during the colonial era, when a foreign force invaded a segment of society, interfered in its lifestyle, and transformed it into a political élite controlled by those in power.

Thereafter, two societies operated side by side in Tunisia: that of the countryside, an old rural society which used all of its power to preserve the traditional values on which it was raised; and a modern society set on the French blueprint of modernization, which faces specific problems with regard to its relationship with religion.[1]

For Ghannouchi, the period of French domination between 1882 and 1956 fractured Tunisian society by introducing foreign values that have since been adopted by some Tunisians. He believed the solution was to return to the ideological coherence that existed prior to colonization.

This perception of the past denies the evidence of history and views culture as an atemporal element. Ghannouchi's reasoning leads to the idea of one section of society emerging as a subproduct of foreign influence; this section of society cannot be authentically Tunisian and so either must become authentic all over again or must cease to exist politically. He goes even further in questioning the nationalist credentials of Habib Bourguiba, whom he accuses of completing the victory of Western values over the Arab-Islamic civilization of Tunisia. According to Ghannouchi, nationalism under the leadership of Bourguiba implemented a historic stratagem designed to bring Tunisia under the influence of the Western way of life, of which laicity is a major expression. He fervently believed that a minority elite, formed after independence, had deliberately strangled the Arab/Muslim culture and manners of the old Tunisia. On the pretext that it was competent to run a modern state, this elite apparently imposed ideological orientations imported from Europe. In an interview given in 1992 to François Burgat, Ghannouchi described this process as a "de-Islamization" carried out by a regime that deliberately ignored the spiritual references of the people:

For the generation brought up within the Arab Muslim culture which frequented the Zitouna and other traditional institutions, the process of Tunisia's westernization was a violation. This generation was repressed and traumatized; and yet it was a majority. At independence, those attending establishments dependent on the Zitouna numbered between 25,000 and 27,000, while those studying in the secondary schools created under the French occupation numbered between 4,000 and 5,000. So the majority felt marginalized by the minority. Laicity and westernization were not backed by any popular movements. What had happened was this: an active minority had been able to marginalize a passive majority because it alone had the capacity to understand the West, to understand what was happening abroad, and to communicate with the new international order. The majority did not have that knowledge. So it was perfectly natural that it should be intellectually marginalized.[2]

Ghannouchi underestimates the Arab-Islamic dimension of Arab nationalism, of which Bourguiba was the central figure in Tunisia. After independence, Bourguiba applied the program of the nationalist movement, which had promised to achieve the modernization denied to Tunisians by the French colonial power. He had a plan to create jobs in agriculture, industry, and the service sector. Like other nationalist leaders, he implemented ambitious education policies. Bourguiba's measures enabled hundreds of thousands of children to learn classical Arabic at primary school and a foreign language at secondary level. So it is hard to sustain the claim that the postcolonial nationalist elites meant to "de-Islamize" society, especially when we know that one of their ideological references was Al-Nahda. The first president of independent Algeria, Ahmed Ben Bella, stated his belief that socialism was invented by Islam—not by Karl Marx. His successor, Col. Houari Boumediene, made a speech at the 1974 meeting of the World Islamic Organization in Lahore, Pakistan, that "no Muslim should go to paradise on an empty stomach." He surprised the Muslim heads of states present at the conference, trying to justify the priority he was giving to the industrialization of his country. Arab leaders like Boumediene, Gamal Abdel Nasser, and Habib Bourguiba can hardly be accused of hostility to Islam. By outlawing polygamy in Tunisia, Bourguiba relied on a personal reading of the Qur'an, pointing out that the crucial verse on the subject enjoins men to be fair to their wives—and doubts that they can be. The dynamic of postcolonial social change was in many ways unstoppable, carrying with it all the contradictions that the Islamist movement was later to express. The present leaders of the Islamist movement are all university educated, although they come from ordinary working-class backgrounds. They are the contradictory product of a genuine modernization process to which they now seek to add the element of religious symbolism.

The army is concerned with the survival of the regime, with the social peace, and of course the privileges enjoyed by the officers. Ideologically, the army is neither in favor of nor against the Islamists as far as they recognize their authority over the state and their legitimacy to be the source of power. In Egypt, Algeria, Libya, and Syria the army took power in the 1950s and 1960s, at a time when military officers gave themselves the mission of ensuring the political independence and managing the economic development. In identifying themselves with the regimes that they created, these military officers acquired a habitus—in the sense that Pierre Bourdieu has given to the notion—that structured the political culture. They cannot now imagine a state in which the army is not the ultimate source of power, and they consider the Islamists, when they win elections, to be a serious danger to civil peace. Moreover, united by their esprit de corps, senior military officers have come no closer to accepting a civil power that might impose accountability on the army's budget and that would perhaps put an end to the privileges they currently enjoy both during their careers and their retirement. The army in Egypt has built up an economic domain that is not limited to the military industry. Having diversified, it controls textile manufacturing companies, factories for transforming agricultural products, farms, tourist services, and so on. These economic activities have generated a new aristocracy made up of retired officers appointed as chief executives of army-owned businesses dependent on labor that is practically free of charge.[3]

In Algeria the army is not directly involved in economic activities as it is in Egypt, but it has the last word on how money derived from the export of oil and gas is divided within the state budget. Using its secret services, it also keeps a close eye on the signing of domestic contracts with foreign companies; this naturally generates widespread corruption involving senior officers. They use the pretext of the ideological division of society to present themselves as the one institution that can guarantee national unity and civil harmony. To this end, they need the support of those social groups that may be hostile to the Islamists, since they seem threatened by religious intolerance. Thus, the press becomes a strategic resource in the struggle against an opponent who must be discredited in the eyes of public opinion. Journalists write editorials explaining why the authoritarianism of the army is a lesser evil than Islamist intolerance. In a world where information is globalized, this strategy of communication is essential if public opinion is to accept a repression conducted outside any legal framework. It may even go as far as the manipulation of Islamists to commit shocking assassinations.[4]

In this political game for three players, the strategy of the army consists of continually preventing the two other protagonists from becoming allies. They are ready to make compromises with the Islamists or with their opponents, who are given ministerial offices in the government, but they are adamantly opposed to any alliance between the two that would damage the interests of the army. The Italian non-governmental organization Community of Sant'Egidio, which was close to the Catholic Church, organized a meeting in Rome in January 1995 between Algerian representatives of the Islamist and non-Islamist factions, both of which were under pressure from the security services. By agreeing to talk with representatives of non-Islamist groups, the Islamists showed that they recognized the political and ideological diversity of society; this was clearly against the political interests of the regime. The army is willing to go as far as possible in political openness and compromise, both with the Islamists or with their adversaries, on the one unshakable condition that it remained the only institution that endows the executive branch with legitimacy, which produces the same cycle of violent protest, repression, and manipulation. As in Syria, the army is not ready to let the civilians be in charge of the political field or the state.

As such, the high-ranking officers are not ready to give up their political role in the state.[5] Yet the de-politicization of the military is part of the problem of democratic transition, which consists of installing a civil power emanating from electoral competition. The highly political nature of the army is a real obstacle to transition, which does not only depend on the issue that divides the various ideological currents. The military are trained to wage wars, not to run the state. In their culture, any opponent must be defeated by using either state violence or the judiciary system. From this standpoint, Tunisia, which does not have a politically powerful army and has no significant oil resources, had more chance of bringing off a successful transition than Egypt or Algeria, both of which have armies to which history has given a political role by identifying them with the regime in place. It is no coincidence that, following the election victory of the Tunisian Islamists in 2012, Tunisia did not experience a military coup d'état. In the face of determined minority opposition in the national assembly, the Islamists had to accept compromises on the new constitution, which enshrined the principle of freedom of conscience. Facing a social unrest in the cities that threatened the economy, the Ennahda Party, led by Rachid Ghannouchi, opted for pragmatic realism rather than a trial of strength. The party even accepted the formation of a government of technocrats in order to lower political tensions. The real danger for Ennahda lay in the radicalization of a section of its base, which was attracted by the *salafist* discourse accusing Ghannouchi of capitulating to the secular parties. If the *salafists* can be neutralized, Tunisia will become the first Arab country, apart from confessional Lebanon, in which the executive power has serious electoral legitimacy. The future of democracy in the Arab world is being played out in Tunisia, whose experience may prove to be an example that Algeria and Egypt will one day follow.

A positivist approach would perceive an antagonism between tradition and modernity, a conflict between individualist liberalism and holistic conservatism, fighting for the nation's cultural identity. The reality on the ground, however, is more complex, full of contradictory tendencies that directly affect every group within society. It is no longer a question of wealthy social classes attached to modernity and poor social classes mired in tradition. If there is tension in society, that tension is constantly present in the minds of individuals. Among the Islamists are many medical doctors and engineers whose scientific knowledge cohabits with representation of the past—one that accepts, for example, that a woman should inherit only half of what her brother inherits. Today the medieval cleric and the modern engineer find themselves living together in the same social environment and even in the same person. Nasr Abou Zeid has pinpointed this contradiction:

The Muslim world exists within a kind of intellectual and social schizophrenia, split as it is between conflicting epochs: that of the technological progress achieved by Europeans, which has invaded every aspect of the daily lives of Muslims, and that of the past era of religion which has not changed significantly since the 10th century. For example, a Muslim doctor is perfectly capable of carrying out an *in vitro* fertilization procedure without remotely adjusting his view of life and of himself. He will do advanced scientific work in his laboratory but all other aspects of his existence are ruled by mythology.[6]

As early as the 1970s, Paul Pascon, an anthropologist from Morocco, addressed the heterogeneity of social practices in relation with modernity and tradition. He developed the concept of the composite society in which values are manipulated for personal and group purposes.[7]

Fieldwork research would address the crucial questions: who is modern in Arab societies? What is authenticity, what is modernity, and how do they conflict? The reification of concepts will certainly not help to address a historic situation in which the modernity of one section of society is largely ambiguous, and the conservatism of the rest of it is undermined by modernizing trends. The parties that claim to follow tradition do not follow tradition alone; nor do those who embrace modernity, embrace modernity alone. The secular parties claim to represent national ideological values, calling for a modernization of the cultural heritage conveyed by the Arabic language and by the Amazigh language in North Africa that is a part of the tradition. Meanwhile, the Islamist parties do not reject industrialization or wage earning; they do not express a wish to go back to the self-sufficient economy of traditional society. It is a striking fact that the debates between these two camps are marked by polemic and caricature. Very few intellectuals attempt to demonstrate to the reading public that modernity, as a corpus of universal values relative to the freedom of the individual, is not hostile to religion; nor do they try to show that the sacred texts have a broad capacity to accept and even to justify these universal values. The expression of views on these subjects is regularly compromised by prejudice and misunderstanding, as if modernization were an idea that had to be condemned by some and supported by others. Yet the experience of Europe shows that modernity is not, after all, opposed to tradition; what it does is reinterpret and submit tradition to the idea of a world structured around the individual rather than around the group, as it was before.

The debate about the supposed opposition between tradition and modernity is skewed as soon as the two notions cease to be linked to the aspirations and social practices of ordinary daily life. They are historically and epistemologically bound together; neither means anything without the other as far as Muslim societies are concerned. It is interesting to analyze the tension that characterizes them within their respective fields of meaning and within the historical context of national construction. Some consider that the priority is to strengthen the nation culturally, whereas others think that it should first be developed economically. Beyond all this complexity, which deserves advanced ethnographic research, it is interesting to note that the two sides are divided by the conflict between two ways of being one's self while also belonging to a collectivity. Some champion modernity with implicit reference to the European experience, underestimating the cultural richness of the Muslim heritage. Others advocate authenticity designed forever by the ancestors (the *salafs*), formally rejecting universal values because they come from the dominant West. These two projects are a caricature of modernity and authenticity (or tradition). The question is as simple as it is complex: How can we be ourselves and be modern at the same time? What parts of ourselves do we have to sacrifice to be modern? Is there any interpretation of Islam that can accept freedom of conscience—and, if so, what is it? These questions create a climate of confrontation: the modernists say the traditionalists ignore the lessons of history and prevent the nation from acquiring the strength to take up the challenge of the West. The traditionalists retaliate by saying the modernists are bent on weakening the cultural identity of the nation. These views are so passionately held that the protagonists see each other's position as insensitive to history or to identity accordingly.[8]

The same ideological questions are being asked today in a context where foreign interference is favored by globalization, which has the effect of making both camps even angrier. The globalization of information hardens these ideological positions because there are no more national frontiers to protect the symbolism of the sacred. A verdict handed down in a Pakistani or Sudanese court condemning a woman to death for adultery makes headlines in European and American newspapers and mobilizes nongovernmental organizations that launch petitions denouncing injustice against women in Islamic countries. A humorous caricature of the Prophet Mohammed published in Denmark causes riots in Indonesia and Morocco. The Islamists believe a worldwide conspiracy has been mounted against Islam, with the complicity of local forces. The Muslim origin of Salman Rushdie has convinced many Islamists that the secular elites are working on behalf of the West. For the moment, there is no hope that this gulf that divides Muslim society will be closed any time soon. Would its closure involve political violence? This can only be avoided if the protagonists accept real ideological diversity within society and bow to the decisions of the people expressed in free elections. Such a prospect is bound to collide in the Arab republics with the interests of the army, which, for historical reasons, has managed to play a political role whereby it has imposed itself as the ultimate source of legitimacy, except in Tunisia.

Paradoxically, the force of political change in the republics is essentially made up of the Islamist current, invariably opposed by armies whose regimes are exhausted. The masses have been disappointed and are now attracted by a religious discourse promising a just and strong state that protects the weak and the poor. When used against an administration rotted by corruption, this discourse gives strength to the Islamists who are candidates to replace historically exhausted regimes that ensure their survival through state violence, oil revenues, and the support of Western powers. The secular parties do not have sufficient potential for a popular mobilization to force the army back into its barracks, preferring the status quo to an experiment with Islamist government that might lead to a theocracy, to which they can imagine no end.

Such static politics is peculiar to republics in which disappointments following bright promises have been far more prevalent than in monarchies. The monarchies, of course, have never promised anything. They cleave to tradition while trying to accommodate the forces of modernization. Their main concern is to keep the reigning family at the head of the state. Protected by the religious symbolism of which they make political use, the monarchies have managed to neutralize Islamist protest by preventing it from gaining the popularity it has acquired in the republics. The house of Saud bases its legitimacy on Wahhabism, which is inspired by the thought of Ibn Taymiyyah and even further back by the tradition of Ibn Hanbal.[9] Morocco's king genealogy goes back to the Prophet Mohammed through his daughter Fatima, whose descendent, Idriss, took refuge in the Maghreb, where he founded a dynasty in Fez.[10] The King of Jordan traces his ancestry back to the tribe of the Prophet through his grandfather Sharif Hussein, who was driven out of the Arabian Peninsula by the Saud family in the early 1920s.

The religious symbolism deployed by the dynasties competes with the Islamist language of legitimacy. Islamism has been more effectively contained in Saudi Arabia and Morocco than in Egypt and Algeria, where it came close to taking power by ballot—or by bullet.[11] Because of their political/ideological nature, the monarchies have a greater capacity to integrate the Islamists into their institutions than the republics. In the republics, the Islamists actively look for a clean break; in the monarchies, they seek to carry out "rectifications" for a better application of sharia. On this register, it is difficult for them to compete with the Sauds, who cut off the hands of thieves and forbid women to drive. The Moroccan dynasty is more exposed to the Islamist than the Saudis because of the difference in the social fabric and the economic structure in both countries. For historical reasons, secular social groups in Morocco are more numerous than in Saudi Arabia. This forces the king of Morocco to look for the fragile point of balance between the modernist aspirations and religion from which he draws his political legitimacy. As far as they feel protected by the religious legitimacy of the monarchy, the secular social groups cannot be accused by the Islamists of "hostility" to Islam. The king portrays himself as the protector of all Moroccans, including those who belong to the secular urban middle classes. For the sake of the survival of the monarchy, he would never accept laws that might lead to the rebellion of one particular sector of society.[12]

Al-Nahda, Sufism, and Islamism

The underestimation of theology that needed to be built on new intellectual bases has had grave political consequences. The nationalist elites did not understand that the old theology, inherited from many centuries back, would continue to be the source of ordinary representations and knowledge among the population. Islamism has thrived on this cultural heritage, which it has politicized. Religion is not simply a religious belief in nonsecular societies; it is a cultural system that organizes the cognitive perception of the environment surrounding a person and that articulates the subjectivity of the believer with the objective world as humanized by faith.[13] From this standpoint, Islamism is part of a culture that has a history and that has evolved through contact with European domination. Islamism in Arab countries reactivates a religious culture whose two main components are Sunni orthodoxy and Sufi mysticism. Both are buried in the collective memory and transmitted in different degrees of complexity through many generations.

The second half of the nineteenth century saw the advent of Al-Nahda, or "rebirth," a movement whose objective was to show that the Qur'an was not the cause of Muslim societies' failure to keep up with Europe. Al-Nahda was a direct response to the clichés of orientalists who described Islam as a religion completely closed to progress. The leaders of the Al-Nahda movement, principally Jamal al-Din al-Afghani and Mohammed Abdu, feared that a section of the of Arab elite would be attracted by secularization and would drive religion to the private space. They argued that the Qur'an is open to scientific progress and that Muslims had no need to follow the example of Europe, which had long since de-Christianized itself and lost all spirituality. Muslim societies may have lagged behind a Europe that had turned to the new gods—namely, science and technology—but the gap is not the fault of the Qur'an. The fault lay in bad interpretation of the sacred texts and in the lethargy of Muslim religious thought that did not use for centuries the tradition of *ijtihad* (personal effort to understand the Qur'an using reason). The solution, they said, is to go back to the original Islam, that of the *salafs*, after purging it of the pagan influences that had stifled its humanity and its openness of spirit. The ulemas of Al-Nahda condemned the cult of saints, which they accused of infantilizing believers and interceding between them and God, a practice formally forbidden by the Qur'an. As figures in popular Islam and the avatars of Sufism, the saints were accused of exploiting the naivety of believers and keeping them in a state of ignorance. The ulemas of the cities found in this a splendid opportunity to take revenge on rural Islam, which it viewed as decadent and backward.[14] The condemnation of ecstatic religious manifestations (*moussems, zardates, ziarates*, etc.) by Al-Nahda was consistent with the economic crisis in the rural world, which had seen the power of the brotherhoods and religious orders dwindle dramatically.

The critiques of Al-Nahda were formulated at a time when the peasant farmers of the countryside were undergoing a process of pauperization following the rapid concentration of farmland into larger parcels (in fewer hands) and the spread of monetary exchange. The new nationalist elites, who were city-born or city-acculturated, grasped the ideological advantage in the critiques of Al-Nahda, which were aimed at local religious hierarchies who were jealous of their autonomy and tended to waste social energies on rivalries of prestige and honor. The nationalists were opposed to the brotherhoods, accused of obstructing the nascent national consciousness. They rejected the model of sainthood, finding among the ulemas of Al-Nahda a religious approach that corresponded to the universalism of the nation-state they wanted. It is true that the tribal spirit—what Ibn Khaldun called the 'acabiya—did not sit well with nationalist ideology, which is supposed to transcend the frontiers of brotherhoods, villages, and tribes.[15]

Because of the changes brought about by monetary exchange, rural exodus, and the crisis of traditional agriculture, the Sufi brotherhoods lost a part of their sociological and economic base. This made it easier for the ulemas to discredit them since they were an obstacle to the religious reforms they advocated. The reform program of Mohammed Abdu consisted of reorganizing Sunni orthodoxy to give impetus to a religious attitude that gave believers the sense of responsibility they lacked. The goal was to escape the fatalism to which society had become adapted while preparing it to accept the technological progress of the West by explaining that God gave man reason in order that he might understand and master the complexities of nature. Abdu stated that the Europeans were so strong because they used reason, which Muslims had abandoned. He claimed that to meet the challenge of the Europeans and to catch up with them, Muslim societies should avoid the secular way and rediscover the rational virtues of the Qur'an. These would nurture renewed intellectual audacity and spiritual enterprise in the full respect of the laws laid down by God to protect both the human character of society and man's longing for spirituality. The ideas of Abdu are summarized in his principal theoretical work *Rissalat et Tawhid,* which hinges on the hypothesis that man has a responsibility in the conduct of his life, and thus the decline of Muslim civilization is attributable to human causes.[16]

Although he accepted European empirical sciences, Abdu neither broke with the theological knowledge of the past nor attempted to construct a new theology. He was content to reorganize the legacy of the past by introducing reason into the equation—although he never gave reason priority over the revelation. He sought to bring Muslim philosophy back to life, in its original form prior to its twelfth-century banishment by orthodox theologians. He argued that Muslim civilization was at its most brilliant when philosophy was in full flower. He suggested a reactivation of the thought of Avicenna and Averroes to provoke the rebirth—*nahda* in Arabic—that was necessary for an emancipation of Muslim peoples. But he underestimated history and the progress in philosophy since the sixteenth to seventeenth centuries, ignoring that Europe had made intellectual breakthroughs that influenced even theology. It is as if Abdu was putting back the clock of Muslim thought to the time of Abū Hāmid al-Ghazali, the Muslim equivalent of Thomas Aquinas. Rehabilitating Muslim philosophers like Avicenna and Averroes, even if in their time they were among the precursors of modern philosophy, was to mistake the immensity of the intellectual leap forward that had occurred since then. Abdu was not aware that Averroes's philosophy was not any more intellectually relevant regarding the progress that happened since his time. He was not aware that the medieval philosophy was consistent with the Sufism he fought.

The Al-Nahda movement did not deprive Sufism from its philosophical roots, hence the vacuum that would be later filled by Islamism. While the social manifestations of Sufism have gradually lost their relevance, the Sufi representation has remained active in religious culture. It is no coincidence that the first Islamist organization in Egypt, founded in 1928, called itself the Muslim Brotherhood. The founder of the organization, Hassan al-Banna, belonged to a Sufi brotherhood. There is a clear continuity between Sufism and Islamism; the difference, however, is that the Islamists politicized mysticism, transforming it to ideological utopia. The Sufi ideal has not been extinguished, giving birth to a social energy that nurtures Islamism.

Islamism reactivates the collective memory by making sacred certain profane words (*da'wa, sahwa, majless echoura, irchad, islah*) and secularizing certain sacred ones (*inqad, tawba, sharia, imen*). In doing this, it seeks to replace the present false and corrupt society in which we live now with the right and perfect one to be performed by the Islamic state. The social energy of the Sufi imagination, drawn from the will of a group to affirm its identity and its ethos, has produced an Islamism that modifies the Sufi doctrine on two points. The first is that salvation is no longer individual or personal but collective, and the second is that salvation will not be achieved by the mystic way but by the political one. After the defeat of sainthood orders, the old religious ecstasy of the rural world succumbed to the puritanism of the ulemas, giving birth to an Islamism inclined to use violence to protect the faith. Al-Nahda ideologized religion by claiming that Islam had a scientific basis; Islamism, its byproduct, made religion a political issue linked to the construction of the nation and the state.

The collective rituals and ecstatic traditions of the past have been replaced by demonstrations that bring together tens of thousands of people repeating incantations about the state of Islam and sharia. Islamists have no desire, unlike the old Sufis, to withdraw from the world or to break with it; they aim, rather, to reorganize it by following the generation of *salafs* who supposedly built at their time an ideal society. These blessed ancestors supposedly lived like angels in the world of Platonician ideas and essences, outside historic time. Like the Sufis, the Islamists have a dual model: the norm and the anti-norm, the eschatological ideal and real life on Earth. By political means and by using violent and authoritarian methods, they seek to deliver the Muslim world from the anti-norm (history) and admit it to the norm (utopia). In the absence of a modern theology, Islamists took over the legacy of Al-Nahda, adding fervor and utopia. The urban masses have annexed the Islam of the ulemas, which used to be quietist and puritanical, by adding to it the millenarian fervor of a religious ideal. The continuity between contemporary Islamism and Al-Nahda has been ensured by the postcolonial schooling system that trained the new generations with medieval religious culture. Far from secularizing society, Al-Nahda managed to revive the old concept of *salafiya*, which idealized the past and upbraided believers for turning away from the true word of God.[17]

The problem of religious culture in Muslim countries is that it has not renewed its intellectual approach of the sacred in the light of the progress of modern philosophy. Having been influenced for so long by the Ash'arite doctrine, this culture was taught for centuries to successive generations of students, still taught throughout the educational systems of the present. Millions of young people today have absorbed the teachings of classical Muslim theology that gave birth to Islamism. Mohammed Abdu fell short because he did not have Martin Luther's vision: the purpose of life on Earth is not to serve the sacred. The failure of Al-Nahda and of Abdu himself can be traced to their inability to modify the relationship between God and the faithful and, hence, to drain the metaphysical roots of Sufism in the religious culture. The saints have lost their power while the authority of the ulemas has been contested by younger generations they themselves have trained. All this has led to a profane mobilization of the sacred that has completely redefined the purpose of religion. The crisis in Muslim society is worldwide, total, and profound; it affects the very essence of a social bond whose ethic has not been reformulated for many centuries. What Muslim culture still lacks, above all, is a modern philosophy.[18]

THREE CURRENTS OF RELIGIOUS MUSLIM THOUGHT

Between the eighth and twelfth centuries there were rich intellectual debates among the *mutakallimun* (specialists of the *kalam*, the word of God), the philosophers (principally *mu'tazilas*), and the Sufis, whose mystical thought reached its apogee with the work of Ibn 'Arabi—the Sheikh Al-Akbar, as he was called. It is useful to recall the history of the currents of thought that structured the popular representations legitimized by religious knowledge. A deconstruction of Islamic reasoning shows that this was shaped by the controversies that took place between orthodoxy (Ibn Hanbal), philosophy (Al-Kindi, and later, the *mu'tazilas*), and Sufism. To understand what was at stake during these debates, we need to identify the protagonists. There were three main intellectual currents of opinion. There were first the specialists of the *kalam*, the word of God, known as *mutakallimun*, theologians who rejected the concept of theology (*lahoutia*, or *ilahyate*, the study of God) because they considered it blasphemy for man to presume to study God. As far as they were concerned, men could only study the word or the message of God. Then, second, there were the philosophers who used the Greek *logos* to assert the veracity and rationality of the Qur'anic message. Third, there were the Sufis, whose devotion to Platonician philosophy verged on caricature. The intellectual destiny of the Muslim world was settled when the *mutakallimun* excommunicated philosophy, imprisoning the *kalam* in a poor intellectual framework. The aridity of the *kalam* gave rise to a strong mysticism in the form of Sufi brotherhood. Yet intellectually all three currents flowed from a single philosophical source: the Platonician paradigm. The *mutakallimun* were Platonists without knowing it; the philosophers were Platonists and knew it; and as for the Sufis, they had contrived to push Platonism to the brink of alienation.

Abū Hāmid al-Ghazali (the Thomas Aquinas of Islam) reconciled the three currents by building a balance between the *kalam*, Sufism, and philosophy. This doctrine avoided the exclusion of Ibn 'Arabi from Islamic tradition and made moderate use of philosophy but still defined limits for both, beyond which they dared not go. The big loser in the compromise was philosophy, which was not actually suppressed so much as prevented from evolving. Deprived in this way of a living philosophy, the *kalam* degenerated into a fixed discourse that blocked any reasonable understanding of the world. It stepped back from living reality; consequently, the mass of Muslims turned to Sufism, which at least offered human faces of the sacred.

The teaching of philosophy was abandoned at the revered University of Al-Azhar in Cairo from the thirteenth century onward because of the suspicion that it might lead to atheism. *"Mane mantaqa zandaqa"* (he who uses logic approaches atheism), repeat the ulemas quoting Ibn Taymiyyah. The fall of the Abbasid Dynasty after the foreign invasions from Asia and from Europe (the Crusades) hardened Sunni orthodoxy in the mold of Ibn Taymiyyah's theology. Muslim culture today is paying the price of the rout of philosophy all those centuries ago, and that rout is symbolized by a revealing testimony offered by Ibn 'Arabi in one of his books. Ibn 'Arabi, Sheikh Al-Akbar, known also as Ibn Flatoun (Plato's son), recounted his sadness when he saw in Marrakesh the corpse of Averroes tied to a donkey heading to the cemetery. One the greatest thinkers of the Middle Ages, a sage whose stature equaled that of Aristotle and Plato, did not receive at his death the homage he deserved.

The decline of Islamic culture is synonymous to the victory of the Hanbalist *salafiya*. *Salafiya* emerges as an opposition to the use of Greek philosophy suspected of distorting the heritage of the *salafs*, which must at all costs be restored to its full purity. The masterminds of *salafiya* are Ibn Hanbal and Ibn Taymiyyah who, perceiving the link between Sufism and Platonism, fought tooth and nail against both. They failed to defeat Sufism, which has indelibly marked the thought and practice of Islam, but they did succeed in banning philosophy. They locked Muslim theology into a circular discourse and into axioms that were self-sufficing. They deprived Muslim thought of the philosophical reasoning about the existence of God, impoverishing intellectually the *kalam*, which has depended ever since on the sacredness of barren commentaries made in the distant past. With time, Muslim culture has been shaped by two main currents of thought: Hanbalism, which is the majority opinion among the ulemas of Sunni Islam, and Sufism, which provides ordinary believers with ecstatic warmth and a human face of God.[19] With the decline of Sufism, Hanbalite orthodoxy took over the religious discourse.

Eventful Regression

The discourse of political Islam was principally worked out by Abul A'la Mawdudi and Sayyid Qutb, who resorted to the religious corpus to make believers aware of a geopolitical context that was threatening Islam with the help, they assumed, of local elites attracted by Western values. This discourse was part of an intellectual continuity in religious Sunni thought that had not seen any great theologians for many centuries. Al-Nahda had attempted to revive the rich tradition of classical Islamic theological debate but was unable to reverse a tendency that had been dominant for a very long time. Although it claimed kinship with it, the Islamist discourse did not carry on the project of Al-Nahda; instead, it went backward by comparison with the work of Mohammed Abdu in Egypt, Abdelhamid Ben Badis in Algeria, Allal al-Fassi in Morocco, Tahar Haddad in Tunisia, and others whose work was an attempt to make modernity compatible with the sacredness of the word of God. Mohammed Abdu's commentary on the Qur'an was an invitation to use reason to understand the sacred text and above all to escape the verbal one-upmanship of the ulemas, who competed to appear more loyal to the dogma—and did so without a trace of personal originality about what had been written in the past. Abdu tried to introduce an element of originality through *ijtihad*. He fought to desacralize the commentaries and inject freshness into the meaning of the Qur'anic verses by taking account of historic developments since they were revealed. His disciple in Algeria, Abdelhamid Ben Badis, welcomed the abolition of the caliphate by Mustafa Kemal, perceiving that the caliphate had been a form of central power outdated by different nations to which he gave a religious blessing. He also opined that Algerians belong to three entities: humanity, the Muslim *umma*, and the Algerian nation.[20] Recognizing and accepting the changes of history, he focused on what appeared to him to be essential within

Islam: faith in the oneness of God. Like Abdu, Ben Badis was aware of historical cause and effect and of the extent of the intellectual gulf between Muslims and Westerners. Of course, neither Abdu nor Ben Badis wished the secularization of society, but their work made Islam compatible with nationalism. Their dream was to catch up with Europe, but they underestimated the intellectual advance of Europe.[21] They ignited a process that radical Arab nationalism was unable to manage and that Islamists dismissed.

Qutb expressed respect for Abdu but regretted that he went so far in the defense of reason to the detriment of revelation. He thought Abdu's rationalism endowed man with autonomy to the point of forgetting "another principle of the Koranic vision, which is that God's will and omnipotence are limitless."[22] Through these lines written in the 1950s we can assess the absolute dogmatism of Qutb's refusal to interpret the revelation of the Qur'an using human reason. He went even further back to al-Ash'ari, whose doctrine was a balanced compromise between the partisans of the primacy of the revelation and those who argued for the primacy of reason. It is nevertheless true that the foundation of the work of Abdu was not solid enough because it did not break cleanly with medieval culture and the traditional corpus. Instead he exposed himself to correction by conservative thinkers who demanded that he show greater respect for the dogmas of the *salafs*. Nevertheless, we should acknowledge that in his time Abdu opened a breach of sorts, even though the intellectual and political conditions of Arab societies did not allow that breach to be enlarged. It was quickly closed again by the ulemas of Al-Azhar when they condemned Sheikh Ali Abderrazak's work on politics and Islam and praised Rashid Rida, whose pupil was Hassan al-Banna, the founder of the first Islamist organization in Egypt, the Muslim Brotherhood.

The post-Al-Nahda interval (between the death of Abdu in 1905 and the foundation of the Muslim Brotherhood in 1928) was crucial to the history of contemporary Muslim religious thought insofar as the reformist parentheses was closed and classical Hanbalite tradition reinstated. There was no open rejection of Mohammed Abdu and no condemnation of his work. On the contrary, he was recognized as a great theologian by the official authorities of Islam. Nevertheless, all that survives of his thought is his apology for the natural sciences and his condemnation of the ecstatic rituals of the rural Sufi brotherhoods. Wahhabis also condemn these rituals, which has led to confusion among the mass of Muslim believers who stand somewhere between Abdu and Wahhabism. His legacy has been appropriated by the ulemas of Al-Azhar, both to stifle his reformist dynamic and to prevent secular thinkers to refer to him.

Abdu failed to connect the cultural form of the divine revelation to history. The result is that Muslim culture today has difficulty in accepting freedom of conscience and equality of citizenship among Muslims and non-Muslims from the same nation and between men and women. The Muslim states have some difficulty regarding the Universal Declaration of Human Rights adopted by the United Nations in 1948. If the ulemas have trouble accepting this text of international law, it is because, as Mohsen Kadivar has pointed out, their interpretation of Islam is incompatible with the philosophy of human rights.[23] The very notion of a different interpretation is rejected by the ulemas, who claim that there is only one way of reading the Qur'an, which is the univocal word of God addressed to the whole of humanity and to every generation. They do not accept the idea that God may have spoken in the language and culture of the Arabian Peninsula in the seventh century. Today the sermons of the imams, delivered at Friday prayers, repeat that the verses of the Qur'an have an absolute and univocal meaning independent of culture and history, and that the word of God, confirmed by the scientific discoveries of the Europeans, must be respected to the letter. Despite the work of Mohammed Abdu, who tried to introduce flexibility into the rigid discourse of the ulemas, the latter considered Wahhabism to be the dogma that reflected the Qur'an most faithfully. Even Abdu's closest disciple, Rashid Rida, betrayed the teachings of his master by turning to Wahhabism, which for many years remained the doctrinal source of the Islamists from Hassan al-Banna to Abul A'la Mawdudi.[24]

This ideological and intellectual impasse weighs heavily on any prospect of democratic transition. What is to be done about the Islamists who have such deep-rooted support among the electorate? Should they be prevented from taking over if they win elections under the pretext that they are a mortal danger to secular social groups and even to society itself? Without them there can be no democratic transition, given their electoral strength. They are part of a society that seeks emancipation and progress on which, quite understandably, they wish to stamp their identity. Again, the Islamist is saying essentially this: "I want progress, but not without Islam; I want my daughter and my sister to be emancipated, but in the respect of the sharia." This discourse and this hope cannot be separated from the context of societies undermined by profound contradiction: on the one hand, they are prisoners of a Hanbalite reading of the Qur'an; on the other hand, they wish to develop and modernize themselves, believing that they only need to apply sharia and every obstacle will disappear because of the magic of the Word. As long as ideology remains unconfronted by reality, it will see itself as reality. In the course of history, a moment has always come when the followers of an ideology, even the most utopian ideology, have encountered disenchantment and have been forced to face reality. By reality is meant the eternal political contradictions and divisions within human anthropology.

Islamism is neither a far-reaching religious doctrine nor a coherent political theory; it is a revolutionary ideology. Within the context of the history of Arab societies, it expresses the people's current frustration and dread of absorption by an alien civilization. This dynamic will play itself out when Islamist elites, elected fair and square, are forced to face the reality of government—having believed and having made others believe that it would be enough to go back to the "true Islam" for happiness and well-being to be assured. Once they enter state institutions by way of elections, the Islamists will move away from their former allusive language to discover that of government. They will also discover the profound gap set between the possibilities and their discourse. When they are ruled by elected Islamist governments, Muslim societies will quickly become disenchanted and reawaken to the hard reality of *mou'amalates*. They will realize that there is no such thing as one true Islam, and they will discover that there are not bad and good Muslims but that human beings are simultaneously good *and* bad. And the only way to have a peaceful social life is to set up a secularized rule of law. The contradiction between ideology and history will oblige the Islamists to adjust to the process of secularization, of which they will be the agents in spite of themselves. The rigid interpretation of Islam will lose its influence when Islamists find themselves responsible for the management of a flesh and blood Muslim society, the society of the *mou'amalates*. Paradoxically, only an Islamist government elected freely will put an end to the religious utopia because it will have to choose between utopia and reality. Once they are the ones with responsibility to run the state, they will be forced to face the limitations of their utopian ideal. The social expectations are so big that any party running for office will at last disappoint the electorate.

In the short period during which they governed the state of Egypt, the Egyptian Islamists severely disappointed a good part of their supporters. But by overthrowing President Mohamed Morsi, who had been democratically elected, Gen. Abdel Fattah el-Sisi saved the Islamist utopia, which will continue to flourish in the dreams of millions of Egyptian electors who will be more than ever convinced that the forces of evil will stop at nothing to prevent the victory of

Islam. By deposing Egypt's Islamist president, the Egyptian army chiefs disastrously interrupted the democratic process of transition, through which Egypt was soon to learn the hard way about multiparty politics and electoral alternation. The country had never experienced political pluralism, although before Nasser the semblance of a formal multiparty system existed under the monarchy. The challenge for Egypt and for all Arab countries after the insurrections of 2011 was to bring the Islamists into the mechanisms of electoral alternation and not to exclude them.

Islamists are at their strongest when they are protesting corrupt authoritarian regimes. They are skilled in the expression of popular discontent to which they give religious credentials. But they are infinitely less efficient when it comes to running a government themselves. Condemning corruption, denouncing poverty, appealing to public morality in the name of a utopian ideal that proclaims that all believers are brothers—these tasks are a much more consensual business than managing the machinery of state, and more especially when an oath has been sworn in the court not only to solve the problem of unemployment but also to establish full equality between citizens. These promises are not just demagoguery of the type used by all oppositions to win power; they honestly reflect the contradictions of society.

The Islamist electoral offer is a response to the people's electoral demand loaded by contradictions that today seem insurmountable. Islamism is itself a contradictory product of modernity because it offers the masses access to politics but is incapable of institutionalizing that access. The movement is unable to install constitutional counterweights to guarantee the public character of authority, as the experience of President Morsi has shown all too clearly. The principal characteristic of the rule of law, which ensures the political participation of citizens, is the separation of powers. The purpose of the separation of powers is to protect individual liberties, among which is religious freedom. The rule of law is by no means a neutral administrative apparatus; it is firmly based on its own ideological foundation, with the notion of civil liberties at its heart.

The state is much more than an institutional infrastructure; it is a political cultural entity that guarantees that society will remain the source of power while delegating sovereignty to elected representatives who can make laws in its name. In short, the state offers political autonomy, which means freedom, among other things, from the tyranny of dubious religious interpretation. But the Islamists still refuse to accept the specificity of politics, and this in turn prevents them from acting with realism if they do take over the state. For the moment, they lack the intellectual capacity either to embrace political modernity or to manage a rule of law.

As we have seen, the utopian ideal rejects the shift from faith lived openly and in public to faith that is a private matter for the individual. It relies on the state simultaneously to protect individual liberties and to apply sharia, a medieval system of law for which crime and sin are one and the same thing. The Islamists carry this contradiction within themselves; they do not oppose votes for women who are not equal to men in civil law. In short, the Islamists still think that it is possible to build a modern state based on a medieval interpretation of religion. But will this state represent citizens or believers? This was the crucial question asked by Mohamed Harbi, and it has yet to be answered.[25]

All this brings us back to where we are today—in a phase of historic chaos marked by deep contradictions that have been publicly and brutally laid bare by the failure of radical Arab nationalism. The latter had contrived to lock society into a compromise that was in denial of its own ideological contradictions. The coup d'état of General el-Sisi showed an ominous will to return to this fatal compromise whereby society was prevented from confronting historical reality and, hence, from evolving positively in one way or another.

The military communiqué whereby Mohamed Morsi was abruptly deposed described him as the representative of an ideological sensibility within Egyptian society, not as the elected president and supreme chief of the armed forces. Emboldened by the vociferous protests of Morsi's political opponents, the army forced a return to the authoritarian model based on a compromise that made concessions to the Islamists and liberals while refusing to follow through on the building of a political space honestly regulated by elections. The coup d'état of el-Sisi dealt a blow to this process of disenchantment, through which Egyptians were beginning to learn that a workable state must be neither religious nor antireligious but nonreligious. The Egyptian military chiefs denied their country an experience of eventful regression, which might have set free the entire political arena. They obeyed the same blinkered reflex as their Algerian counterparts, who canceled the elections won by the FIS in January 1992. The Algerian state is still under the control of the military and the secular social groups continue to suffer from the stark intolerance of Islamists. No coup d'état will ever settle the Islamist question. In the end—just as before—the military will reach a static modus vivendi with the Islamists by telling them: leave us the state and all its material wealth, and you can have society and its utopian dreams.

Notes

1. Noureddine Jebnoun, *Tunisia at the Crossroads: An Interview with Sheikh Rached al-Ghannouchi* (ACMCU Occasional Papers, Georgetown University, April 2014), 18.

2. François Burgat, *Face to face Polical Islam* (London: I. B. Tauris, 2003), 50.

3. See Tewfik Aclimandos, "De l'armée égyptienne: Eléments d'interprétation du 'grand récit' d'un acteur du paysage national," *Revue Tiers Monde* 2, no. 22 (2015).

4. Deserters from the Algerian army have revealed that the secret service created the GIA (Armed Islamist Group), which specialized in the assassination

of civilians, purely to discredit the Islamists and convince the population not to support them. See Mohammed Samraoui, *Les années de sang* (Paris: Denoël, 2003); and Habib Souaidia, *La sale guerre* (Paris: La Découverte, 2000). A survivor of the massacre of the village of Bentalha, where 497 people were killed and 1,000 wounded, gave a version of what happened that flatly contradicted the official version reported by the newspapers. See Nasrallah Yous, *Qui a tué à Bentalha* (Paris: La Découverte, 2000). On a smaller scale, Egypt also saw manipulations of this type. The attack on the Coptic Church in Alexandria on December 25, 2010, which left 25 dead and 68 wounded, leaves many questions unanswered.

5. On political armies, see Kees Koonings and Dirk Kruijt, eds., *Political Armies: The Military and Nation-Building in the Age of Democracy* (London: Zed, 2002); and Lahouari Addi, "Army, State and Nation in Algeria," in *Political Armies: The Military and Nation-Building in the Age of Democracy*, ed. Kees Koonings and Dirk Kruijt, 179–203 (London: Zed, 2002).

6. Nasr Abou Zeid, *Critique du discours religieux*, trans. from Arabic by Mohamed Chairet (Arles: Sindbad Actes Sud, 1999), 200.

7. See Paul Pascon, "Le concept de société composite," Actes du colloque international du CENECA, Paris, March 3–4, 1971.

8. The modernity/tradition debate first emerged publicly in the nineteenth century. At that time, it was marked by the circumstances of European domination, which distorted the issue. Fearing that Rifa'a al-Tahtawi's secular aspirations would spread through Arab social élites, al-Nahda tried to reform some aspects of religious life, but it did not create a modern theology. With the coming of independence in the second half of the twentieth century, al-Nahda's compromise reached its outer limits about the relationship of religion to the state and to the rights of individuals. The Islamists and their secular-leaning nationalist adversaries fought over the legacy of Mohammed Abdu, who had disciples in both camps. Some concluded that Abdu's priority was the defense of Islam in a threatening international environment, whereas others emphasized his attempt to reform the social practice of religion. See Saoud Ramzi, "La portée épistémique du réformisme de Mohammed Abdou et le processus de modernisation dans le monde arabo-musulman: une critique d'ordre philosphico-théologique" (PhD thesis, Institut d'Etudes Politiques de Lyon, December 2013).

9. On the Islamist opposition in Saudi Arabia, see Stéphane Lacroix, *Awakening Islam: The Politics of Religious Dissent in Contemporary Saudi Arabia* (Cambridge, MA: Harvard University Press, 2011).

10. On the relationship between the Islamists and the monarchy in Morocco, see Mohammed Tozy, *Monarchie et Islam politique au Maroc* (Paris: Presses de sciences politique, 1999); and Malika Zghal, *Les Islamistes Marocains* (Paris: La Découverte, 2005).

11. I borrow this expression from William Quandt, *Between Ballots and Bullets: Algeria's Transition from Authoritarianism* (Washington, DC: Brookings Institution Press, 1998).

12. Moroccan women's associations demonstrated for changes in the Mudawana (code of personal status) that would ensure better legal protection for women. Given the widespread support for this demand, the king appointed a commission made up of jurists, ulemas, and women to improve the status of women in legal family disputes.

13. To develop my thesis on Muslim societies, I have referred to the work of religious anthropology carried out by Clifford Geertz. See Lahouari Addi, *Deux anthropologues au Maghreb: Ernest Gellner et Clifford Geertz* (Paris: Les Editions des Archives Contemporaines, 2013).

14. Ernest Gellner has formed a theory based on this opposition between the puritanical, literate Islam of the cities and the ecstatic Islam of the illiterate tribes. The former is represented by the ulemas in the cities and the latter by the saints in the countryside. Gellner deduces that the scripture-based Islam of the ulemas is closer to Protestantism in its plain religious practice, which predisposes it to be receptive to the modern ideas of state and nation. Conversely, Islam of the saints is close to Catholicism in its way of placing intermediaries between God and the faithful. Attached as it is to local religious chieftains, to whom believers gave their allegiance to the detriment of the central power, this tribal Islam was stubbornly resistant to nationalist ideas of equality. But Gellner's theory exaggerates the doctrinal resemblance between Protestants and ulemas. The latter do not accept what is the main originality of Protestantism—namely, the doctrine of predestination. For a critique of this model, see Talal Assad, *Genealogies of Religion: Discipline and Reason of Power in Christianity and Islam* (Baltimore: Johns Hopkins University Press, 1993).

15. Some brotherhoods called for jihad against the European military presence, but this resistance tended to be very localized; the fragmented social fabric of the rural world made it easy for colonial powers to play on the divisions between brotherhoods.

16. Sheikh Mohamed Abdu, *Rissalat et Tawhid: Exposé de la religion musulmane*, French trans. B. Michel and Sheikh Mustapha Abdel Razik (Paris: Geuthner, 1925).

17. "*Salafiya*" is a word that goes back to the time of Ibn Hanbal. It was used by his disciples to denounce the philosophers for having made use of Plato and Aristotle, both of whom had been raised to the rank of prophets in commentaries on the Qur'an. Since Ibn Hanbal's time, the word "*salafiya*" has underpinned the debating strategy of delegitimizing opponents by accusing them of abandoning the way indicated by the *salafs*, who belonged to the blessed generation of the Prophet himself. The word does not pertain to a coherent doctrine behind it; it merely defines a self-satisfied stance that accuses other people of not following

the example of the *salafs*. Extremist Islamists call themselves *salafists* to set themselves apart from other currents of opinion that are viewed as moderate. Thus, discredit is cast upon other people's ways of believing, arising from the desire to imitate the salafs, the pious ancestors, as if the believers of past centuries were not good Muslims.

18. I address this subject in my forthcoming book *La crise du discours religieux musulman: Le nécessaire passage de Platon à Kant.*

19. On Muslim philosophy, see Fakhry Majid, *A History of Islamic Philosophy* (New York: Columbia University Press, 1983), and Hernadez Miguel Cruz, *Histoire de la pensée en terre d'islam*, trans. from Spanish by Roland Behar (Paris: Editions Desjoinières, 2005).

20. See Ali Merad, *Le réformisme en Algérie* (Paris: Mouon, 1967).

21. The scientific and economic advance of Europe followed the intellectual revolution of the sixteenth to eighteenth centuries, which moved humanity into another age. The German philosopher Karl Jaspers viewed this upheaval as an "axial transformation" whose consequences were no less important than the appearance of agriculture in human history. See his book *Origin and Goal of History*, translated from German by Michael Bullock (London: Routledge and K. Paul, 1953).

22. Sayyed Qutb, *Fi Zila al qur'an* (Beirut: Dar ech-chourouk, 1982), v. 6, T.6.

23. Mohsen Kadivar, "Human Rights and Intellectual Islam," in *New Directions in Islamic Thought: Exploring Reform and Muslim Tradition*, ed. Kari Vogt, Lena Larsen, and Christian Moe, 47–73 (London: I. B. Tauris, 2009).

24. The Islamists agree with the Wahhabi doctrine but they are troubled by the position of Saudi Arabia on the Palestinian question. They do not understand how the heirs of Muhammad 'Abd al-Wahhab can be allies of the United States, the protector of Israel.

25. Mohamed Harbi, *Croyants ou Citoyens?* (Paris: Éditions Arcantère, 1989).

Conclusion

Born out of a response to European domination, radical Arab nationalism won over many segments of society with its goal of establishing modern, independent nations that would earn international respect. It promised to close economic, scientific, and military gaps with the West in order to improve social conditions—employment, housing, education, health, and so on—for the poorest members of society. Not only did this dream not become a reality but radical Arab nationalism went on to become a barrier standing in the way of civil peace and national cohesion, as demonstrated in the tragic case of Syria. The social and political situations in Egypt, Algeria, and especially Syria provide their own assessment of these regimes, which had once inspired so much hope.

Radical Arab nationalism failed for two reasons. The first reason is that the army militarized nationalism's political objectives. Once soldiers took over the state, they hindered the creation of a civil society—the expression of a political modernity and a necessary condition to achieve rule of law. This military thirst for power returned Arab countries to the feudal political culture of the Mamluks and Janissaries of Ottoman tradition. The basis of a modern state is primarily the economy and the law, not the army. This brings us to the second reason that Arab nationalism failed. It did not recognize the intellectual specificity of the progress of Europe, which, during the seventeenth and eighteenth centuries, had moved on from the medieval metaphysics still present in Arab culture. From the 1920s to the 1940s, Arab ideologists and leaders such as Sati al-Husri, Michel Aflaq, Chakib Arslan, and Messali Hadj did not place any emphasis on the intellectual progress made in the West regarding personal freedom. They were too captivated by the political future of the group that had to be freed from foreign domination. This is how the Arab state was built: by ignoring civil rights and individual freedoms. The idea that a state's power is first and foremost intellectual cannot be understood by the military, for whom the future of nations is determined by weaponry. Indeed, the West was not understood as a special experiment in the cycle of human history but rather as a space in which science had emerged by pure chance to give Westerners an advantage over everyone else. The essentialist crystallization of a radical difference between "us" and "them" shows that radical Arab nationalism is just as foreign to historical consciousness as Islamism, with which it shares the same cultural paradigm.

It was the failure of Arab nationalism that made Islamism so popular. If radical nationalism militarized politics, the Islamists politicized religion to delegitimize their opponents. In doing so, they are making the same mistakes, ignoring the cultural and political basis of Western civilization, which, in their perception, has been reduced to a single dimension: imperialistic domination. But the will to power and domination is not unique to Westerners; it is a trait of human nature. The demonization of the West obscures its contributions to world civilization, especially at the political level. Civil society, social equality, freedom of thought, and civil rights are European innovations that enrich the human heritage. Even though the West was the stage for two of the world's deadliest wars and used weapons to dominate and ravage its colonies, this is no reason to view Westerners as one dimensional. Like all other humans, they are both good and evil at the same time. Radical evil is neither European nor Arab; it is an inherent trait of human nature.

Anarchy and an imbalanced international order must be understood through the lens of humankind's aggressive nature. A legal system to establish a peaceful community, at a national or international level, is thus indispensable. The objective of the twenty-first century is to build a global legal system based on cosmopolitanism. An individual has, in fact, two identities: one relative to her cultural origins, and one relative to her value as a human being, with natural and universal rights. The medieval interpretation of Islam, defended by the ulemas and Islamists, stands in opposition to the cosmopolitan nature of Muslims with their natural, universal rights.

Note

This conclusion was translated by Christopher Pitts.

Index

Arabic names beginning with the prefix "al-" or "el-" are alphabetized by the subsequent part of the name.

Abbasid Dynasty, 238–39
Abd al-Hamid Kishk, 175
'Abd al-Wahhab, Muhammad, 20, 22, 27
Abderrazak, Ali, 75, 136, 193, 214n16, 214n18, 241
Abdu, Mohammed: on the caliphs, 214–15n23; ideology of, 31–32, 75, 127, 145, 233–34; on interpretation of the Qur'an, 194–96, 214n22, 232, 240; legacy of, 236, 248n8; Qutb and, 129, 241; rejection of, 242–43; *Rissalat et Tawhid*, 234; on Sufism, 217–18; ulemas and, 188–89; on violence, 166n5
Abou Zeid, Nasr, 76, 165, 226–27
Abrahamic monotheism, 141, 147, 200
abrogation (*naskh*), 211
Abu al-Hasan al-Ash'ari, 27–28, 136–37, 166n9
Abu Bakr, 156
Abū Hāmid al-Ghazali, 27, 137, 234, 238
acculturation, 11, 29
Al Adl Wa Al Ihssane, 158
adultery, 206, 208, 215n27
Afghan-Soviet war, 152
Aflaq, Michel: Baathists and, 39, 40; on Mohammed, 75; political dissent by, 112–13; populism and, 61; revolutionary change and, 118; shared identity and, 86

"ahl el hal oual 'aqd" (those who have power to bind and unbind), 146, 192
AKP (Justice and Development Party), 161–62
Alawites, 99
'alem, 149, 192. *See also* ulemas
Algeria: *arch* structure in, 81n12; assassinations in, 224, 247–48n4; colonialism in, 69; confessionalism and, 100; corruption in, 80–81n4; economic model of, 6–7, 55–56; elections in, 55, 218, 220; health care in, 90; Islamism in, 7, 218, 219–20, 225, 247; military regimes in, 87, 93, 224, 225, 247; national charter of, 46, 91; National Liberation Army and, 81n8; political parties in, 155–57, 219–20; post-Islamism in, 155–57; reforms in, 6–7, 55–56; repression in, 113; right of succession in, 215n29; scholars in, 82n19; single-party system in, 48, 55; sociology in, 78; utopianism and, 212n2; violence in, 96, 151, 152; Western Sahara and, 213n11
Ali, Muhammed, 5, 17, 20–21, 28, 111
all power belongs to God slogan. *See al hakimiyya li Allah* (all power belongs to God) slogan
Almohad Empire, 43n1

Amazigh language, 227
amir el mou'minine (Commander of the
    Faithful), 169n45
ancestry, 22, 111, 230. *See also salafs*
anthropological optimism, 130, 166n6
anthropological pessimism, 166n6
anthropology: denial of, 135; econo-
    mic, 54, 71; linguistic, 165n1;
    political, 71, 120n11; study of Isla-
    mism and, 121, 122; synchronic
    approach to, 109–10
Aquinas, Thomas, 234
Arabian Peninsula: Muhammed Ali's
    sack of, 20–21; creation of a centra-
    lized authority in, 16, 18–19, 21–25;
    economic sterility of, 24; Ottoman
    Empire and, 16; Prophet Mohammed
    and, 142–43; Qutb on, 142–43; Al
    Saud monarchy in, 17, 18–25
Arabic language: Arab nationalism and,
    85; Baathists and, 39, 40; debt and
    religion in, 213n13; diachronic
    changes in, 191; modernization of,
    227; in mosques, 177; political
    concepts in, 115; sharia and, 202; al-
    Tahtawi and, 28–29
Arab identity, 32
Arabi Pasha, 32, 166n5
Arab nationalism: Arabic language
    and, 85; conservative, 25; cultural
    populism and, 38; emergence and
    development of, 11–13, 15–43,
    85–86; European domination and,
    2–3, 15–17, 98–99; Ghannouchi on,
    221–22; Islamic theology and, 136;
    liberal, 28–34; middle class and, 40;
    military regimes and, 88; modernity
    and, 92–93; postcolonial, 12–13, 15;
    precursors of, 25; shared identity
    and, 85, 86; in Turkey, 162; ulemas
    and, 12; utopian societies and, 115–
    16; Westphalian order and, 115–16.
    See also radical Arab nationalism
Arab Revolt (1916), 2, 37, 43n4

Arab society: cultural heterogeneity of,
    218–31; destructuring of, 123; evolu-
    tion of, 2–3; historic origins of, 2;
    ideological breakup of, 217–18; intel-
    lectuals in, 72, 76, 77, 136–37, 152,
    226–27, 238; modernity/tradition
    debate in, 226–29, 248n8; moderni-
    zation of, 122, 123; predemocratic
    stage in, 182, 213n6; religious culture
    in, 236–37; three currents of dis-
    course in, 237–39; two types of, 3;
    violence of the 1980's in, 94, 96–97
Arab Spring uprisings (2010-), 4, 56, 97,
    154
Arab street, 41
arch structure, 81n12
Arendt, Hannah, 97, 130
Aristotle, 89, 249–50n17
Arkoun, Mohammed, 165
Armed Islamist Group (GIA), 247–48n4
the army: Arab nationalism and, 40;
    assassinations by, 224, 247–48n4;
    de-politicization of, 225–26; as the
    embodiment of the nation, 113;
    Islamism and, 219, 223; legitimacy
    of, 219; populism and, 63–64; pri-
    vileges enjoyed by, 223–24; strategy
    of, 224–25. *See also* military regimes
Aron, Raymond, 165–66n2
Arslan, Chakib, 86
al-Arsuzi, Zaki, 39, 40, 61, 85
Ash'arite doctrine, 236
al-Ash'ri, 27, 28, 136–37, 166n9, 241
Assad, Bashir, 48, 99
al-Assad, Hafiz, 3, 47
assassination, 139, 151, 167n24, 224,
    247–48n4
associationism (*chirk*), 27
atheists, 154, 238
authoritarianism: anthropological opti-
    mism and, 166n6; divine sovereignty
    and, 184–85; failure of nationalism
    and, 13, 45–46; vs. the ideal state,
    177; in Iran, 160; Islamism and, 123,

187; legitimacy of, 187; Mawdudi on, 149–50; of military regimes, 5–6, 89–90, 112–13, 115, 224; modernization and, 91; populism and, 34, 180; sovereignty and, 111, 114; of the sultans, 69; traditional societies and, 60–61. *See also* populism

Averroes, 234, 239

Avicenna, 234

El-Awa, Selim, 152

Al-Azhar: Abderrazak and, 75, 214–15n23, 241; Abdu and, 242; Qutb and, 167n24; al-Tahtawi and, 30

Al-Azhar University, 128, 136, 238

Azoury, Najib, 35

Baathists, 5, 39–40, 42, 61

banking system, 50

al-Banna, Hassan, 152, 153, 164, 235, 241

barbarity (*jahiliyya*), 131–32, 143–44, 145

Barth, Frederik, 102

Bayat, Asef, 159–60

Bedouins, 16, 20–21, 37

Béji, Héli, 128

Ben Badis, Abdelhamid, 166n5, 240–41

Ben Bella, Ahmed, 93, 113, 222

Benhadj, Ali, 155–56

Bentalha massacre, 247–48n4

Berger, Peter, 125, 166n3, 182

beylik, 69

Bible, 139, 213n1

bin Laden, Osama, 8–9

Bismarck, Otto von, 85

al-Bitar, Salah, 40, 113

Bled Echam (historical Syria), 34–36

Bodin, Jean, 198

Bonaparte, Napoleon, 2–3, 11, 28

Boudiaf, Mohamed, 113

Boumediene, Houari: death of, 4; on health care, 90; ideology of, 3; national charter of, 46; on the people, 65, 81n7; popularity of, 116; repression

by, 113; single-party system and, 48; World Islamic Organization speech by, 222–23

Bourdieu, Pierre, 126, 165–66n2, 212n2, 223

bourgeoisie: Arab Spring uprisings and, 56; democracy and, 90, 178; in Egypt, 62, 91; emergence of, 57; monetary, 56; state-controlled economy and, 91; al-Tahtawi and, 34

Bourguiba, Habib, 118, 215n31, 221, 222

Boussof, Malika, 219

Bouteflika, Abdelaziz, 156

the British, 17–18, 24, 32, 33, 37–38, 148. *See also* European domination

brotherhoods, 232–33, 235, 249n15. *See also* Muslim Brotherhood

Burgat, François, 221

el Bustani, Butros, 35

caliph, title of, 196, 214–15n23

capital, 52–53, 56, 91

The Capital (Marx), 73

capitalism: Arab socialism and, 48; British opposition to, 33; Islamist's rejection of, 138; primitive accumulation of, 73; speculative, 56; traditional societies and, 60–61; in Turkey, 161–62. *See also* market economy

capital punishment, 209

Carré, Olivier, 167n23

Catholic Church, 119n3, 135, 185, 213–14n14

chauvinsim, 102, 103

chirk (associationism), 27

cho'oubia, 12

Christians and Christianity: European domination and, 98–99; Al-Nahda and, 31; one-upmanship in, 119n3; pan-Arabism and, 35–36; private practice of faith and, 135; Qur'an on, 140–43; Qutb on, 139–40, 141–42; in Syria, 35; al-Wasat Party on, 154

citizenship, 104, 108, 154, 242
civic nationalism, 105–6
civil rights, 13, 46, 66, 161. *See also*
    human rights
civil society: corruption and, 80–81n4;
    economic development and, 62, 74;
    market economy and, 53; military
    regimes and, 97; modernity and,
    73–74; the nation and, 13; non-
    capitalist development and, 80n2;
    populism and, 64; socialism and, 48;
    state-controlled economy and, 51
clientelism, 90, 100–101
collective community: Arab society as,
    228; aspirations of, 95; civil society
    and, 73–74; vs. individuals, 135; Islam-
    ism and, 235; of nations, 100–101,
    103, 106; political, 84, 86, 100–101,
    103, 104; populism and, 65; tolerance
    and, 156; utopianism and, 5
collective memory, 81n12, 232, 235
colonialism, 12–13, 16, 32, 69, 118–19,
    143–44. *See also* European domin-
    ation
Committee of Union and Progress
    (CUP), 36
communism, 48, 80n2, 89, 145, 150
community. *See* collective community;
    umma
Community of Sant'Egidio, 225
competition, 52, 54, 56, 81n5, 91–92
Conference of Non-Aligned Nations
    (1974), 78
confessionalism, 34–35, 38–39, 40,
    99–100, 226
conflict-free society, 91–92, 97, 159
conscience: freedom of, 94, 105,
    135, 182, 226, 228, 242; individual
    and, 74; moral order and, 166–
    67n10; secularization and, 134,
    182, 203
consciousness: false, 65, 125; historical,
    252; national, 233; social, 134, 182;
    values and, 126

conservatives, 25, 30–31, 40, 94, 241. *See
    also* monarchy
conspicuous consumption, 65, 81n7
constitutional law, populism and,
    67–68, 81n10
Copts, Egyptian, 98, 153, 154, 247–48n4
corporal punishment, 206
corruption: economic development and,
    133; Islamism against, 229–30, 245;
    state-controlled economy and, 53, 69,
    80–81n4
cosmopolitanism, 253
Council of the Ulemas, 8, 9. *See also*
    ulemas
crime: penal law and, 211–12; sharia on,
    200–201, 206; vs. sin, 131, 132, 208,
    246
cultural identity, 119–20n6
cultural nationalism, 105–6
cultural representations, 99, 125–27,
    138, 151, 165n1, 179
culture and cultural change: economism
    and, 72–73; heterogeneity of, 218–31;
    Islam and, 75–77, 82n17; Nasser and,
    62; postnationalism and, 96; reli-
    gions and, 231–32. *See also* Muslim
    culture
CUP (Committee of Union and Pro-
    gress), 36
currency manipulation, 50, 51

darura (necessity), 149
debt, 189, 213n13
decolonization, 41–42, 78, 107
dehumanization, 58
de-Islamization, the people and, 221–22
democracy: Abdu and, 194; authorita-
    rian opposition to, 114; Benhadj on,
    155–56; bourgeoisie and, 90, 178; as
    defeat of the others, 220; definition
    of, 212–13n4; economic development
    and, 181; historical background of,
    177–78; Islamic theology and, 178;
    Islamism and, 183–84; Mawdudi on,

146; middle class and, 180, 182; military regimes on, 92; non-Muslims and, 146; the people in, 81n10; political participation and, 177; populism on, 89–90; post-Islamism and, 153; poverty and, 180, 182; prerequisites of, 182; Saudi Arabia and, 182–83; transition to, 225–26, 245; in Tunisia, 226; Western culture and, 98

democratic threshold, 181–82, 212–13n4

Descartes, René, 74, 77, 128

Le désenchantement national (Béji), 128

determinism, 126

developing countries, 57, 78–79, 91, 107, 109–10, 200

dhimmi (inferior status), 140, 141

divine sovereignty: Abdu on, 194–96; *al hakimiyya li Allah* slogan and, 184–87, 191, 192–93, 197; leaders and, 184, 213n10; monotheism on, 198; Qutb on, 144

divorce, 171, 204

Du'at la Qudat (Preachers, not judges), 167n24

Durkheim, Emile, 70, 213n10

economic anthropology, 54, 71

economic development: background of, 74–75; civil society and, 62, 74; democracy and, 181; military regimes and, 94, 224; populism and, 75, 161–62; promise of, 1–2, 43; religious duties and, 133; society and, 71–72

economic reform, 6–7, 55, 57–58

economism, 53, 72–80

economy. *See* market economy; state-controlled economy

education: confessionalism and, 34–35; on foreigners, 106; mass, 76–77, 150, 174; Mawdudi on, 150; populism and, 72–73; postcolonial, 235; role of, 86; for true Islam, 201; in Tunisia, 222

Egypt: Muhammed Ali and, 15, 17, 28; Bonaparte's expedition to, 2–3; bourgeoisie in, 62, 91; civil society in, 64; economic model of, 6, 55–56; elections in, 33–34, 55, 110, 163–64, 218, 220; elites in, 16, 28–29, 33; employment in, 90; Free Officers coup in, 4–5, 18, 87–88, 113, 119n1; al-Husri and, 39; Islamist victory in, 218, 220, 244–45; liberal nationalism in, 28–34; middle class in, 34; military regimes in, 4–5, 34, 87–88, 218, 220, 224, 246–47; modernization in, 17; monarchy in, 18, 41, 87–88, 111; Morsi and, 218, 244–45, 247; National Action Charter of 1962, 46, 55, 93; National Assembly membership in, 90; October Charter of 1974, 55; Ottoman Empire and, 16; parliamentary regime in, 33–34; political parties in, 153–55, 163–64, 168n36; populism and, 61–64, 77–78; radical Arab nationalism in, 4–5, 17–18; reforms in, 5, 6, 55–56; repression in, 113; rural populations in, 30, 33; secularization and, 30, 31; single-party system and, 48; state-controlled economy in, 6, 63–64; Tahrir Square demonstrations in, 154; al-Tahtawi and, 17–18, 28–30, 33, 34; United Arab Republic and, 41–42. *See also* Nasser, Gamal Abdel

Egyptian Copts, 98, 153, 154, 247–48n4

elections: in Algeria, 55, 218, 220; Benhadj on, 156; in Egypt, 33–34, 55, 110, 163–64, 218, 220; Islamism and, 155, 183–84; Islamist victories in, 218, 219, 220, 223, 243; Mawdudi on, 147; military regimes on, 92; post-Islamism and, 159; rigged, 68; social class and, 179–81; sovereignty and, 81n10, 199; in Tunisia, 225–26 elites: Bonaparte's expedition and, 2–3; civilian vs. military, 92; denial of sovereignty by, 107; in Egypt, 16, 28–29, 33; European influence and, 11, 16; German, 85; republican, 3; social inequalities and, 9; al-Tahtawi and, 28–29, 33; in Tunisia, 220–21; ulemas and, 94; Wahhabism and, 25. *See also* leaders

employees, state, 42, 48, 63, 64, 90

Enlightenment, 75, 108–9

Ennahda Party (Tunisia), 155, 163, 226

Erbakan, Necmettin, 161

Essay on Revolution (Arendt), 97

ethnocentrism: in the Arabian Peninsula, 19; *cho'oubia* and, 12; Hussein and, 37; nationalism and, 84, 102–3; orientalism and, 117; Wahhabism and, 20–21; in the Western world, 106, 117

ethnographic research, 228

ettahrir (liberation), 115

Europe: axial transformation of, 250n21; development of democracy in, 177–78; emergence of nation-states in, 84, 97, 98, 104–6, 213n6; ethnocentrism and, 117; failure to keep up with, 162, 195, 233, 241; intellectual transformation in, 74, 75–77, 85, 127–28, 132, 151, 251–52; modernity in, 73; nationalism in, 85; right-wing thinkers in, 119–20n6; secularization in, 85, 185. *See also* scientific and technological innovations; Western world

European domination: Arab identity and, 32; emergence of Arab nationalism and, 2–3, 15–17, 98–99; Ghannouchi on, 221; Hussein and, 37–38; marginalization of sharia by, 203; modernity/tradition debate and, 248n8; Qutb on, 143–44; radical Arab nationalism and, 18, 61–62; roots of Islamism and, 127–28; Saudi Arabia's avoidance of, 24; struggle against, 3, 12–13

everyday life: Islamist ideology and, 138; modernity and, 228; Othmani on, 158; of the poor, 180; secularization in, 133–35, 166n9; theological relevance to, 28, 136

evil, vs. good, 142, 201, 202

exchange rate, 50, 54

executive branch, 45–46, 225

external economies, 58

extreme right-wing, 67, 119–20n6

eye for an eye (*lex talionis*), 208

failed states, 107

fake gospel, 167n14

false consciousness, 65, 125

family, 204–5, 207, 208, 215n29. *See also* marriage

Farouk (King), 111

fascism, 119–20n6

al-Fassi, Allal, 118, 240

fatalism, 195, 233–34

fatalist conception (*qadirite*), 194–96

feudal system, 33, 53, 80n2, 88, 100, 251

Fichte, Johann Gottlieb, 39, 85

fikh (Muslim law): creation of, 191–92; on '*ibadates* vs. *mo'amalates*, 164–65; lack of advances in, 209–10; modernization of, 210–11; modifications to, 206–7; penal law of, 211–12; Qutb on, 144; vs. sharia, 201–2

FIS (Front Islamique du Salut), 155, 193–94, 195, 218, 219

foreign domination. *See* European domination; Western world

foreigners, integration of, 105–6

fortuna, 119n1

France: civic nationalism of, 105–6; Egypt and, 32; Hussein and, 38; Ibn Saud and, 24; sovereignty and, 198–99; Tunisia and, 221. *See also* European domination

INDEX

freedom: Abdu on, 195; of conscience,
94, 105, 135, 182, 226, 228, 242; fear
of, 184; of individuals, 12–13, 115,
117; of the press, 6, 180; religious, 94,
117, 141, 246; of speech, 94, 155, 164,
212–13n4
Free Officers coup (1952), 4–5, 18,
87–88, 113, 119n1
French language, 28–29
French Revolution (1789), 111, 198–99
Front de Libération Nationale (National
Liberation Front), 61, 113
Front Islamique du Salut (FIS), 155,
193–94, 195, 218, 219
fuqahas (religious lawmakers), 137, 191–
92, 199, 203, 208

Gaddafi, Muammar, 43, 89
Galileo, 77, 82n17
Geertz, Clifford, 102–3, 109–10, 165n1,
202
Gellner, Ernest, 105, 108–9, 249n14
Germany, 3, 39, 85, 105–6
Ghannouchi, Rachid, 155, 158, 220–22,
226
GIA (Armed Islamist Group), 247–48n4
globalization, 75, 121, 217, 229
global legal system, 253
God: allegiance to, 213n1; enemies of,
139–40; Islamism on, 131–32, 138–
39; judgment by, 213–14n14; as
omnipresent, 189; representatives of,
214–15n23; transcendent power of,
194. *See also* divine sovereignty
God's will (*qadr*), 27–28
good: vs. evil, 142, 201, 202; myth of, 135
goods, nonmarket, 58
Gospel of Barnabas, 167n14
government: centralized, 16, 18–19,
21–25; in democracies, 81n10, 220;
freedom to criticize, 51; *hukuma* as,
190; lack of experience in, 1, 155,
244, 245; by technocrats, 76, 226. *See
also* nation-states; the state

government-controlled economy. *See*
state-controlled economy
government power. *See* state power
The Great Transformation (Polanyi),
59–60
"Green Book" (Gaddafi), 89
Gulen, Fethullah, 161

Habermas, Jürgen, 48, 180
Al Hakem, 189–90
hakimiyya, 147, 189–91, 194, 195
al hakimiyya li Allah (all power belongs
to God) slogan, 147, 184–97; divine
sovereignty and, 184–87, 191, 192–93,
197; Islamism and, 193–94; Mawdudi
and, 147, 188, 189–93, 197; modernity
and, 184
Hanbalism, 27, 136–37, 165, 211, 237–39,
242
Harbi, Mohamed, 246
Hashemites, 38, 43n4
health care, 90, 180
Hegelian historicism, 118–19
Heikal, Mohamed Hassanein, 63–64
Herder, Johann Gottfried von, 39, 85
hereditary legitimacy, 22, 111, 230
heresy, 1, 23, 26–27, 210
Hindus, 146
Hizmet movement, 161
Hobbes, Thomas, 64–65, 115
al horiya (liberty), 115, 131
al-Hudaybi, Hassan, 145, 167n24
huddud rules, 206, 212
hukm, 190, 194, 213–14n14, 214n16
hukuma, 190
humanist culture, 75, 77, 142, 177
human rights, 150, 155, 157, 164–65,
242
human sovereignty, 191–92, 198
Hume, David, 60
hunger riots, prevention of, 51
al-Husri, Sati: Arab language and, 85;
army officers and, 40; ideology of, 39,
61; on intellectual progress, 252;

INDEX

al-Husri *(continued)*
  revolutionary change and, 118; shared identity and, 86
Hussein, Saddam, 99, 160
Hussein, Sharif, 2, 24, 25, 36–38, 40, 230
hypocrites, 139, 140, 142

'ibadates (religious obligations), 164–65, 189, 200, 208, 213n13, 215n30
Ibn 'Arabi, 26, 237, 238, 239
Ibn Hanbal, 20, 26–27, 28, 230, 239, 249–50n17
Ibn Khaldun, 195, 233
Ibn Rushd, 136
Ibn Saud, Abdulaziz, 9, 21, 23–25, 212
Ibn Taymiyyah, 26, 230, 238–39
Ibn Toumert, 43n1
ideal state, 175, 177
identity: Arab, 32; colonialism and, 12–13; cultural, 119–20n6; ethnocentrism and, 102–3; integration of, 98–99, 104–5; local patriotism and, 102–3; national, 98–99; political, 89; shared, 85, 86
ijtihad, 232, 240
Ikhwan, 9, 21–24, 25
imagined community, 103
imarat, 158, 169n45
IMF (International Monetary Fund), 4, 7, 57–58
immigration, 105, 107
India, 146, 149
individualism: vs. families, 208, 215n29; Islamism and, 126, 134–35, 166–67n10; restrictions of, 132; rule of law and, 68, 131; society and, 134–35
individuals: civil society and, 74; freedom of, 12–13, 115, 117; vs. the group, 12, 135; the state and, 68, 81n11
Indonesia, 110
industrial development, 47, 51–52, 62. *See also* economic development
Industrial Revolution, 75
inferior status *(dhimmi)*, 140, 141

infitah ("opening of the door"), 6
inheritance, 133, 149, 168n30, 171, 215n29
integrist trend, 149, 150–51
intellectuals: in Arab society, 72, 76, 77, 136–37, 152, 226–27, 238; marginalization of, 222; secular, 154, 160
intellectual transformation, European, 74, 75–76, 85, 127–28, 132, 151, 251–52
intelligence services, 176
intermediary bodies, 79
International Congress of Sociology (1974), 78
international law, 107
International Monetary Fund (IMF), 4, 7, 57–58
Iran, 151, 159–60
Iraq: invasion of Kuwait by, 8; militarization of, 88; monarchy in, 41–42, 111; repression in, 113; traditional societies in, 99; war with Iran, 160
irchad, 154, 235
ISIS (Islamic State in Iraq and Syria), 121
Islam: cultural change and, 75–77, 82n17; fake gospel on, 167n14; integrist trend in, 150–51; Mawdudi on, 146; modernity and, 11–12, 117; Al-Nahda and, 31–32; nationalist, 12; one-upmanship in, 119n3; puritanical doctrine of, 128; on separation of religion and state, 166–67n10; social and political place for, 11–12; traditional, 130–31; "true," 128–29, 201, 244; universalistic, 17, 19, 21–24; al-Wasat Party on, 153–54. *See also* Islamic theology
Islamic law. *See fikh*; sharia
Islamic Salvation Front, 218
Islamic state, 152–53, 155, 157, 158, 171, 235
Islamic State in Iraq and Syria (ISIS), 121
Islamic theology: classical, 137, 236; decline of, 166n9; divine sovereignty

and, 188; interpretation of, 179, 212n3; Kharijite orientation of, 151; lack of advances in, 75–77, 135–37, 151, 209–10; medieval interpretation of, 76–77, 86, 93, 178, 231, 253; modernization of, 93, 136, 151, 164–65, 169n53; Al-Nahda and, 75, 128; norms provided by, 179; 7th century Arabian Peninsula and, 165; three currents of, 237–39

Islamism, 1, 138–53; in Algeria, 7, 218, 219–20, 225, 247; authoritarianism and, 123, 187; against corruption, 229–30, 245; cultural representations of, 125–27, 138, 165n1; cultural roots of, 127–37; discourse of, 240–47; divisions in, 126–27; in Egypt, 218, 220, 244–45; elections and, 155, 183–84, 218, 219, 220, 223, 243; electoral victories of, 218, 219, 220, 223, 225–26, 243; evolution of, 4, 163–64; future obstacles to, 162–63; goal of, 171; *al hakimiyya li Allah* slogan and, 193–94; ideological and political perspectives of, 121–23, 217–18, 235–36; ideological naivety of, 162–63; increasing popularity of, 4, 7; individualism and, 126, 134–35, 166–67n10; interpretation of the Qur'an by, 128–29, 178; knowledge of Islamic theology by, 137; leaders of, 223; Madg's vision of, 152–53; Mawdudi's ideology of, 123, 126, 138–39, 145–50, 157, 178, 240; military regimes and, 89, 218–19; moderate, 8, 250n17; modernity and, 1, 123; monarchies and, 8, 196–97, 230–31; on moral order, 129–30, 131–32; on national sovereignty, 185, 213n11; political participation and, 172–84; political parties of, 147, 179–81; populism and, 80; Qutb's ideology of, 123, 126, 138–45, 151, 157, 167n23, 178, 240; radical Arab nationalism

and, 7, 123; religious culture and, 231–32; republics and, 8–9, 230–31; research on, 121; in Saudi Arabia, 8–9; secularization and, 132, 218, 244; sharia and, 171, 209; as a social representation, 122; Sufism and, 231–32, 235; vs. traditional Islam, 130–31; utopian vision of, 123, 134–35, 159, 173–75, 177, 202, 243–45, 246; violence of, 128, 129, 151–52; Wahhabism and, 243, 250n24; on wealth distribution, 69; Western world and, 7, 129, 138
Islamization, 221
Israel, 4, 40, 139, 250n24

jahiliyya (barbarity), 131–32, 143–44, 145
jalalat el Malik, 197
Jamal al-Din al-Afghani, 32, 75, 145–46, 232
Jamiat-e Islami, 147, 149
Jaspers, Karl, 250n21
Jeddah Treaty (1927), 24
Jesus, 139, 140, 167n14
Jews: Palestinian home for, 38–39, 250n24; pan-Arabism and, 35–36; Qur'an on, 140–43; Qutb on, 139–40, 141–42; al-Wasat Party on, 154
jihad, 37, 142, 144, 151, 249n15
jizya (tax), 140
Jordan, 159, 199
judgment, 190, 213–14n14
judiciary branch, 45, 49–50, 52, 80–81n4, 157, 212–13n4
justice, 131, 132, 205–6
Justice and Development Party (AKP), 161–62
Justice and Freedom party (Egypt), 154–55, 164

Kacem, Abdul Karim, 114, 116
Kadivar, Mohsen, 242
kalam, 237, 238, 239

INDEX

Kamil, Mustafa, 33, 34
Kant, Immanuel: influence of, 119;
  Islamism and, 128; on nations, 108–9;
  on pacification, 106–7; on the rule of
  law, 71, 74; Schopenhauer on, 165–
  66n2; on secularization, 85
Kemal, Mustafa, 38, 161, 240
Keynes, John Maynard, 181
Keynesian economics, 57
Khalifa Affair, 80–81n4
Khan, Wahiduddin, 149
Kharijite theology, 151
Khatab, Sayed, 167n24
Khomeini, Ruhollah, 151
Kuwait, 8, 9

labor, value creation and, 56, 57, 80n3
Laroui, Abdallah, 76
Latin America, 60–61
Lavoisier, Antoine, 128
leaders: divine sovereignty and, 184–87,
  213n10; of Islamism, 223; legitimacy
  of, 88–89, 113–14, 144; Mawdudi on,
  146; providential, 115; as a symbol,
  95
Lebanon, 99
Lefort, Claude, 116
legal system, 101, 206, 253. See also rule
  of law
legislative branch, 45–46, 92, 188, 200
legitimacy: of the army, 219; hereditary,
  22, 111, 230; of leaders, 88–89, 113–
  14, 144; of military regimes, 88–89,
  113–14; of the monarchy, 8, 111, 192,
  230–31; religious, 22, 33, 37, 183, 192,
  199, 215n23, 231; of the Al Saud
  family, 183, 230, 231
Lenin, Vladimir, 144–45, 150, 167n23
Lewis, Bernard, 117
lex talionis (an eye for an eye), 208
liberalism: advance of, 3; in Egypt,
  28–34; military regimes on, 116; Al-
  Nahda and, 32; neoclassical theory
  and, 57–58; pan-Arabism and, 35–36,

38; radical Arab nationalism and, 61;
  in Syria, 35–36; ulemas on, 116
liberation (ettahrir), 115
liberty (al horiya), 115, 131
Libya, 43
linguistic anthropology, 165n1
Lipset, Seymour, 182
Luckman, Thomas, 125, 166n3
Luther, Martin, 236

Machiavelli, Niccolò, 64–65, 115, 119n1
Magd, Ahmed Kamal Aboul, 152–53
malik, 188, 190, 196–97
mamlaka, 196–97. See also monarchy
market economy: balance of power in,
  53; inequalities of, 6; modernity and,
  73; neoclassical theory and, 57–59;
  poverty and, 180; price system and,
  60; radical Arab nationalism and, 46,
  47–56; rule of law and, 59; society
  and, 59–60, 71. See also capitalism
marriage: legal age for, 205, 215n24;
  Mawdudi on, 149, 168n30; sharia on,
  171, 203–5, 215n24
Marshall, Alfred, 58
Marx, Karl, 57, 65, 67, 73, 85
Marxism, 3, 78–79, 80n2, 145
materialism, 129–30, 138
Mawdudi, Abul A'la: al hakimiyya li
  Allah slogan and, 147, 188, 189–93,
  197; Islamist ideology of, 123, 126,
  138–39, 145–50, 157, 178, 240;
  knowledge of classical Islamic theology, 137; on slavery, 215n26
Mecca verses, 211, 216n33
mechanical solidarity, 13, 105
Medina verses, 211, 216n33
memory, collective, 81n12, 232, 235
merchant sector, 46, 57. See also market
  economy
Messiah, 202
middle class: democracy and, 180, 182;
  in Egypt, 33, 34; liberalism and, 32;
  Al-Nahda and, 127; postindepen-

dence, 174; poverty of, 50, 96; secular, 231; World War II and, 40

Middle East, 13, 16, 31, 34

militarization, of politics, 87–97, 251

military regimes: in Algeria, 87, 93, 218, 224, 225, 247; assassinations by, 224, 247–48n4; authoritarianism of, 5–6, 89–90, 112–13, 115, 224; civil society and, 97; conflict-free society and, 91–92, 97; in developing countries, 91; economic development and, 94, 224; in Egypt, 4–5, 34, 87–88, 218, 224, 246–47; Islamism and, 89, 218–19; legitimacy of, 88–89, 113–14; modeled on European armies, 18; political power and, 112; popularity of, 116; repression by, 5–6, 89–90, 112–13, 115; single-party system and, 90; sovereignty and, 87, 92, 110, 111–14; strategy of, 90, 224–25; survival of, 223–24

minorities, religious, 35–36, 102, 135, 150

moderate Islamism, 8, 250n17

modernity and modernization: Arabic language and, 227; aspirations for, 1, 139, 171; authoritarianism and, 91; civil society and, 73–74; compatibility with religion, 240; of *fikh*, 210–11; *al hakimiyya li Allah* slogan and, 184; ideological discourses on, 189; Islam and, 11–12, 117; of Islamic theology, 93, 136, 151, 164–65, 169n53; Islamism and, 1, 123; of Muslim societies, 122, 123; Al-Nahda and, 31, 127–28, 145–46; nationalism and, 92–93; populism and, 73, 79–80; radical Arab nationalism and, 5, 43, 70; religion and, 227–28; Al Saud family and, 23–24; secularization and, 11; state-controlled economy and, 51–52; state power and, 92–93; vs. traditional societies, 226–29, 248n8

Mogul Dynasty, 149

Mohammed (Prophet): Aflaq on, 75; Arabian Peninsula and, 142–43; divine sovereignty and, 193; Gospel of Barnabas on, 167n14; Mecca and Medina verses on, 211, 216n33; monotheism of, 139, 141; Moroccan monarchy and, 230; penal law and, 211–12; two qualities of, 193, 214n18

Mohammed V, 110

monarchy: Arab Spring uprisings and, 4; Council of the Ulemas and, 8; in Egypt, 18, 41, 87–88, 111; historic origins of, 2, 3–4, 8; in Iraq, 41–42, 111; Islamism and, 8, 196–97, 230–31; in Jordan, 199; legitimacy of, 8, 111, 192, 230–31; in Morocco, 158, 196–97, 199, 230, 231; overthrow of, 87–88; political sovereignty of, 199; relegitimization of, 42–43; vs. the republics, 4, 42–43; in Saudi Arabia, 17, 18–25, 111; sovereignty and, 110–11, 185, 198; wealth distribution and, 43; Western world's relationship with, 42

monotheism, 139–40, 141, 147, 197–98, 200

moral order, 129–30, 131–32, 151, 166–67n10, 172, 201

Morocco: Council of the Ulemas in, 8; French control of, 32; Geertz on, 110; monarchy in, 158, 196–97, 199, 230, 231; Ottoman Empire and, 169n45; personal status code in, 249n12; political parties in, 157–58; post-Islamism in, 157–58, 159; Western Sahara and, 213n11

Morsi, Mohamed, 218, 244–45, 247

Moses, 139, 141, 167n14

mou'amalates (social relationships), 136, 164–65, 200, 208, 215n30, 244

mu'tazilas, 27, 165

Mubarak, Hosni, 95, 154, 168n36

Muslim Brotherhood: founding of, 152, 162, 235, 241; Justice and Freedom party of, 154–55, 163, 164; mission of, 145; Qutb and, 145, 167n24; al-Wasat Party and, 153, 154

Muslim culture: concept of state in, 115; Ghannouchi on, 221; intellectual transformation of Europe and, 127–28; Islam and, 75–77, 82n17; lack of change in, 75–77; modern philosophy and, 237, 238, 239; patriarchy in, 204, 207; postnationalism and, 96; radical Arab nationalism and, 47; *siba* (stateless) and, 64, 69; sovereignty and, 195, 199; in Tunisia, 221–22

Muslim law. *See fikh*

Muslim society. *See* Arab society

Muslim theology. *See* Islamic theology

mutakallimun, 237, 238

Al-Nahda: critiques of, 233; Ghannouchi and, 155, 222; ideology of, 232, 235; modernity and, 31, 127–28, 145–46; reforms attempted by, 75, 248n8; on scientific and technological innovations, 31, 127–28; on Sufism, 217–18; ulemas of, 30–32, 33. *See also* Abdu, Mohammed

naskh (abrogation), 211

Nasr, Sayyed Vali Reza, 148

Nasser, Gamal Abdel: on Arab socialism, 3; assassination of Qutb by, 139, 167n24; on employment, 90; Free Officers coup and, 87, 113, 119n1; National Action Charter and, 46, 93; pan-Arabism and, 41; popularity of, 116; populism and, 61–64; Qutb on, 144; reforms by, 5; single-party system and, 48; as a symbol, 95

the nation: collective community and, 100–101, 103, 106; complaints against, 113; concept of, 13; definition of, 86; formation of, 83–86;

Gellner and Kant on, 108–9; historico-political context of, 104–6; lack of sovereignty in, 109–19; mechanisms of integration and, 104–5; vs. nationalism, 83, 84, 103–7; pacification of, 106–7; Tahtawi and, 29; theoretical model of, 100–101; as a tribe, 89; universalism and, 99–100, 109. *See also* nation-states

National Action Charter of 1962 (Egypt), 46, 55, 93

National Assembly (Egypt), 90

National Charter (Algeria), 91

national identity, 98–99

nationalism: aggressive nature of, 98–107, 108; civic, 105–6; cultural, 105–6; divisive nature of, 101–3; ethnocentrism and, 84; in Europe, 85, 119–20n6; local patriotism and, 102–3; vs. nations, 83, 84, 103–7; political power and, 13, 68; as a source of conflict, 104. *See also* Arab nationalism

National Liberation Army (Algeria), 81n8

National Liberation Front (Front de Libération Nationale), 61, 113

national sovereignty: the army and, 87; authoritarianism and, 114–15; in France, 198–99; Islamism on, 185, 213n11; military regimes and, 112–13; vs. popular sovereignty, 86; Westphalian order and, 199, 200

Nations and Nationalism (Gellner), 108–9

nation-states: collectivity and, 100–101; developing countries and, 107; European emergence of, 84, 97, 98, 104–6, 213n6; formation of, 85–86; local structures and, 68; Mawdudi on, 148; vs. *umma*, 12; Westphalian order and, 15, 84

nature: laws of, 126, 130, 147, 148, 206; positivist view of, 77; reason and, 31, 127, 233; sovereignty and, 197; Wahhabism and, 26

necessity (*darura*), 149
neoclassical theory, 57–59
neoliberalism, 58, 59
Nietzsche, Friedrich, 85, 132
non-capitalist development, 48, 80n2
nonconflictual society, 91–92, 97, 159
non-exploitative property, 91
nonmarket goods, 58, 59
non-Muslims: authority of, 32, 149; democracy and, 146; equality for, 242; integration of, 105–6; pan-Arabism and, 35; sharia on, 153; al-Wasat Party on, 154. *See also* Christians and Christianity; Jews
norms, 74, 179, 210
North Africa, 16, 42, 43n1, 181, 227
al-Nour Party (Egypt), 163, 164
Nu'ami, Mohammed Manzur, 149

October Charter of 1974 (Egypt), 55
oil revenues: Algeria and, 224; as capital, 52–53; price increases and, 43; Saudi Arabia and, 25, 183; wealth distribution and, 17, 45
Omar Ibn al- Khattab, 175–76, 210
"opening of the door" (*infitah*), 6
optimism, anthropological, 130, 166n6
organic solidarity, 13
orientalism, 117, 134, 178, 230
Othman (Caliph), 156
Othmani, Saadeddine, 157–58, 169n45
Ottoman Empire: Arabian Peninsula and, 16, 19, 20–21; *beylik* administration, 69; confessionalism and, 99; decline of, 2, 3, 11; Egyptian elites and, 16; Ibn Saud and, 24; individuals in, 68; Morocco and, 169n45; partition of, 38; Syria and, 35, 36; Young Turks and, 36, 162
oumma (unity), 12, 126

pacification, Kant on, 106–7
Pakistan, partition of, 149
Palestine, 38–39, 250n24

pan-Arabism: Baathists and, 40; al-Husri and, 39; liberalism and, 35–36, 38; Nasser and, 41–42; vs. Pan-Germanism, 85; in Syria, 34–36
Pan-Germanism, 39, 85
paradise, entrance into, 189, 201, 213n13, 223
paramilitary groups, 151
parliamentary model, 33–34, 90, 147
Parti de la justice et du développement (PJD), 157–58
Pascon, Paul, 227
Pasteur, Louis, 128
patriarchy, 204, 207
patriotism, 16, 35, 102–3
peasants, 29, 30, 60, 79, 233
penal law, 211–12
the people: Boumediene on, 65, 81n7; elections and, 81n10; power for, 193–94; vs. society, 46, 65–68; sovereignty of, 114, 115–16, 118; the state and, 46, 116, 184; states' relationship with, 46, 184; in wartime, 67, 81n8
People of the Book, coexistence with, 141
personal status code, 207, 249n12
pessimism, anthropological, 166n6
philosophy: Abdu on, 128, 234; absence of, 136; controversies with, 237–39, 249–50n17; Islamic theology and, 166n9; modern, 237
PJD (Parti de la justice et du développement), 157–58
Platonism, 238, 239, 249–50n17
pluralism: juridical, 192; political, 163–64, 182, 245
Polanyi, Karl, 58, 59–60, 71
political anthropology, 71, 120n11
political autonomy, 15–16, 246
political collectivity, 84, 86, 100–101, 103, 104
political dissent, 48, 89–90, 112–13, 115, 123
political economy, 53–54, 56–60, 74, 80n3

political identity, 89
political Islam, 96, 150, 240–47. *See also* Islamism
political participation: democratic threshold and, 181–82, 212–13n4; fictional, 101; Islamism and, 172–84; political resource and, 172–73, 212n1; populism and, 63, 181–82; social class and, 179–81, 182
political parties: in Algeria, 155–57, 219–20; in Egypt, 153–55, 163–64, 168n36; in India, 149; Islamist, 147, 179–81; military regimes and, 88; Morocco, 157–58; Muslim Brotherhood and, 154–55; political philosophy of, 5; post-Islamist, 153–57, 161–62, 163–64, 168n36; secular, 220, 226, 230; in Tunisia, 155, 163, 226; in Turkey, 161–62. *See also specific parties*
political pluralism, 163–64, 182, 245
political police, 176
political power: divine sovereignty and, 185; the *fuqahas* and, 192; Ikhwan and, 21–24; Mawdudi on, 146, 188, 190; military regimes and, 112; Nasser on, 62; nationalism and, 13, 68; private nature of, 92, 97; for society, 116; wealth and, 72. *See also* state power
political resource, 172–73, 212n1
political science, role of, 71
political sovereignty, 86, 188, 189, 199, 213n1
politics: apolitical representation of, 132–33, 150; autonomy of, 132, 154; legitimacy of, 136, 164; militarization of, 87–97, 251; populism's rejection of, 63; society and, 71–72
polygamy, 205, 207, 208–9, 215n31, 223
polytheism, 27
popular representations, 138
populism: in Algeria, 7; the army and, 63–64; authoritarianism and, 34, 180; constitutional law and, 67–68, 81n10; cultural, 38, 72–73; democracy and,
89–90; economic development and, 75, 161–62; economic model of, 54, 55; Egypt and, 61–64, 77–78; Islamism and, 80; legitimacy of, 65; market economy and, 58–59; modernity and, 73, 79–80; political dissent and, 89–90; political participation and, 63, 181–82; poverty and, 50–51, 72; on the Qur'an, 173–74; radical Arab nationalism and, 61–66, 70, 80; society and, 60–61, 65–68; state-controlled economy and, 63–64; state power and, 66; traditional societies and, 60–61; universities and, 77–79, 82n19; utopianism and, 173–74
positivism, 77, 82n17, 128
postcolonialism, 12–13, 15–16, 118–19, 151
post-Islamism, 153–65; in Algeria, 155–57; Bayat on, 159–60; elections and, 159; in Morocco, 157–58, 159; shift toward, 163–64; in Tunisia, 127, 155, 158–59; in Turkey, 161–62
postnationalism, 95–96
poverty: democracy and, 180, 182; Islamism on, 130; populism and, 50–51, 72; republican ideology and, 9; state-controlled economy and, 55; utopian beliefs and, 173, 212n2
power: for the people, 193–94; science of, 64–65; sovereignty and, 86, 185. *See also* political power; state power
predecessors (*salafs*), 26, 173, 228, 232, 239
predemocratic stage, 182, 213n6
predestination, 249n14
Preobrajensky, Yevgeni, 60
prepolitical phase, 97
pre-Ricardian theory, 53, 54
the press, 6, 45, 79, 174, 180, 224
price system: global, 46, 59; goods and, 58; market economy and, 60; public economic sector and, 49; rational, 81n5; state-controlled economy and, 47–48, 50, 52, 54–55, 59, 81n5

the prince, 64–65, 192
prisoners of war, 215n26
productivity, 6, 50, 52, 54, 58, 59
professional associations, 51, 79, 81n4
profits, 50, 52, 80n3. *See also* wealth
   accumulation
property: inheritance of, 149, 168n30,
   171, 215n29; *mamlaka* and, 196–97;
   non-exploitative, 91
Protestantism, 135, 249n14
protonationalism, 2
public economic sector, 47, 49–50, 54–55
Public Liberties in the Islamic State
   (Ghannouchi), 155
public space, 108, 116, 120n7
punishment: for adultery, 208, 215n27;
   capital, 209; corporal, 206; by God,
   140, 188; penal law and, 211–12;
   Qur'an on, 208

qadirite (fatalist conception), 194–96
qadr (God's will), 27
al-Qaeda, 8–9, 121, 159
Qur'an: Abdu on, 194–96, 214n22, 232,
   240; on divine sovereignty, 193; fatalist
   conception of, 194–96; on God's
   power, 194; Hanbalism on, 165; *hud-*
   dud rules of, 206; Islamism and,
   128–29, 131; on Jews and Christians,
   140–43; literal interpretation of, 178;
   Mawdudi on, 147–48; new interpretations of, 136–37, 242; on obedience,
   174; on polygamy, 208–9, 215n31;
   populist reading of, 173–74; on punishment, 208; on Ramadan, 133; reason
   and, 241; on repentance, 208–9; on
   sharia, 200; Wahhabism and, 27; on
   women, 207. *See also* Islamic theology
Qutb, Sayyid: on Abdu, 129, 241; assassination of, 139, 167n24; El-Awa on,
   152; Islamist ideology of, 123, 126,
   138–45, 151, 157, 167n23, 178, 240;
   knowledge of classical Islamic theology, 137; as a martyr, 167n24;

Mubarak regime on, 168n36; on
   universalism, 150

radical Arab nationalism: in Egypt,
   4–5, 18; European domination and,
   18, 61–62; failure of, 1–2, 4, 43,
   45–46, 139, 241, 246–47, 251–52; historic origins of, 1, 2–3; ideological
   limitations of, 45–47; Islamism and,
   7, 123; market economy and, 46,
   47–56; modernity and, 1, 5, 43, 70;
   populism and, 61–66, 70, 80; promise of, 5–6, 45, 251; rule of law and,
   77–78; secularization and, 75–77;
   social inequalities and, 9; society
   and, 5–6; state-controlled economy
   and, 51–56; in Syria, 34–43. *See also*
   Arab nationalism
radicalization, 3, 61, 128–29, 145, 226
Ramadan, 133, 215n30
rapport de force, 11, 17, 52, 94–95, 183
Al Rashid family, 21, 25
Rassemblement pour la Culture et la
   Démocratie (RCD), 219
reality: harshness of, 173, 174, 212n2;
   social construction of, 125–26, 131,
   166n3; vs. utopia, 244, 246
reason, 27, 31, 129, 233–34, 241
relativists, 116–17
religion: culture and, 231–32; divisive
   nature of, 101–2, 119n3; freedom of,
   94, 117, 141, 246; politicalization of,
   252; as a social construct, 12; universalism and, 29–30; Westphalian
   order and, 84
religious duties (*'ibadates*), 133
religious lawmakers (*fuqahas*), 137,
   191–92, 199, 203, 208
religious legitimacy: Al Saud family
   and, 183; ancestry and, 22; Sharif
   Hussein and, 37; of monarchs, 192,
   199, 215n23, 231; al-Tahtawi and, 33
religious minorities, 35–36, 102, 135,
   150

religious obligations (*'ibadates*), 164–65, 189, 200, 208, 213n13, 215n30
Renan, Ernest, 105–6
rent, 50, 53–55, 56, 59, 69, 80n3
repentance, 208–9
representations: apolitical, 132–33, 150; cultural, 99, 125–27, 138, 151, 165n1, 179; heuristic concept of, 125, 165–66n2; popular, 138
republics: elites and, 3; fragility of, 4; historic origins of, 3, 4; ideology of, 9; Islamism and, 8–9, 230–31; vs. monarchy, 4, 42–43; revolutionary nationalism of, 42; static politics in, 229–30
repudiation, 203, 204
researchers, 78–79, 82n19, 121
revolutionary change: in France, 105; Hegelian historicism and, 118; Islamism and, 130–31, 243–45; Mawdudi on, 146–47; militarization and, 91; populist utopia and, 173–74
revolutionary councils, 111–12
Ricardo, David, 53, 57, 58, 80n3
Rida, Rashid, 241, 243
right-wing groups, extreme, 67, 119–20n6
Rissalat et Tawhid (Abdu), 234
robbery, 206
Roy, Olivier, 160
rule of law: Abdu on, 194; anthropological pessimism and, 166n6; based on religion alone, 172–73; Benhadj on, 156–57; civil society and, 74; in developing countries, 109–10; development outside of Europe, 117–18; individualism and, 68, 131; market economy and, 59; peace and, 253; radical Arab nationalism and, 77–78; separation of religion and state with, 245–46; society and, 67–68, 71, 86, 116, 244
rural populations: Al-Nahda and, 232–33; Ottoman Empire and, 36–37;

peasants in, 29, 30, 60, 79, 233. *See also* traditional societies
Rushdie, Salman, 229
Russia, 60

Sadat, Anwar, 4, 55–56, 110, 151
Sadi, Saïd, 219
saints: Sufi, 232, 233, 236; Wahhabism on, 21, 26–27
salafiya, 235, 239, 249–50n17
salafs (predecessors), 26, 173, 228, 232, 239
salvation, 190, 213–14n14, 235
Saud, Abderrahmane, 21
Al Saud family: Arabian Peninsula and, 17, 18–25; Ikhwan and, 21–24; legitimacy of, 183, 230, 231; modernization and, 23–24; Wahhabism and, 20, 230
Saudi Arabia: adultery in, 215n27; avoidance of colonialism by, 24; centralized government of, 16, 18–19, 21–25; democracy and, 182–83; Islamism in, 8–9; Jeddah Treaty of 1927 and, 24; monarchy in, 17, 18–25, 111; origins of, 18–25; Palestinian question and, 250n24; al-Qaeda and, 8–9; ulemas in, 8, 9, 183; United States and, 9, 25
sayyada, 195, 214n22
Schmitt, Carl, 104
scholars, 77–79, 82n19. *See also* intellectuals
Schopenhauer, Arthur, 165–66n2
Schumpeter, Joseph A., 212–13n4
scientific and technological innovations: Abdu on, 234; Al Saud family and, 23–24; Arab society's lack of, 75; of Europe, 250n21; Al-Nahda and, 31, 127–28; state-controlled economy and, 51–52. *See also* intellectual transformation
secularization: Catholic Church and, 185; conscience and, 134, 182, 203; in Egypt, 30, 31; in Europe, 85, 185;

in everyday life, 133–35, 166n9; Hanbalism and, 165; Iran and, 160; Islamism and, 132, 218, 244; Islamization of, 1; Mawdudi on, 146, 148; modernization and, 11; nationalism and, 1; national sovereignty and, 199; pluralism and, 182; political science and, 71; process of, 109; radical Arab nationalism and, 75–77; rejection of, 203; social differentiation and, 123; of the state, 171–72; syncretism and, 93; in Tunisia, 220–21; in Turkey, 161

secular political parties, 220, 226, 230

self, representation of, 77

self-sufficiency, 61, 69

semantics, 125, 165n1

separation of religion and state: as heresy, 1; Islam on, 166–67n10; Mawdudi on, 146; post-Islamism and, 160; rejection of, 115, 122, 132, 219; rule of law and, 245–46

sermons, of opposition imams, 175–77

Shahrur, Muhammad, 169n53

shared identity, 85, 86

sharia, 200–212; as chief source of the law, 116; concept of, 200–201; on crime, 200–201, 206; on divorce, 171; on family law, 207; vs. *fikh*, 201–2; idealization of, 203; implementation of, 155, 246; on inheritance, 171; interpretation of, 210; Islamists on, 171; on justice, 205–6; as a legal system, 206; marginalization of, 203; on marriage, 171, 203–5, 215n24; Mawdudi on, 149, 150, 168n30; ordinary believers on, 201–2; on polygamy, 205; on slavery, 206; the state and, 135, 152–53; utopianism and, 202

Shayagan, Daryush, 82n17

Shiites, 22, 89, 99, 101, 104

siba (stateless) culture, 64, 69

sidi, 214n22

sin: vs. crime, 131, 132, 208, 246; original, 137; sharia on, 200–201

single-party system: in Algeria, 48, 55; delegitimization of, 174; Mawdudi on, 149; military regimes and, 90; Sadat and, 55; socialism and, 48

el-Sisi, Abdel Fattah, 220, 244–45, 246–47

slavery, 206, 215n26

Smith, Adam, 57, 58, 71, 74

social class, 4, 34, 91, 179–81, 182, 226

social consciousness, 134, 182

social differentiation, 70–72, 123

social inequality: authoritarianism and, 166n7; capitalism and, 138; Islamism on, 129; military regimes and, 89; populism and, 65, 67; republican ideology and, 9; sharia and, 201

socialism, 48, 80n2, 93, 138, 222

social relationships (*mou'amalates*), 136, 164–65, 200, 208, 215n30, 244

social status, 90. *See also* personal status code; social inequality

society: Arab countries as, 72; composite, 227; conflict-free, 91–92, 97, 159; cultural representations of, 125–26; God at the heart of, 138–39; historical construction of, 71–72; individualism and, 134–35; market, state and, 59–60; modernity and, 73; national unity and, 45–46; vs. the people, 46, 65–68; political power for, 116; populism and, 60–61, 65–68; radical Arab nationalism and, 5–6; rule of law and, 67–68, 71, 86, 116, 244; state-controlled economy and, 52. *See also* Arab society; civil society

sociological Muslims, 142

sociology, 78–80, 121, 122–23, 165–66n2, 213n10

soldiers, politicization of, 88–89. *See also* the army

solidarity, 13, 100, 105, 134

Soroush, Abdolkarim, 160

sovereignty: authoritarianism and, 111, 114; denial of, 107; elections and, 81n10, 199; of *fuqahas*, 191–92; of God, 144; historical dimensions of, 197–200; human, 191–92, 198; Mawdudi on, 147, 191; military regimes and, 87, 92, 110, 111–14; of monarchs, 110–11, 185, 198, 199; a nations lack of, 109–19; of the people, 114, 115–16, 118; the people and, 81n10; political, 86, 188, 189, 199, 213n1; popular, 86; power and, 86, 185; of Saudi Arabia, 25. *See also* divine sovereignty; national sovereignty
Soviet Union, 58
speculation, 7, 56
speech, freedom of, 94, 155, 164, 212–13n4
Spengler, Oswald, 195
Spinoza, Baruch, 74
the state: administrative concept of, 91–92; concept of, 115; development outside of Europe, 117–18; failed, 107; ideal, 175, 177; individual dependence on, 68, 81n11; market, society and, 59–60; modernity and, 73; the people and, 46, 116, 184; political autonomy and, 246; political economy and, 74; secularization of, 171–72; sermons against, 174–75; sharia and, 135, 152–53; violence by, 112–13
state-controlled economy: banking system in, 50; bourgeoisie and, 91; capital and, 52–53; corruption and, 53, 69, 80–81n4; in Egypt, 6, 63–64; employees of, 42, 48, 63, 64, 90; industrial development and, 47; judiciary branch and, 49–50; market in, 69; necessity for, 46; political dissent and, 48; populism and, 63–64; price system and, 47–48, 50, 52, 54–55, 59, 81n5; radical Arab nationalism and, 51–56; wealth distribution and, 46, 47

state employees, 42, 48, 63, 64, 90
stateless (*siba*) culture, 64, 69
state power: authority of, 64, 113; clientelism and, 100–101; confessionalism and, 99–100; executive branch and, 45–46; intellectual progress and, 252; market economy and, 53; modernity and, 92–93; populism and, 66; privatization of, 97; rule of law and, 77–78; science of, 64–65
state sociology, 78–80
succession, right of, 21, 207, 215n29
suffrage, universal, 219
Sufism: Abdu on, 217–18, 242; controversies with, 237–39; Hizmet movement and, 161; Islamism and, 231–32, 235; Al-Nahda on, 217–18; representation of, 234–35; saints and, 232, 233, 236; Wahhabism and, 21, 26–27, 242
Sukarno, 110
sultan, 195, 196
Sunnis, 27, 99, 231–32, 238–39
Sykes-Picot Agreement (1916), 3, 37–38, 43n4
symbolic violence, 129–30, 153
syncretism, 93, 110
Syria: Baathists takeover in, 42; confessionalism and, 99; coup d'état in, 40; militarization of, 88; pan-Arabism in, 34–36; radical Arab nationalism in, 34–43; religious minorities in, 35–36; repression by, 112–13; traditional societies in, 99; United Arab Republic and, 41–42; uprisings of the 1980's in, 151

taghout (tyrant), 144
Taha, Mahmoud Mohammed, 136, 211
Tahrir Square demonstrations (2011), 154
al-Tahtawi, Rifa'a, 17–18, 28–30, 33, 34, 248n8
takfir oual hijra (theory of the vanguard), 144–45

INDEX

talion, 211–12
"Tawakkalna 'ala Allah," 189, 191
taxes, 69, 94–95, 140
technocrats, 76, 226
technological innovations. *See* scientific
  and technological innovations
terrorism, 121, 152
theocracy, 150, 184, 185–86, 192, 230
theory of the vanguard (*takfir oual
  hijra*), 144–45
13th Political Science Congress (1999),
  152
those who have power to bind and
  unbind (*"ahl el hal oual 'aqd"*), 146,
  192
Tocqueville, Alexis de, 68
Tönnies, Ferdinand, 70, 71
traditional societies: apolitical representation of politics in, 132–33;
  confessionalism and, 99; Islamism
  and, 122; vs. modernity, 226–29,
  248n8; populism and, 60–61
tribes, 19, 20–21, 69, 89
"true" Islam, 128–29, 244
Tunisia: Arab Spring uprisings and, 4;
  de-Islamization in, 221–22; education in, 222; elections in, 225–26;
  Ennahda Party in, 155, 163, 226;
  Islamist victory in, 225–26; polygamy in, 207, 215n31, 223; post-
  Islamism in, 127, 155, 158–59; secularization in, 220–21
Turkey, 161–62, 207
Turkish Federation of Businessmen and
  Industrialists, 161
Turkish language, 36
tyrant (*taghout*), 144

ulemas: Abdu and, 188–89; authority of,
  94, 199, 236–37, 242; of the *cho'oubia*,
  12; dependence on, 76; Gellner on,
  249n14; knowledge of the texts by,
  210, 211; on liberalism, 116; Mawdudi
  and, 146, 149, 150, 151; monarchies

and, 8; of Al-Nahda, 30–32, 33; nationalist Islam and, 12; plural of, 192;
  on Qutb, 151; in Saudi Arabia, 8, 9, 183
umma, 30, 40, 143, 213n11
unions, 48, 51, 52, 80n2, 81n5
United Arab Republic, 41
United Nations, 25, 107, 242
United States, 9, 25, 191, 213n1
unity (*wahda*), 12, 126
Universal Declaration of Human Rights,
  242
universalism: of French society, 106; of
  man, 165; Mawdudi's influence in,
  150; nations and, 99–100, 106; process of, 109; Qutb's influence in, 150;
  rejection of, 228; relativists on, 116–
  17; religious, 29–30
universalistic Islam, 17, 19, 21–24
universities: modernization and, 174;
  populism and, 77–79, 82n19; research
  themes at, 78–79; violence of the
  1980's in, 96
US Treasury Department, 57–58
utopianism: Arab nationalism and,
  115–16; belief in, 173, 212n2; divine
  sovereignty and, 184–85; Islamism
  and, 123, 134–35, 159, 173–75, 177,
  202, 243–45, 246; nonconflictual
  society and, 91–92, 97, 104, 159;
  populism and, 173–74; poverty and,
  173, 212n2; vs. reality, 244, 246;
  sharia and, 202

value, 50, 56–57, 80n3
violence: Abdu on, 166n5; in Algeria,
  96, 151, 152; in everyday life, 134;
  Islamism and, 128, 129, 151–52; of
  the 1980's, 94, 96–97; populist utopia
  and, 173–74; Qutb on, 145; social
  class and, 179; by the state, 112–13;
  symbolic, 129–30, 153

Wafd (political party), 98
wages, 50, 81n5, 208

273

Wahhabism: in the Arabian Peninsula, 16, 18–25; description and concepts of, 26–28; ethnocentric appeal of, 20–21; Islamism and, 243, 250n24; Al-Nahda and, 31; puritanical doctrine of, 20, 22, 25, 26–28, 43n1; Al Saud family alliance with, 20, 230; Sufism and, 21, 26–27, 242; ulemas on, 243; universalistic Islam and, 19, 21–24

Walras, Léon, 54, 60

warlike verses, 211

War of 1967, 42

wartime, the people in, 67, 81n8

al-Wasat Party (Egypt), 153–55, 163–64, 168n36

Washington Consensus on economic reform, 57–58

watan. See the nation

wealth accumulation, 91, 95

wealth distribution: competition and, 91–92; Islamism on, 69; monarchies and, 43; political economy and, 57; public economic sector and, 49; Al Saud family and, 17; state-controlled economy and, 46, 47

Weber, Max, 70

Western domination. *See* European domination

Western Sahara, 213n11

Western world: Arab nationalism and, 2–3; democracy and, 98; demoniza-tion of, 252–53; ethnocentrism in, 106; Islamism on, 7, 129, 138; mate-rialism of, 129–30, 138; Mawdudi on, 146, 148; monarchies support for, 42; Muslims living in, 168n30; political science in, 71; Qutb on, 143–44; al-Tahtawi and, 28–30; universalism and, 117. *See also* Europe; European domination

Westphalian order: Arab nationalism and, 115–16; emergence of, 15, 110; Abdulaziz Ibn Saud and, 24; military regimes and, 112; national sover-eignty and, 199, 200; nation-states and, 15, 84

"What Is a State if It Is Not Sovereign?" (Geertz), 109–10

will, 125, 165–66n2

women: adultery and, 206, 208, 215n27; personal status code and, 249n12; status of, 207. *See also* marriage

World Bank, 57–58

World Islamic Organization, 223

World Trade Organization, 57–58

World War I, 24, 36–37

World War II, 40

Yassine, Abdessalam, 8, 158

Zaghloul, Saad, 33, 34, 118

za'im (unquestioned leader), 88–89

About the Author

Lahouari Addi is a professor at the Institut d'études politiques at the University of Lyon and a research fellow at the Centre de recherche en anthropologie sociale et culturelle in Oran, Algeria. He is the author of numerous books and articles on North Africa and political Islam, including *Deux anthropologues au Maghreb: Ernest Gellner et Clifford Geertz* (Les Editions des Archives Contemporaines, 2013) and *L'Algérie et la démocratie* (La Découverte, 1995).

CPSIA information can be obtained
at www.ICGtesting.com
Printed in the USA
BVOW08s2222200717
489881BV00002B/48/P